# PRAISE FOR MAKING OF MARTYRS

'They were products of the same colonial experience which both nurtured and angered them; they inspired many and were hated by many more. They each rose to unmatched heights of political power, offered India, Pakistan and Bangladesh a vision for social and economic change and were each afterwards assassinated by political opponents. Their legacies remain intertwined with the contemporary realities of modern South Asia. They fell from power in the 1970s within a few months of each other; yet their stories are seldom told together. I am delighted that Dr Faisal Khosa has told the stories of Indira Gandhi, Zulfikar Ali Bhutto and Sheikh Mujibur Rahman together in this important and original book. This book will be an invaluable teaching resource for South Asian studies.'

—**Matthew McCartney, PhD**
Bestselling Author,
Director of South Asian Studies 2011–2018,
Associate Professor of Political Economy and Human
Development of South Asia,
University of Oxford,
Oxford, United Kingdom.

'Dr Faisal Khosa has written an original and thought-provoking book that provides new insights and perspectives on three of South Asia's most important twentieth-century leaders.'

—**David Lewis**
Bestselling Author,
Professor of Social Policy and Development,
Department of Social Policy,
London School of Economics and Political Science,
London, United Kingdom.

'While South Asia's triad of populist-martyrs—Zulfikar Ali Bhutto, Indira Gandhi and Sheikh Mujibur Rahman—have attracted insightful scholarly analysis in the past, this is the first comprehensive comparative study of their politics and personalities. Engaging and accessible, this is a welcome addition to the field that will be read widely.'

—**Ayesha Jalal**
Bestselling Author,
Mary Richardson Professor of History,
Director, Center for South Asian and Indian Ocean Studies,
Tufts University,
Medford, Massachusetts, USA.

'The book is a must-read for anyone who cares about governance and leadership pattern in the subcontinent and, therefore, a more stable subcontinent. Khosa brilliantly explores and explains the psyche of leadership styles and the age-old conundrum—how leaders of the subcontinent and others are influenced and changed. As an informed citizen and a reader, it is intriguing from the book that family dynasty in the subcontinent is an impediment to flourishing democracy.'

—**Golam M. Mathbor, PhD**
Bestselling Author,
Professor, Monmouth University,
President, American Institute of Bangladesh Studies,
Former President, Canadian Association for the Study of International Development,
New Jersey, USA.

'This admirable book tackles a topic that has had far too little attention in studies of politics in and beyond South Asia—political assassinations and their impact. It also offers clear, enlightening accounts of lives and untimely ends of three crucial leaders. It deserves careful attention from specialists and non-specialists alike.'

—James Manor
Bestselling Author,
Emeritus Professor of Commonwealth Studies,
Institute of Commonwealth Studies,
School of Advanced Study,
University of London,
London, United Kingdom.

'Faisal Khosa has produced a very timely and necessary historical re-examination of three major figures of South Asia, each doomed to die a violent death, and whose actions continue to reverberate in the history of the region to this day. Zulfikar Ali Bhutto, Indira Gandhi and Sheikh Mujibur Rahman were towering figures on their domestic landscape. By juxtaposing their stories, Khosa has helped clarify lessons for scholars and politicians in South Asia today to avoid the pitfalls of hubris and to place the needs of their people first. If this book produces introspection, then Khosa will have succeeded in his quest.'

—Shuja Nawaz
Bestselling Author,
Distinguished Fellow, South Asia Center,
Atlantic Council,
Washington DC, USA.

'Faisal Khosa gives us the complex diplomatic history of the Indian subcontinent in a clear, coherent and fascinating form through the personalities of its three most remarkable politicians: Indira Gandhi, Zulfikar Ali Bhutto and Sheikh

Mujibur Rahman. Their conflicting agendas and political styles make for high drama, and the results of their interactions continue to reverberate in the twenty-first century.'

—**Brooke Allen**
Bestselling Author,
Bennington College,
Vermont, USA.

'Making of Martyr's in India, Pakistan and Bangladesh: Indira, Bhutto and Mujib not only presents a novel examination of the important developments of foundational South Asian history through the prism of three pivotal leaders, but is also an interesting personality study of Zulfikar Ali Bhutto, Indira Gandhi and Sheikh Mujibur Rahman in those great events.'

—**Julian Schofield, PhD**
Bestselling Author,
Associate Professor of Political Science,
Concordia University,
Montreal, Canada.

'Insightful sketches of three charismatic South Asian leaders, all of whom met an untimely end. Particularly interesting are the parallels between the figures and the varying perspectives each figure had in various regions of the subcontinent and among different factions, whether constituents or opponents.'

—**Douglas T. McGetchin, PhD**
Bestselling Author,
Associate Professor of History,
Florida Atlantic University,
Florida, USA.

'Khosa's book is well researched and lucidly written. It triangulates Pakistan, India and Bangladesh and three key leaders of these countries: Z.A. Bhutto, Indira Gandhi and Sheikh Mujibur Rahman. The book interweaves the stories of these three leaders to create a historical narrative that is 'South Asian'. Not narrowly defined by the nationalist histories of Pakistan, India or Bangladesh, the book will appeal to the public in all three countries as well to specialists in South Asia and across the globe.'

—Matthew A. Cook, PhD
Bestselling Author,
President, American Institute of Pakistan Studies,
Professor of Postcolonial and South Asian Studies,
Department of History,
North Carolina Central University,
North Carolina, USA.

'At a time when populist politics are sweeping much of the world, Faisal Khosa explores the closely connected careers of three earlier South Asian leaders—Indira Gandhi, Zulfikar Ali Bhutto and Sheikh Mujibur Rahman—whose populist legacies still resonate across the region as a whole. His accessible, joined-up reassessment challenges the image of a deeply divided subcontinent by drawing attention to what India, Pakistan and Bangladesh have in common as far as their respective political histories are concerned.'

—Sarah Ansari
Bestselling Author,
Professor of Department of History,
Royal Holloway University of London,
Egham, United Kingdom.

'Faisal Khosa's book is smartly written and makes for very enjoyable reading. The focus on assassinated leaders in India, Pakistan and Bangladesh turns out to be an ideal way to introduce the politics and cultures of South Asia. I foresee Making of Martyrs being widely read by those interested in South Asia and being widely adopted in comparative politics and South Asia courses (I will use Faisal Khosa's book in my Politics of South Asia courses). The book is a highly significant work.'

—**Christopher Candland**
Bestselling Author,
Associate Professor of Department of Political Science,
Director, South Asia Studies Program,
Wellesley College, Wellesley,
Massachusetts, USA.

'Three national leaders who redefined postcolonial South Asia. Three tragic figures who met with unnatural death. Beyond the individual role and the intertwined destinies of Zulfikar Ali Bhutto, Indira Gandhi and Sheikh Mujibur Rahman, Faisal Khosa recaptures with talent and insight the tense times of the 1970s and the 1980s, which saw not just the South Asia map redrawn, but also challenged the nature and continuity of democracy in the subcontinent.'

—**Jean-Luc Racine, PhD**
Bestselling Author,
Emeritus CNRS Senior Fellow at the Centre for South Asian Studies,
Centre for South Asian Studies,
School for Advanced Studies in Social Sciences,
Paris, France.

'I am sure it will win many classroom adoptions as a key text on an important subject.'

—**Edmund Burke**
Bestselling Author,
Professor Emeritus,
Research Professor of History,
Founding Director of Center for World History,
University of California Santa Cruz,
California, USA.

'Lucidly written and well-documented, this book captures not only the political biographies of the three pivotal leaders of South Asia but also sheds valuable light on the politics of India, Pakistan, and Bangladesh during the watershed period from the 1960s through the 1980s.'

—**Habibul Haque Khondker, PhD**
Bestselling Author,
Professor of Social Sciences,
Zayed University,
Abu Dhabi, United Arab Emirates.

'Faisal Khosa's comparative analysis of three most important leaders of modern South Asian history—Indira Gandhi, Sheikh Mujibur Rahman and Zulfiqar Ali Bhutto—not only shows their similarities and differences but also reveals how their policies have shaped the contemporary political milieu. He has weaved a story that is gripping and informative, at once. This book deserves attention of anyone interested in understanding South Asian politics.'

—**Riaz Ali, PhD**
Bestselling Author,
Distinguished Professor of Political Science,
Illinois State University, USA.

'Kudos to Faisal Khosa for penning a remarkably well-researched and illuminating book about three dynamic political leaders of Bangladesh, India and Pakistan. Their followers held them up on a pedestal and literally worshipped them. Their critics portrayed them as power-hungry, ruthless and tyrannical leaders. It's a must-read for anyone interested in historical facts and the indelible mark these three contemporaries left. The reader will be informed about the "truth" and find much to ponder over.'

—**Sanjiv Chopra, MD, MACP**
Bestselling Author,
Professor of Medicine,
Harvard Medical School,
Massachusetts, USA.

# MAKING OF MARTYRS IN INDIA, PAKISTAN AND BANGLADESH: INDIRA, BHUTTO AND MUJIB

To my parents for instilling the belief that
anything is possible.
To Sabeen, Rania, Mikyle & Nyle for making
everything possible.

I would like to thank everyone on the Bloomsbury India
team who have supported me throughout this process and
a special thanks to Paul Vinay Kumar,
my ever patient Publisher.

# Making of Martyrs in India, Pakistan and Bangladesh: Indira, Bhutto and Mujib

## DR FAISAL KHOSA

# BLOOMSBURY

NEW DELHI • LONDON • OXFORD • NEW YORK • SYDNEY

BLOOMSBURY INDIA
Bloomsbury Publishing India Pvt. Ltd
Second Floor, LSC Building No. 4, DDA Complex, Pocket C – 6 & 7,
Vasant Kunj, New Delhi 110070

BLOOMSBURY, BLOOMSBURY INDIA and the Diana logo are trademarks of
Bloomsbury Publishing Plc

First published in India 2021
This edition published 2021

ISBN: HB: 978-93-88630-84-9; ebook: 978-93-88630-86-3

2 4 6 8 10 9 7 5 3 1

Typeset in Sabon LT Std by Manipal Technologies Limited
Printed and bound in India by Thomson Press India Ltd.

To find out more about our authors and books visit www.bloomsbury.com and
sign up for our newsletters

# ZULFIKAR ALI BHUTTO

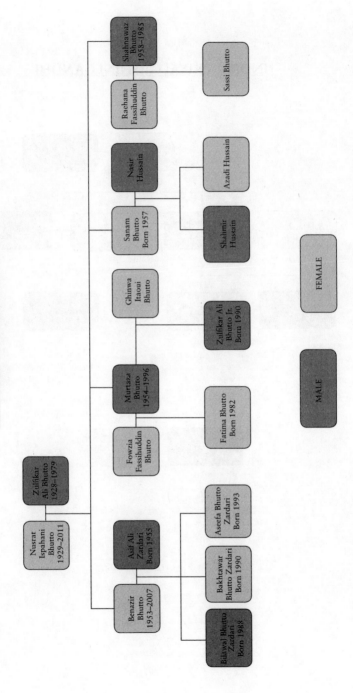

# INDIRA PRIYADARSHINI GANDHI

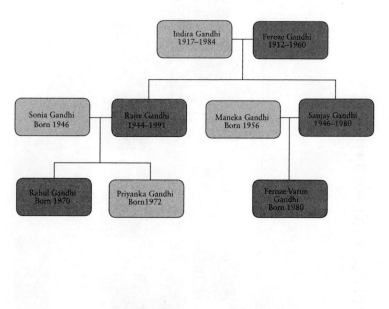

# SHEIKH MUJIBUR RAHMAN

```
                                    Sheikh
                                    Mujibur
                                    Rahman
                                   1920–1975
                    Sheikh
                    F. Mujib
                   1927–1975

Sheikh Russel          Shafiq Siddiq      Sheikh Rehana      Sheikh Jamal      Sheikh Kamal       Sultana Kamal      M.A. Wazed        Sheikh Hasina
1964–1975                                  Born 1957         1954–1975         1949–1975          1952–1975          Miah              Wazed Born 1947
                                                                                                                    1967–2009

                      Tulip                Radwan                                                                    Saima Wazed        Sajeeb
                      Rizwana              Munib                                                                     Hossain            Ahmed
                      Siddiq               Siddiq                                                                    Born 1972          Wazed
                                                                                                                                       Born 1971
```

FEMALE

MALE

# TIMELINE

- The partition of the Indian subcontinent and subsequent independence of Pakistan (14 August 1947) and India (15 August 1947)
- First Indo-Pak War: 1947–1948
- Mohandas Karamchand Gandhi's assassination: 30 January 1948
- Muhammad Ali Jinnah's death: 11 September 1948
- Second Indo-Pak War: 1965
- Third Indo-Pak War: 1971
- Bangladesh's independence (separation from Pakistan): 16 December 1971. What was known as East Bengal at the time of Independence, in 1947, was renamed East Pakistan in 1954, and it later became Bangladesh in 1971.
- Mujib's assassination: 15 August 1975
- Bhutto's hanging (judicial murder): 4 April 1979
- Indira Gandhi's assassination: 31 October 1984

# CONTENTS

*To an extent, leadership is like beauty: It is hard to define, but you know it when you see it.*

—Warren Bennis[1]

| | | |
|---|---|---|
| *Preface* | | xix |
| *Introduction* | | 1 |
| 1 | Individual Leader's Personality, Politics and Leadership Style | 3 |
| 2 | The History of Independence of India and Pakistan | 23 |
| 3 | Mujib's Rise to Power; Bhutto's Rise to Power | 44 |
| 4 | Pakistan's and India's General Elections: The Lead-up to War | 66 |
| 5 | Bengali Liberation Movement Leading to Third Indo-Pak War | 105 |
| 6 | Welcoming the Enemy: Meetings Between Bhutto, Mujib and Indira | 141 |
| 7 | Resolving the Differences and Getting Along | 160 |
| 8 | How the Mighty Fall: Downfall and Martyrdom | 182 |
| *Epilogue* | | 209 |
| *Bibliography* | | 211 |

[1] Will Yakowicz, 'Lessons from Leadership Guru Warren Bennis,' *Inc.,* 4 August 2014, https://www.inc.com/will-yakowicz/7-leadership-lessons-from-late-warren-bennis.html (accessed 10 May 2019).

# PREFACE

*Making of Martyrs in India, Pakistan and Bangladesh: Indira, Bhutto and Mujib* examines the influence and controversies surrounding three leaders—Indira Gandhi (1917–1984), Zulfikar Ali Bhutto (1928–1979) and Sheikh Mujibur Rahman (1920–1975)—and their legacies, which continue to fuel political animosities to this day. What is perhaps most interesting are the conflicting stories and accounts of their political roles. Depending on whom one asks, there is always a unique 'Indian', 'Pakistani' and 'Bengali' version of the story, and each story has its own protagonist(s) and antagonists.

This book seeks to connect each of these versions and attempts to provide—for arguably the first time—an individual-focused, unabridged and objective political portrait of the three leaders. Drawing on the proverb 'Let him who is without sin cast the first stone', I have refrained from making judgements on their private lives and have intentionally steered clear of discussing their personal failings or family lives, except when it involved incidents that related to or later influenced their politics. My aim is to reveal the political individual in each of these legendary figures as well as compare, contrast and shed light on their roles in shaping the history of their respective nations.

# INTRODUCTION

Three elected leaders of the erstwhile Indian subcontinent have left indelible marks on its politics, and though decades have passed since their deaths, their names still hold political clout. Each of these leaders was tactical and strategic in their rise to power. In other words, they knew how to play the right cards at the right time. Indira Gandhi, Zulfikar Ali Bhutto and Sheikh Mujibur Rahman have been simultaneously loved and hated in equal measure. Their followers, admirers and loyal supporters have idolised and romanticised them, turning them into objects of pathos—remembered as heroes and martyrs. In the eyes of their critics, they were ruthless, power-hungry tyrants—partisan villains who left dark marks on their nations' histories.

The relative nature of public opinion is evident within this historical narrative where the line between reality and misapprehension can be imperceptible and can even change over time. This book, therefore, will work through these conflicting accounts and diametrically opposed opinions in a way that will allow room for its readers to draw their own conclusions. The concept of a complete and objective truth is illusory, clouded by ambivalent evidence and biased perceptions. Our knowledge of any past event can never be complete, for obvious reasons, even if we were at its epicentre. There are at least two sides to every story and the reality of what transpired changes with individual expectations and experience.

This book examines the populist leaders of India, Pakistan and Bangladesh—Indira Gandhi, Zulfikar Ali Bhutto and Sheikh Mujibur Rahman—and how their leadership styles influenced postcolonial nation-building in their respective countries.

# 1

## INDIVIDUAL LEADER'S PERSONALITY, POLITICS AND LEADERSHIP STYLE

*The very essence of leadership is that you have to have vision. You can't blow an uncertain trumpet.*

—Theodore Hesburgh[1]

## INDIRA GANDHI: DUMB DOLL TURNED GODDESS OF WAR

*In the age of Indira, the Indian people came of age.*

—Srinath Raghavan[2]

Also known as Mother India, Indira Gandhi[3]—the only woman prime minister in Indian history until now—is referred to as the 'Iron Lady' of India. To quote journalist Oriana Fallaci, 'Many people didn't like her. And they called her arrogant, cynical, ambitious, ruthless. They accused her of ideological inconsistency, of demagoguery, of playing a double game. Many, on the other hand, liked her to the

---

[1] BrainyQuote, 'Theodore Hesburgh Quotes', https://www.brainyquote.com/quotes/theodore_hesburgh_126341 (accessed 10 May 2019).

[2] Srinath Raghavan, 'Indira Gandhi: India and the World in Transition' in Ramachandra Guha edited, *Makers of Modern Asia* (Cambridge: Harvard University Press, 2014), 217.

[3] It should be noted that Indira's last name was taken from her marriage to Feroze Gandhi; neither Indira nor Feroze was related to Mohandas Karamchand Gandhi aka Mahatma Gandhi.

point of falling in love with her... They called her strong, courageous, generous, brilliant.'[4]

Indira Gandhi was the second-longest serving prime minister, after her father Jawaharlal Nehru—the first prime minister of an independent India. Indira served as the prime minister from 1966 to 1977, and then again from 1980 until her assassination in 1984. She is known not only for downright dominating both the Congress party and the Indian Parliament but also for ushering in the culture of political populism in Indian politics.[5]

## Indira's Early Life and Background

Unlike Zulfikar Ali Bhutto and Sheikh Mujibur Rahman, Indira Gandhi had been in the political spotlight since birth. Born on 19 November 1917, Indira Priyadarshini Nehru was the only child of Jawaharlal Nehru.

Indira's exposure to politics at a rather young age influenced her greatly. As a child, while playing, she would divide her dolls into two teams—'freedom fighters' and 'bad guys'. She would stage confrontations between these two groups, with the freedom fighters defeating their opponents each time. Her role model was Joan of Arc and just like her, Indira, too, wanted to lead her people to freedom. She treated the various challenges in her life as blessings and used them to learn resourcefulness, self-reliance and resilience.[6]

Indira's family's involvement in national politics had an adverse effect on many aspects of her life, especially childhood. Her formal education suffered greatly due to

---

[4] Oriana Fallaci, *Interview with History* (Boston: Houghton Mifflin, 1977), 153.
[5] Sourabh Singh, 'Unraveling the Enigma of Indira Gandhi's Rise in Indian Politics: A Woman Leader's Quest for Political Legitimacy', *Theory and Society* (No. 5, 2012), 479–504, www.jstor.org/stable/23263480 (accessed 25 January 2018).
[6] Oriana Fallaci, *Interview with History* (Boston: Houghton Mifflin, 1977), 172.

repeated imprisonment of her family members. In 1921, when Indira was only four years old, she accompanied her father and grandfather to Allahabad for a court hearing over their involvement in Satyagraha—the non-violent resistance and independence movement led by Mahatma Gandhi.[7] The event was Indira's first real exposure to the reality of politics. She was witness to her father and grandfather receiving a six-month prison term, an experience Indira was to relive many times.[8] A year later, Indira's family transferred her from the Allahabad Modern School to a new school, only to eventually remove her from school altogether and home-school her instead.[9] The experience at the Allahabad court affected Indira greatly. Indira's father was imprisoned a total of six times, and her mother and grandparents, too, were imprisoned several times. In one instance, a young Indira greeted a group of visitors at her home, telling them matter-of-factly, 'I'm sorry. There's no one at home. My father, mother, grandfather, grandmother, and aunt are all in prison.'[10]

## Indira's Entry into Politics and Rise to Power

Up until now, most people had regarded her gender as a weakness. Lyndon Johnson wanted to 'protect this girl'. Indira was the 'dumb doll' in Parliament. Indira's antagonist Morarji Desai once referred to her as 'this mere *chokri*' (slip of a girl). Journalists called her 'the little woman'. The public said that at least they now had a pretty face to look at on the front page of the newspaper.[11] Indira's

---

[7] Inder Malhotra, *Indira Gandhi: A Personal and Political Biography* (London: Hodder & Stoughton, 1989), 36.

[8] Ibid., 36–37.

[9] Ibid., 39.

[10] Oriana Fallaci, *Interview with History* (Boston: Houghton Mifflin, 1977), 154.

[11] Katherine Frank, *Indira: The Life of Indira Nehru Gandhi* (London: HarperCollins, 2001), 303.

transformation was brought to light during her first five years in the government—first as an information and broadcasting minister and later as prime minister. The former position earned her the demeaning nickname '*Gungi Guriya*' (dumb doll). However, within five years, Indira showed the Indian society her prolific ability and earned a new, noble moniker—'Durga', the invincible goddess of war in Hindu mythology.[12]

Indira Gandhi's political career took off while her father was the prime minister of India. She joined the Congress party's working committee in 1955 and was elected as its president in 1959. Following her father's death in 1964, Indira was appointed as a minister of information and broadcasting as part of Prime Minister Lal Bahadur Shastri's cabinet. It is alleged that one of the main reasons Indira accepted the cabinet portfolio was because of her need for a salary.[13] As a minister, Indira made more of an impact outside her ministry's jurisdiction than inside. During the language riots in Madras, in 1965, she hopped onto a plane to Madras to assure those protesting against the Hindi language and helped restore peace. Indira was in the midst of another controversy in Kashmir in August 1965. Ostensibly, she flew to Srinagar on 8 August for a holiday even as she was aware of the volatile situation in Kashmir. She was urged to take the next flight back to Delhi but she refused. Not only did she stay back, she even flew to the battlefront when hostilities broke out between Indian and Pakistani forces at the start of the 1965 Indo-Pak War. She told a crowd in Srinagar, 'We shall not give an inch of our territory to the aggressor.' This bravado enthralled the Indian press, which

---

[12] Biography.com, 'Indira Gandhi Biography', http://www.biography.com/people/indira-gandhi-9305913 (accessed 29 December 2016).

[13] Ramchandra Guha, *Makers of Modern Asia* (Cambridge: Harvard University Press, 2014), 220.

acclaimed her as 'the only man in a cabinet of old women'.[14] These actions showcased that Indira would not shy away from controversy or life-threatening situations.

It was Shastri's sudden death two years later, in January 1966, that provided a golden opportunity to Indira. It opened up the door for her to what would eventually become a magnificent expedition towards power—a journey that would sadly end with her death. Indira is best remembered in South Asia for her role in the dismemberment of Pakistan when in 1971 she supported and facilitated the Bengali freedom fighters and approved military incursions in East Pakistan in support of the Bengali Liberation War. During her reign, India achieved self-sufficiency in agricultural production as well as made significant advancements in nuclear and space technology.[15]

## Indira's Politics and Leadership Style

> My father was a statesman. I am a political woman.
> My father was a saint. I am not.
> —Indira Gandhi[16]

In the words of biographer Pupul Jayakar:

> There was something special in the manner in which Indira
> Gandhi confronted a major crisis. As the assault against
> her increased in velocity, she instinctively avoided any
> reflexive reaction... [waiting] till the energy of the attack
> had abated and her opponents felt a false sense of security...

[14] Katherine Frank, *Indira: The Life of Indira Nehru Gandhi* (London: HarperCollins, 2001), 281.

[15] Sourabh Singh, 'Unraveling the Enigma of Indira Gandhi's Rise in Indian Politics: A Woman Leader's Quest for Political Legitimacy', *Theory and Society* (No. 5, 2012), 479–504.

[16] BrainyQuote, 'Indira Gandhi Quotes', https://www.brainyquote.com/quotes/indira_gandhi_389576 (accessed 30 April 2019).

*[nonetheless], her ears were open... She observed people's faces, their glances, their gestures... [and] when the time was right, she struck when [a blow] was least expected.*17

As a politician, Indira Gandhi was anything but ordinary and predictable. She was a trailblazer and a trendsetter, being the first woman in the subcontinent to assume a top political position, that too more than once. While Bhutto and Mujib were master orators skilled in rhetoric, Indira, in contrast, could captivate her audience with mere silence.

In September 1960, Indira's husband Feroze Gandhi suffered a fatal heart attack at 48 years of age. Married since 1942, she and Feroze had their share of marital disagreements and were parents of two young children. Although she recalled his death as one of 'the saddest days of her life',[18] Indira did not let it get in the way of her political aspirations and continued on her political journey. She proved to be more than just 'Nehru's daughter'. Her critics often overlook the fact that, despite her admiration for her father's politics, Indira did not blindly follow in his footsteps—both before and after assuming power. In reality, Indira was quick to express criticism towards many of her father's policies of reconciliation, accommodation and compromise. At the height of the language movement of the 1950s, she wrote to her father:

*[You] are tending more and more to accept almost without question, the opinions of certain people with regard to certain parts of the country. Morarjibhai for Bombay, Gujerat, Maharashtra etc, Bidhan Babu for Bengal, Bihar, Kamaraj for Tamilnad. These are very fine men and our top*

---

[17] Pupul Jayakar, *Indira Gandhi: An Intimate Biography* (New York: Pantheon Books, 1992), 207.

[18] Inder Malhotra, *Indira Gandhi: A Personal and Political Biography* (London: Hodder & Stoughton, 1989), 71.

*leaders, but no one is big enough or detached enough to be the only word on matters of their area.*[19]

Indira took this sentiment further during the Kerala crisis (1957–1959) when she wrote to a friend that her father was 'incapable of dictatorship or roughshodding over the views of his senior colleagues'.[20] According to one of her close colleagues, Indira identified her father's 'weakness' as his 'virtuousness', and that she was resolute not to be held back by similar qualities—by 'what she called public-school morality'.[21] Unlike her father, Indira reportedly 'did not mind her critics calling her amoral and ruthless'.[22]

## ZULFIKAR ALI BHUTTO—PAKISTAN'S JOHN F. KENNEDY

> *Zulfikar Ali Bhutto was a political phenomenon. In a country where the majority of politicians have been indistinguishable, grey and quick to compromise, he stalked among them as a Titan.*
>
> —Salman Taseer[23]

Zulfikar Ali Bhutto (1928–1979), also known as *Quaid-e-Awam*—leader of the masses—was the founding father of Pakistan People's Party (PPP), the fourth president of Pakistan (1971–1973) and the ninth prime minister of Pakistan (1973–1977). Educated at the University of Southern California, the University of California, Berkeley

---

[19] Srinath Raghavan, 'Indira Gandhi: India and the World in Transition' in Ramachandra Guha edited, *Makers of Modern Asia* (Cambridge: Harvard University Press, 2014), 221–22.

[20] Ibid., 222.

[21] P. N. Dhar, *Indira Gandhi, the 'Emergency', and Indian Democracy* (New York, New Delhi: Oxford University Press, 2000), 123.

[22] Ibid.

[23] Salmaan Taseer, *Bhutto: A Political Biography* (London: Ithaca Press, 1979), 3.

and Oxford University, Bhutto remains an essential part of the history of Pakistan.

Bhutto's political ingenuity was unparalleled in Pakistani politics, where he sat staunch and unwavering. His ultimate desire was to unite and empower the dispossessed and marginalised communities in Pakistan against the ruthless exploitation they had endured under corrupt politics and leadership. In December 1967, he announced the creation of PPP and proclaimed, 'Islam is our faith, democracy is our polity and socialism is our economy, and all power to the people.' In fact, in its election campaign in 1970, PPP promised *'roti, kapra aur makaan'* (food, clothing and shelter) to all Pakistanis if it came into power.[24] Although noble in theory, it was a radical vision that paved the path to Bhutto's execution.[25] It is evident that Bhutto's influence as a politician has extended to this day, with his simultaneous legacy and infamy affecting government actors. Therefore, it is not surprising that there is no consensus on his role in Pakistani society. Depending on who is asked, he is either a legendary and heroic figure or a reviled antagonist. Despite his polarising personality, Henry Kissinger described him as 'undoubtedly the most brilliant man in Pakistani politics'.[26]

Bhutto was a member of one of the wealthiest and most powerful families in Sindh[27] that held strong ties with similar, influential families of Karachi in Pakistan as well as the Middle East.[28] Italian journalist Oriana Fallaci compared Bhutto's background to that of former US president John F. Kennedy, saying, '[He] reminds you of

---

[24] Zulfikar Ali Bhutto popularised this slogan ahead of Pakistan's general elections in 1970.

[25] Fatima Bhutto, *Songs of Blood and Sword: A Daughter's Memoir* (New York: Nation Books, 2010), 54.

[26] Henry Kissinger, *The White House Years* (Boston: Little, Brown and Co., 1979), 851

[27] Spelled 'Sind' prior to 1980.

[28] Salmaan Taseer, *Bhutto: A Political Biography* (London: Ithaca Press, 1979), 35.

John Kennedy. Like Kennedy, [Bhutto] grew up in the kind of wealth for which nothing is impossible, not even the conquest of political power, cost what it may. Like Kennedy, he had a comfortable, happy, privileged childhood. Like Kennedy, he began his rise to power very early.'[29] Bhutto was also graced with charm and good looks, and that allowed him to garner power.

Upon completing his education abroad, Bhutto returned to Karachi in 1953 and started legal practice at the Sindh High Court. Bhutto's Oxford and Berkeley education provided him with 'the right intellectual equipment'[30] with which to weave himself into Pakistani society. Though he had been trained as a lawyer, Bhutto had little, if any, interest in practising law. As a young man, Bhutto easily built connections with the Pakistani elite. Speaking fluent Sindhi, a provincial language, he mixed in naturally with old family friends and politicians[31] by exuding charm, grace and eloquence. A family friend recalls, '[Bhutto] was good-looking in rather a sensuous way, always very polite and courteous and seeming to know the correct things to say at all occasions.' Another recalls, '[Bhutto made] it a point to seek out senior politicians and to be excessively attentive to them.'[32] These skills positioned Bhutto favourably in his future reaches for power.

Historians have argued that Bhutto was supremely confident and his 'ego was of cosmic proportions'.[33] In this context, the Bhutto theme is separated into two balancing entities—the angry young politician with a jingoistic sense of nationalism and justice of the pre-Simla Summit time and the peace-seeking statesman of post-Simla days trying

---

[29] Oriana Fallaci, *Interview with History* (Boston: Houghton Mifflin, 1977), 184
[30] Salmaan Taseer, *Bhutto: A Political Biography* (London: Ithaca Press, 1979), 36.
[31] Ibid., 36.
[32] Ibid., 35.
[33] Inder Malhotra, *Indira Gandhi: A Personal and Political Biography* (London: Hodder & Stoughton, 1989), 252.

to resolve intractable problems with skilful diplomacy, persuasion and accommodation.[34] Anthony Howard, writing of him in the *New Statesman*, London, said 'arguably the most intelligent and plausibly the best read of the world's rulers'.[35] His formal and informal education helped him garner the art and science of eloquent speech with which he could win intellectual debates, political discussions and also the hearts and minds of the audience in public forums.[36] Bhutto entered national politics in Pakistan in 1958 at the age of 31 and despite his superior intellect, dazzling way with words and close relationships with the elite in positions of power, Bhutto's appointment as minister of commerce was neither unique nor due to personal character. Rather, it was the 'considered decision' of Iskander Mirza, which led to Bhutto's achievement of this political milestone.[37]

Despite his professed loyalties to Mirza, Bhutto was not the one to bank on his relationships with only one person. When General Ayub Khan ousted Mirza through a subsequent coup and assumed presidency on 27 October 1958, Khan created his own cabinet of technocrats, diplomats and military officers, which included Bhutto as a cabinet minister.[38] Bhutto wasted no time in gaining Ayub Khan's trust and respect. This particular cabinet position would turn out to be much more fruitful for Bhutto, who would eventually go on to become one of Ayub Khan's most trusted allies. It was this very connection that would catapult Bhutto's blossoming political career into the upper echelons of their national government.

---

[34] Kamaleshwar Sinha, *Zulfikar Ali Bhutto: Six Steps to Summit* (Delhi: Indian School Supply Depot, Publication Division, 1972), 10.

[35] Salmaan Taseer, *Bhutto: A Political Biography* (London: Ithaca Press, 1979), 3.

[36] Kamaleshwar Sinha, *Zulfikar Ali Bhutto: Six Steps to Summit* (Delhi: Indian School Supply Depot, Publication Division, 1972), 36.

[37] Inder Malhotra, *Indira Gandhi: A Personal and Political Biography* (London: Hodder & Stoughton, 1989), 252.

[38] General Ayub Khan retained Bhutto as the minister of commerce.

## Bhutto's Personality and Leadership Style

> *I have learnt that if one is to become a successful politician, one has to live by a profitable absence of scruples. We have to do what others do to us, but we must do it before the others have the opportunity.*
>
> —Bhutto[39]

The influence of Bhutto as an individual has been well documented by journalists and political leaders alike. Upon interviewing Bhutto in 1972, Oriana Fallaci—who had interviewed several well-known international political leaders of that era, including Indira Gandhi and Sheikh Mujibur Rahman—wrote, '[Bhutto] is undoubtedly one of the most complex leaders of our time… Anyone will tell you there is no alternative to Bhutto. If Bhutto goes, Pakistan will be erased from the map.'[40] His influence on Pakistani politics is evident—he was essentially equated with the nation's strength and stability.

In 1971, Bhutto had the honour of becoming the first civilian to assume the position of president (fourth) of Pakistan and the only civilian chief martial law administrator to date. Later, following changes to the Constitution, he served as its first elected prime minister (ninth). While in office, he did much to strengthen Pakistani nationalism and national identity and introduced a series of social, constitutional and economic reforms. He was the architect of the 1973 Constitution, in which Bhutto declared bluntly to the world that Pakistan was, and always had been, 'an Islamic state'.[41] However, Bhutto was ousted by a military coup and executed for conspiring to murder a political rival.

---

[39] https://www.thenewstribe.com/2016/01/05/rare-facts-and-photos-of-bhutto/ (last accessed 30 April 2019).

[40] Oriana Fallaci, *Interview with History* (Boston: Houghton Mifflin, 1977), 183.

[41] Christophe Jaffrelot and Gillian Beaumont, *A History of Pakistan and its Origins* (London: Anthem Press, 2002), 11.

In the words of Oriana Fallaci:

*The more you study [Bhutto], the more you remain uncertain, confused. Like a prism turning on a pivot, he is forever offering you a different face, and at the same moment that he gives in to your scrutiny, he withdraws. So you can define him in countless ways, and all of them are true: liberal and authoritarian, fascist and communist.*[42]

In 1965, 14 years before Bhutto's execution, Sir Morrice James, a former British high commissioner to Pakistan (1961–1965), stated that 'Despite his gifts, I judged that one day Bhutto would destroy himself… Bhutto was born to be hanged.'[43] Sir James, like many others who had followed Bhutto's political career—whether out of genuine interest or sheer entertainment—had 'predicted' and foreshadowed Bhutto's downfall. Most people who met Bhutto interpreted him as either an 'extraordinary and captivating leader' or slated him as an 'unethical manipulator'. Sir James offered a more nuanced account, stating:

*Bhutto certainly had the right qualities for reaching [political] heights—drive, charm, imagination, a quick and penetrating mind, zest for life, eloquence, energy, a strong constitution, a sense of humour and a thick skin… [but his flaws were his 'ruthlessness' and 'capacity for ill-doing']… there was, how – shall I put it? – the rank odour of hellfire about him. It was a case of* corruptio optimi pessima *[the corruption of what is best is the worst tragedy]. He was a Lucifer, a fallen angel. I believe that at heart he lacked a sense of the dignity and value of other people; his own self was what counted.*[44]

---

[42] Oriana Fallaci, *Interview with History* (Boston: Houghton Mifflin, 1977), 183.

[43] Nauman Asghar, 'ZAB–An assessment', *The Nation*, 10 April 2015, http://nation.com.pk/columns/10-Apr-2015/zab-an-assessment (accessed 26 May 2016).

[44] Ibid.

This summary illustrates the complex and aggressive nature of Bhutto's politics. His populist politics would ultimately lead to his downfall and eventual execution. During his reign, however, Pakistan developed lasting close relations with China as well as with Muslim nations of the Middle East. He also was the pioneer of Pakistan's nuclear programme.

## Bhutto's Politics and Presidency

Bhutto was a nationalist and socialist who hoped to see the instalment of parliamentary democracy in Pakistan. His democratic socialist platform appealed to the poor, to students and to the working classes. One of the earliest examples of Bhutto's nationalist sentiment was his response to the theft of an invaluable Islamic artefact from a mosque in the Indian-administered territory of Kashmir. Between 28 and 29 December 1963, violent riots had broken out across Srinagar, the summer capital of the northernmost state of Jammu and Kashmir, after a sacred relic associated with Holy Prophet Muhammad (peace be upon him) was stolen from its resting place.[45] Mr Bhutto, the Pakistan foreign minister, alleged on 1 January 1964 that the theft of the relic had been "permitted by the Indian occupation authorities and their puppets as part of India's plan to reduce the Moslem majority in Jammu and Kashmir to a minority, by bringing home to its Moslem population the feeling that the lives, honour and religion of Muslims are not safe, and that therefore they must leave the state".[46]

## SHEIKH MUJIBUR RAHMAN: MAO ZEDONG OF

[45] *The Chicago Tribune,* 'Moslems Riot Over Theft of Sacred Relic', 29 December 1963, http://archives.chicagotribune.com/1963/12/29/page/1/article/moslems-riot-over-theft-of-sacred-relic (accessed 31 October 2016).

[46] Keesing's research report (9), *Pakistan from 1947 to the Creation of Bangladesh* (New York: Charles Scribner's Sons, 1973), 51.

## BANGLADESH

> *I have not seen the Himalayas. But I have seen Sheikh*
> *Mujib. In personality and in courage, this man is*
> *the Himalayas. I have thus had the experience of*
> *witnessing the Himalayas.*
>
> —Fidel Castro[47]

Sheikh Mujibur Rahman (1920–1975)—known colloquially as Sheikh Mujib or Mujib and also known as *bangabandhu* (friend of Bengal)—is best remembered as the founding father of Bangladesh. In 1949, he co-founded the Awami (People's) League, which advocated for the autonomy of East Bengal (later renamed East Pakistan). He led the Awami League to an unparalleled victory in the 1970 general elections, but was imprisoned by the Pakistani military regime in 1971 when civil war broke out the same year. This was the war that led to East Pakistan being separated and renamed Bangladesh. Following his release from prison, Mujib served as the head of state of the provisional government of Bangladesh and later became the prime minister of the country in 1972. On 15 August 1975, renegade army officers assassinated Mujib—and most of his family—during a military coup. Nearly half a century since his death, Bangladeshi society remains divided over his role in the country's history.

## Mujib's Background and Formative Years

While Bhutto and Indira came from affluent, politically influential families, Mujib had a modest upbringing. Born on 17 March 1920 in the village of Tungipara in

---

[47] *The Daily Star,* 'I haven't seen Himalayas but have seen Sheikh Mujib: Castro in 1973', 26 November 2016, http://www.thedailystar.net/politics/i-havent-seen-himalayas-have-seen-sheikh-mujib-castro-1973-1320706 (accessed 7 April 2019).

Bengal, then under the British Raj, he was the third child of a family of four daughters and two sons. As a child, Mujib suffered from several illnesses, one of which was beriberi (vitamin B1 deficiency) that afflicted his heart. As a teenager, he also developed glaucoma that significantly compromised his eyesight.[48]

At an early age, he displayed the qualities that would make him a central figure in the politics of the Indian subcontinent. One was an energetic social conscience, another a paramount passion for politics.[49] Mujib first developed an interest in political activism in 1939 while studying at Gopalganj Missionary School as an intermediate student.[50] During this time, he began attending meetings of the Swadeshi Movement—a political movement that, amongst other things, opposed the British government's decision to divide Bengal into East Bengal (part of Pakistan) and West Bengal, which remained part of India after the Partition in 1947. It was here that Mujib experienced first-hand the suffering, subjugation and exploitation of Bengali people under British colonisers. This experience turned him into a rebel. In 1943, Mujib was elected as councillor of the Muslim League—a representative political organisation of Muslims in the Indian subcontinent.

Mujib became progressively politically active as a member of the All Bengal Muslim Students' League. Later, as a student leader, he rose swiftly within the ranks of the Awami League as a charismatic and persuasive orator. Mujib made speeches supporting the Lahore Resolution, specifically the clause asserting that there were to be 'two Pakistans'—one comprising the Bengal and Assam regions (East Bengal)

[48] Mujibur Sheikh Rahman, *The Unfinished Memoirs* (Karachi: Oxford University Press, 2012), 7.

[49] Anthony Mascarenhas, *Bangladesh: A Legacy of Blood* (London: Hodder & Stoughton, 1986), 12.

[50] Mujibur Sheikh Rahman, *The Unfinished Memoirs* (Karachi: Oxford University Press, 2012), 8.

and the other comprising the Punjab, Balochistan, Frontier Province and Sindh (West Pakistan).[51] Mujib interpreted the Lahore Resolution as stating that East Pakistan and West Pakistan were to be two separate, independent sovereign nations. This was an interpretation that he would later defend vehemently.

In 1947, upon receiving a Bachelor of Arts degree from Islamia College in Kolkata, Mujib became active in preventing the communal riots that broke out in the wake of the partition of the Indian subcontinent. He played a crucial role in protecting fellow Muslims and containing the violence during this volatile period.

## Mujib's Politics and Leadership Style

> When you play with gentlemen, you play like a
> gentleman. But when you play with bastards, make
> sure you play like a bigger bastard. Otherwise you will
> lose.
>
> —Sheikh Mujibur Rahman[52]

Leading up to the Partition in 1947, Mujib had been a strong supporter of Muslim independence. He believed that if Muslims did not create an independent nation, they would be wiped out under the ethnic and religious majorities of India, which comprised primarily of Hindus. An advocate of socialism, Mujib became popular for his opposition to the ethnic and institutional discrimination against Bengalis in the new State of Pakistan. He believed that capitalism was an instrument of oppression used to subjugate, deprive and exploit the working classes. According to Mujib, 'As long as capitalism remained the means of the economic

[51] Ibid., 23.
[52] Anthony Mascarenhas, *Bangladesh: A Legacy of Blood* (London: Hodder & Stoughton, 1986), 5.

order, people all over the world [would] continue to be oppressed.'[53] Anthony Mascarenhas, who was a Pakistani journalist and knew Mujib very well, described his charisma in the following words:

> *Mujib's great strength—and success—lay in an elemental*
> *ability to fathom the full measure of his people's emotions*
> *and to arouse and articulate them with resounding eloquence.*
> *He had the fantastic ability to relate to crowds. Because of*
> *this, his opponents derided him as a rabble-rouser. However*
> *that may be, time and circumstance put a high premium on*
> *his talent and at a crucial moment he became the symbol*
> *and supreme spokesman of a gigantic human upsurge*
> *against discrimination and tyranny. For his pains Mujib was*
> *cruelly hounded, spending 11 ½ years in Pakistani prisons.*
> *Martyrdom, however, only served to enhance his image.*[54]

As a politician, Mujib was headstrong and had an indomitable will. His belief in the Bengali cause was unshakeable, and his love for Bengalis and the nation of Bangladesh was evident in all his struggles: 'As a man, what concerns mankind, concerns me. As a Bengali, I am deeply involved in all that concerns Bengalis. This abiding involvement is born of and nourished by love, enduring love, which gives meaning to my politics and to my very being.'[55]

A notable example of these characteristics was seen during a heated debate with the prime minister of East Bengal, Huseyn Shaheed Suhrawardy, in 1946, in which

---

[53] Mujibur Sheikh Rahman, *The Unfinished Memoirs* (Karachi: Oxford University Press, 2012), 237.

[54] Anthony Mascarenhas, Bangladesh: A Legacy of Blood (London: Hodder & Stoughton, 1986), 13.

[55] Mujibur Sheikh Rahman, *The Unfinished Memoirs* (Karachi: Oxford University Press, 2012).
This excerpt is from Mujib's personal diary and this text is included at the start of his book, *The Unfinished Memoirs*.

Mujib rhetorically asserted that he would 'prove to everyone that [he] was somebody'.[56]

Although Mujib maintained utmost respect for senior Muslim League leaders such as Muhammad Ali Jinnah and Huseyn Shaheed Suhrawardy, his views about junior politicians and other members of the Muslim League were quite the opposite. He believed that most of these politicians were 'influential and affluent' because of perks— land and honorary titles endowed to them by the British in return for their unfettered loyalty to the Empire. Mujib was convinced that it would not be in these politicians' best interests to break away from the laws of the imperialists since this would mean losing all the privileges bestowed upon them. Thus, from early on, his goal had been to break up old power structures and pave the way for equal, value-free representation and an elected government. However, these dreams ultimately came into conflict with Mujib's own quest for power, a detour which he himself was not prepared to deal with.

## Arrests and Relationship with the Pakistani Government

As previously explored, Mujib's steady involvement in political issues made him a well-known figure in Pakistan as well as in the broader Bengali society and politics of East Pakistan. During the 1950s, Mujib progressively rose into the upper ranks of East Pakistani politics. On 9 July 1953, he was elected as the general secretary of the East Pakistan Awami League, a political party he reorganised and transformed following the death of H. S. Suhrawardy, in December 1963.[57]

---

[56] Ibid., 30.
[57] *International Journal of Scientific and Research Publications*, Volume 4, Issue 5, May 2014, Page 3 (last accessed 3 June 2017).

In the summer of 1955, Mujib intensified his role in East Pakistani politics and became much more vocal about his criticism of the national government. In June 1955, he was elected as a member of the constituent assembly. Following his electoral success, Mujib organised a meeting of the Awami League at Paltan Maidan in Dhaka (formerly anglicised as 'Dacca', until 1982) where he put forth a 21-point programme demanding greater autonomy for East Pakistan.[58] In August 1955, Mujib told the Pakistan constituent assembly in Karachi:

> Sir, you will see that they want to use the phrase 'East Pakistan' instead of 'East Bengal'. We have demanded many times that you should use Bengal instead of East Pakistan. The word 'Bengal' has a history and tradition of its own. You can change it only after the people have been consulted. If you want to change it, we have to go back to Bengal and ask them whether they are ready to accept it. So far as the question of one unit is concerned, it can be incorporated in the constitution. Why do you want it to be taken up right now? What about the state language, Bengali? We are prepared to consider one unit with all of these things. So, I appeal to my friends on that side to allow the people to give their verdict in any way, in the form of referendum or in the form of plebiscite.[59]

Though Mujib was comprehensively involved in politics in the 1940s and 1950s, he didn't become the nation's leader until the 1970s. In the aftermath of the third Indo-Pak War, which resulted in the liberation of Bangladesh as a sovereign and independent nation, Mujib was elected as the first president of Bangladesh in 1971, and later became the first prime minister under the new parliamentary form

[58] Mujibur Sheikh Rahman, *The Unfinished Memoirs* (Karachi: Oxford University Press, 2012), XVIII.
[59] Ibid., XIX.

of government. In 1975, following a succession of natural calamities including drought and famine, and perpetual political unrest, he was assassinated during a military coup. This led to the establishment of a military government that ruled through martial law. Mujib's leadership, persistence, perseverance and personal sacrifice made Bangladesh a reality.

## SUMMARY

There are many parallels among the three figures that are profiled here. Apart from their mannerisms and personal attributes, the parallels extend to their dynastic legacies and similarly unnatural and violent deaths. All the three individuals evoked strong emotions in their constituencies with their electorate either revering or reviling them. All three were big in life and metamorphed into giants in death. Each of them was the most popular leader in their respective country. Yet, none of them had a friend or a colleague they could truly rely on. Together they have made significant contributions to the present day subcontinent and played a pivotal role in the dismemberment of Pakistan in 1971, which resulted in the birth of Bangladesh (aka East Bengal and East Pakistan).

# 2

# The History of Independence of India and Pakistan

*Is life so dear, or peace so sweet, as to be purchased at the price of chains and slavery?*
*Forbid it, Almighty God! I know not what course others may take; but as for me, give me liberty or give me death!*

—Patrick Henry[1]

## THE INDIAN PARTITION MOVEMENT

The Indian subcontinent, once regarded by the British as their most valuable asset—the so-called 'Crown Jewel' of the Empire—experienced a hurried departure of the colonising forces and an even swifter transition into nationhood immediately following World War II (WWII). Moreover, it was the decisions and attitudes of past policymakers in the Indian subcontinent that planted the seeds for future conflict between India and Pakistan. These decisions had not been sensitive to the unique demography of the region—the diversity of people, cultures and histories that made up these nations. This is something that would perpetually plague the partitioned nations, ending in mistrust and eternal hostility between India and Pakistan.

---

[1] Colonial Williamsburg, 'Patrick Henry's "Give Me Liberty or Give Me Death" Speech', https://www.history.org/ almanack/life/politics/giveme.cfm (accessed 30 April 2019).

Winston Churchill, who as prime minister led Britain to victory in WWII, had always abhorred the idea and was bitterly opposed to India's Independence. Churchill's embarrassing defeat in the 1945 British elections resulted in a new government and prime minister Clement Atlee, who were in favour of India's Independence. Churchill knew the mindset of the new prime minister and mocked Atlee thus, 'He is a modest man with much to be modest about.'[2] Churchill continued with his opposition to Indian Independence and made a speech in the British Parliament on 12 December 1945 voicing concern over the proposed Indian Independence:

*In handing over the Government of India to these so-called political classes, we are handing over to men of straw of whom in a few years no trace will remain. Many have defended Britain against their foes, none can defend her against herself. But let us not add by—shameful flight, by a premature hurried scuttle—at least let us not add to the pangs of sorrow so many of us feel, the taint and smear of shame.*[3]

The end of WWII financially overdrew Britain, and India was no longer the famous storehouse of rubies and spices that had helped finance Britain's rise to world power. During the war, the British government had instead racked up colossal debts to India—more than £6 billion—as a result of soldiers it had sent to the deserts of north Africa, the boots and the parachutes produced in its factories, the maintenance and care as well as feeding of British troops battling the Japanese in Burma. After the war, the

[2] *The Telegraph,* 'From Churchill to Corbyn: the 40 most brutal British political insults', 15 March 2018, http://www.telegraph.co.uk/books/authors/the-best-british-political-insults-rows-and-putdowns/clement-attlee/ (accessed 6 June 2018).

[3] Leonard Mosley, *The Last Days of the British Raj* (London: Weidenfeld and Nicolson, 1961), 53.

THE HISTORY OF INDEPENDENCE OF INDIA AND PAKISTAN

government had to beg for a $3.75 billion loan from the United States (US); after months of difficult negotiations, the money was approved only in May 1946.[4]

Towards the end of WWII, the Indian subcontinent became a thorn and almost impossible to rule by the British Raj. Strikes were incessant and held by everybody from tram drivers and press workers to postmen and industrial workers in cotton mills, potteries and factories.[5] In 1946, there were 1,629 industrial disputes involving almost 2 million workers and a loss of nearly 12 million worker days.[6] An Indian railway strike, which would have created gridlock in the country, was only narrowly avoided. In March 1946, the military had to be called to control the situation when a police mutiny took place in Bihar, during which police officers broke open a central armoury and rampaged through towns. A similar incident in Delhi involved mutiny by over 300 police officers. Navy mutiny was another one of the frequent rebellions in India in 1946. Several nationwide anti-British protest movements took place in retaliation to firing on the naval mutineers in Bombay, Karachi and Madras. The peasant movement tried to seize control of food committees, resist the authority of wealthy food hoarders and protests against ration cuts.[7] Religious intensity and ethnic cleansing of minorities in most of the Indian cities compounded this chaos, leading to an utter collapse of law and order.

[4] Nisid Hajari, *Midnight's Furies: The Deadly Legacy of India's Partition* (Gloucestershire: Amberley Publishing Limited, 2015), 7.

[5] Sumit Sarkar, *Modern India, 1885–1947* (Delhi: Macmillan, 1983), 405–08.

[6] Amit Kumar Gupta and Nehru Memorial Museum and Library, *The Agrarian Drama: The Leftists and the Rural Poor in India, 1934–1951* (New Delhi: Manohar, 1996), 287.

[7] Yasmin Khan, *The Great Partition: The Making of India and Pakistan* (New Haven: Yale University Press, 2007), 27.

The two major organised political parties in India before Independence were Indian National Congress and All-India Muslim League. While the former was the most popular party that was created in 1885 in Bombay and had over 4.5 million members, the latter, in contrast, was founded in 1906 in Dhaka in East Bengal, which remained its headquarter till 1911 and had over 2 million members. There were 4 main architects of India's Independence: Louis Mountbatten, the last British viceroy; Mohandas Karamchand Gandhi, popularly known as Mahatma Gandhi; Muhammad Ali Jinnah, given the title of Quaid-e-Azam; and Jawaharlal Nehru, Gandhi's disciple and fellow worker. No one except Jinnah and his physician knew that Jinnah had end-stage tuberculosis and he had only months, at most two years, to live.[8] The pre-Partition movements brought with them mixed feelings of triumph and tragedy as political leaders had conflicting views about India's Independence. Mohandas Gandhi was opposed to the partition of India and repeatedly stated, 'Cut me to pieces first, then divide India.'[9] Jinnah was determined to get independence for Pakistan at any cost and his stance remained, 'We shall have either a divided India or a destroyed India.'[10]

Mountbatten took over as the last viceroy of India on 24 March 1947. He had visited India several times and had served as supreme allied commander for Southeast Asia in WWII. Mountbatten and his colleagues had not worked their way up through the hierarchy of British Raj from district to imperial capital. Therefore, his team neither suffered from the curse of knowledge of historic injustices in the Indian subcontinent nor were they familiar with the

[8] Larry Collins and Dominique Lapierre, *Freedom at Midnight* (New York: Simon and Schuster, 1975), 124.

[9] Rajmohan Gandhi, *Mohandas: A True Story of a Man, His People and an Empire* (Haryana: Penguin Books India, 2007), 435.

[10] James Lawrence, *Raj: The Making and Unmaking of British India* (London: Little, Brown & Company, 1997), 607.

anxieties and political gimmicks of its inhabitants. Upon his arrival, Mountbatten denied having landed in India with any prepared plans and road map for independence. Once he and his team were exposed to the political thought process, inflexibility and insecurities of the stakeholders, he was swiftly reconciled with the idea of the Partition. Within a month, and before he had even toured outside Delhi, he realised that India's partition was inevitable and that he had arrived on the scene too late to negotiate or alter the demand for Pakistan.[11]

The dream of a separate independent State for Muslims of India, though initially regarded as impractical and unfeasible, gained significant popularity and support amongst Muslim communities who felt marginalised under predominantly Hindu political elites. Since 1930, Muslim leaders of British India had proposed the idea of a separate Muslim nation called Pakistan (Land of the Pure). Celebrated Urdu poet-philosopher Muhammad Iqbal was amongst those leaders. Iqbal, who presided over Muslim League's meeting at Allahabad in December 1930, called for the amalgamation of Punjab, the North-West Frontier Province, Sindh and Balochistan into a single state where the Muslims of north-west India would reside. A few years later, several students, led by another student Rahmat Ali, at Cambridge University started a national movement of Pakistan, writing widely and circulating pamphlets about Pakistan as the 'Muslim Fatherland' and demanding its immediate creation as a claim based on righteousness and parity.[12]

In response to the growing separatist sentiment, the prime minister of Bengal A.K. Fazlul Huq presented the

---

[11] Yasmin Khan, *The Great Partition: The Making of India and Pakistan* (New Haven: Yale University Press, 2007), 87.

[12] Stanley A. Wolpert, *Bhutto of Pakistan: His Life and Times* (New York: Oxford University Press, 1993), 23.

Lahore Resolution which called for the creation of a group of 'independent sovereign states' for Muslims in the north-western and eastern zones of what was then British India.[13] The All-India Muslim League, in its three-day general session in Lahore, subsequently adopted the resolution on 23 March 1940. These events led to the start of an organised independence movement for a separate Muslim nation. The partition plan drawn up by Mountbatten allowed Punjabi and Bengali legislators the opportunity to vote on a potential split of the provinces of Punjab and Bengal. Additionally, a plebiscite on whether or not they would be joining Pakistan would be necessary for the North-West Frontier Province (NWFP), where a Congress ministry, geographically detached from the rest of India but firmly in favour of a united India, posed a tantalising problem.[14] To add to the complexities, the Sikh community across India felt that their interest had been entirely overlooked. The proposed settlement threatened to put their regional interests in the hands of the Muslim League.[15]

The Partition movement gained momentum in the pre-Partition general elections held in India during 1945–1946, in which over 40 million were eligible voters. The elections explored the formation of the provincial governments and initiated dialogue amongst elected officials on the future of the partition and constitutional matters.[16]

---

[13] Mujibur Sheikh Rahman, *The Unfinished Memoirs* (Karachi: Oxford University Press, 2012), 56.

At a joint convention of the Muslim League's central and provincial councils on 8 April 1946, the original Lahore Resolution was amended and the word 'states' was replaced with 'state'. Thus, the resolution evolved as a demand for a single, unified Muslim state called Pakistan. This resolution was endorsed by Huseyn Shaheed Suhrawardy who was the only Muslim League prime minister in India in 1946.

[14] Yasmin Khan, *The Great Partition: The Making of India and Pakistan* (New Haven: Yale University Press, 2007), 88.

[15] Ibid., 60.

[16] Sho Kuwajima, *Muslims, Nationalism, and the Partition: 1946 Provincial Elections in India* (University of Michigan: Manohar, 1998), 47.

The election campaign was run on the basis of religion (Hindu versus Muslim) and Pakistan (pro- or anti-Pakistan). Muslims were anxious about being subjugated if Pakistan did not become a reality; the same went for Hindus and Sikhs if Pakistan indeed did. These real and perceived threats of exploitation of minorities gave importance to religious identity and led to mass atrocities by all parties before and after the Partition. On 28 March 1946, the outcome of the election was formally announced as a result of which the Congress started governing the Central Provinces, Bombay, Madras, Uttar Pradesh (UP), Bihar, Orissa, Assam and NWFP, while the Muslim League governed Sindh and Bengal with a coalition government in Punjab.[17]

Prior to the Partition, in 1946–1947, communal riots erupted across India, accompanied by intense violence between Hindu, Muslim and Sikh communities in different provinces. This resulted in a significant loss of life and property for all Indians. The two major political leaders in British India—Mohandas Gandhi and Jinnah—issued a joint statement in response to the communal riots, condemning the violence and pleading their supporters not to participate in the uprisings. Despite their pleas, the riots continued and led to modern history's most sizeable mass migration in which over 8.5 million people relocated across the Indian subcontinent in an attempt to escape the atrocities and violence.[18]

The drawing of a boundary between the proposed States was a challenge in itself. Cyril Radcliffe, a British lawyer, was given the charge to lead the two boundary committees and arrange for the Indian Independence Act to be instated. Although he did not have prior experience or expertise with such endeavours, he was to lead the drawing of the borders

---

[17] Yasmin Khan, *The Great Partition: The Making of India and Pakistan* (New Haven: Yale University Press, 2007), 45.

[18] Keesing's research report (9), *Pakistan from 1947 to the Creation of Bangladesh* (New York: Charles Scribner's Sons, 1973), 10.

for the new States of Pakistan and India based on majority, such that as many Hindus and Sikhs remained in India and as many Muslims remained in Pakistan as possible. Radcliffe submitted his partition map on 9 August 1947 that split Punjab and Bengal almost in half. The lines weaved perilously across agricultural land, cut off communities from their sanctified pilgrimage sites, paid no heed to railway lines or the integrity of forests, and disconnected industrial plants from agricultural hinterlands where raw materials such as jute were grown. Radcliffe was aware of the contentious and unsatisfactory nature of his work and admitted as much in the final text of the partition plan itself, saying, 'I am conscious, too, that the award cannot go far towards satisfying sentiment and aspirations deeply held on either side.' The Radcliffe Line (boundary line) was ultimately revealed to the citizens of India and Pakistan on 17 August 1947, three days after the official Independence.[19]

In the weeks leading up to Independence, the majority of the princely states (565) yielded to Indian pressure, granting the right to the new national government to intervene in the matters of defence, foreign affairs and communications. In July 1947, Indian National Congress conveyed to the rulers of these princely states that it did not intend to interfere in any manner whatsoever in the domestic affairs of the states. When the pressure to accede and merge was intensified on the princely states by the new government in the summer of 1947, it caused a volatile situation in the princely states of Kashmir and Hyderabad where national allegiances were not straightforward. Hyderabad had a Muslim ruler but a clear majority of Hindus. The matter was resolved in 1948 when Nehru sent in troops to Hyderabad and ordered a takeover of the state by force.[20]

[19] Yasmin Khan, *The Great Partition: The Making of India and Pakistan* (New Haven: Yale University Press, 2007), 125–26.
[20] Ibid., 98.

Kashmir remains one of the longest-running disputes in the history of the world, with three wars fought over it between India and Pakistan, and without an amicable resolution in sight. The princely state of Jammu and Kashmir, with three quarters of its population being Muslim, was expected to join the new Muslim nation of Pakistan in August 1947. Kashmir's ruler, Maharaja Hari Singh, was a Hindu and at first, tried to keep his state independent of both the newly formed countries. But in early October 1947, Pathan tribal volunteers from Pakistan invaded Kashmir in British lorries. As these volunteers approached Srinagar, the Maharaja fled and later opted to join India. The first undeclared war had broken out and would continue to shroud Kashmir's lovely vale in smoke and induce fighting for more than a year. Governor General Jinnah had tried in vain to hurl Pakistan's entire army against the airborne Indian troops flown into Srinagar from Delhi on Governor General Mountbatten's order. British officers were still in command of the new dominions' armies and Pakistan's commander-in-chief refused to launch his force against troops under Mountbatten's command. Jinnah, having no other choice, authorised an expanded invasion by volunteer forces.[21]

A United Nations (UN) ceasefire agreement was put into effect at the start of 1949. Mountbatten and Nehru both promised a fair and impartial plebiscite after all the fighting had ceased and all the invading forces were withdrawn. Pakistan refused to order the unilateral withdrawal of the invaders as long as Indian troops remained to 'intimidate' the Kashmiris. The UN ceasefire line became a de facto border between the western third of the former unitary state of Jammu and Kashmir, called Azad (free) Kashmir by Pakistan, and the rest of the state, including the capital city of Srinagar and its vale, called Jammu and Kashmir,

[21] Stanley A. Wolpert, *Bhutto of Pakistan: His Life and Times* (New York: Oxford University Press, 1993), 63.

now a territory within India. The UN subsequently sent several of its best mediators to try and resolve the plebiscite deadlock but in vain. A token UN force of monitors remains at checkpoints along the ceasefire line.[22]

As the Independence Day drew nearer, both Nehru and Jinnah tried to dispel the fears of minorities by promising that their rights would be safeguarded in the new state. On 11 August 1947, Jinnah spoke at the opening session of Pakistan's constituent assembly:

*You are free; you are free to go to your temples, you are free to go to your mosques or any other place of worship in this State of Pakistan. You may belong to any religion or caste or creed—that has nothing to do with the business of the State... We are starting with this fundamental principle: that we are all citizens, and equal citizens, of one State... Now I think we should keep this in front of us as our ideal, and you will find that in course of time Hindus would cease to be Hindus, and Muslims would cease to be Muslims, not in the religious sense, because that is the personal faith of each individual, but in the political sense as citizens of the State.[23]*

The Pakistan constituent assembly met on 14 August 1947 in a special session at Karachi (West Pakistan) to hear a message from Viceroy Lord Mountbatten:

*I am speaking to you today as your Viceroy. Tomorrow the Government of the new Dominion of Pakistan will rest in your hands and I shall be the constitutional head of your neighbour, the Dominion of India. [...] Tomorrow two new sovereign States will take their place in the Commonwealth... [Not] immature governments or weak,*

---

[22] Ibid., 63.
[23] Jaswant Singh, *Jinnah: India, Partition, Independence* (New Delhi: Rupa Publications, 2010), 572.

*but fit to carry their great share of responsibility for the peace and progress of the world. The birth of Pakistan is an event in history... All this has been achieved with toil and sweat. I wish I could say also without tears and blood. But terrible crimes have been committed. It is justifiable to reflect, however, that far more terrible things might have happened if the majority had not proved worthy of high endeavours of their leaders, or had not listened to that great appeal which Mr. Jinnah and Mahatma Gandhi together made...*[24]

Nehru spoke to the Indian constituent assembly on the eve of Independence, stating:

*Long years ago we made a tryst with destiny, and now the time comes when we shall redeem our pledge, not wholly or in full measure, but very substantially. At the stroke of the midnight hour, when the world sleeps, India will awake to life and freedom. A moment comes, which comes but rarely in history, when we step out from the old to new, when an age ends, and when the soul of a nation, long suppressed, finds utterance... All of us, to whatever religion we may belong, are equally the children of India with equal rights, privileges and obligations... And to India, our much-loved motherland, the ancient, the eternal and the ever-new, we pay our reverent homage and we bind ourselves afresh to her service.*[25]

At midnight on 14 August 1947, the British Raj came to an end as Britain formally transferred the power to two new sovereign nations—Dominion of Pakistan and Dominion of India. However, the British government's lack of planning and haphazard attempt at the partition left the region in a

---

[24] Keesing's research report (9), *Pakistan from 1947 to the Creation of Bangladesh* (New York: Charles Scribner's Sons, 1973), 1.

[25] Sarvepalli Gopal, *Jawaharlal Nehru: A Biography* (Delhi: Oxford University Press, 2004), 362.

state of chaotic flux. The sense of insecurity heightened by mistrust and coupled with an uncertain future resulted in killing and mass migration before and after the declaration of Independence. The division of assets and liabilities between the two new nations also caused acrimonious exchanges, fuelling further mistrust.[26]

On 30 January 1948, a Hindu shot and killed Gandhi. In all the commotion, someone from the crowd shouted, 'It was a Muslim who did it!' Mountbatten, who was present at the time, had no way of knowing the killer but he did know that this rumour would start a massacre. 'You fool!' Mountbatten shouted. 'Don't you know it was a Hindu?' As it turned out, Mountbatten was right. Nine months later, Jinnah died, too, from heart failure.[27]

After the Partition, democracy in India survived and flourished even in the face of widespread instabilities, communal unrest, famine and war—the same issues which in neighbouring Pakistan and Bangladesh (after the 1971 Liberation War) turned out to be symbolic invitations for uniformed forces, namely the army, to step in and take control. India's first prime minister Jawaharlal Nehru—Indira's father—remained a central figure in Indian politics before and after Independence. He became the prime minister of an independent India in 1947 and held this high office until his death, in 1964. This uninterrupted period of more than 16 years was sufficient in strengthening democratic institutions and other administrative branches of the government. This helped India progress into a sovereign, socialist, secular and democratic republic following Independence in 1947. The political stability in India resulted in the adoption of a

---

[26] Larry Collins and Dominique Lapierre, *Freedom at Midnight* (New York: Simon and Schuster, 1975), 206–08.

[27] Jan Morris, *Farewell the Trumpets: An Imperial Retreat* (London: Faber and Faber, 1978), 493–94.

constitution within three years of its Independence, on 26 January 1950.

## THE BIRTH OF PAKISTAN AND ITS CHALLENGES

On 8 April 1946, at a joint convention of the Muslim League's central and provincial councils, the original Lahore Resolution was amended and the word 'States' was replaced with 'State'. Thus, the resolution evolved into a demand for a single, unified Muslim State called Pakistan. Huseyn Shaheed Suhrawardy of Bengal, who was the only Muslim League prime minister in India in 1946, endorsed this resolution. The hasty retreat of the British from the subcontinent, without proper deliberation for the political structure of the new countries, created a severe power vacuum in Pakistan.[28] This was further compounded by the death of its founding father, Jinnah, in 1948 and the assassination of Pakistan's first prime minister, Liaquat Ali Khan, in 1951.

Between the years of 1947–1957, Pakistan had seven prime ministers in quick succession, each authorised by the Constitution of Pakistan to complete a five-year term, but each was cut short; instead of serving for a total of 35 years, these seven prime ministers collectively served for only 10 years.[29] This rapid turnover, due to political bickering and compounded by the interference of bureaucracy and uniformed services, led to repeated disruption and perpetual political instability in Pakistan.

Further, the territorial borders and geographies of Pakistan that were established during the 1947 Partition did not correspond to existing cultural, social, religious and linguistic concentrations across the region. Multiple

---

[28] Ashok Kapur, *Pakistan in Crisis* (London: Routledge, 1991), 14.
[29] Sidrah Zaheer, 'List of Prime Ministers of Pakistan Since 1947', *Pakistan Insider*, 5 April 2012, http://insider.pk/national/list-of-prime-ministers-of-pakistan-since-1947-with-photos/ (accessed 11 September 2016).

and competing political interests cut across these borders, paving the way for new movements, leaders and ideas. Over 1,000 miles of hostile Indian territory separated the eastern and western wings of Pakistan. Beyond the geographic distance, the two regions were additionally estranged by tremendous social and cultural disparities. West Pakistan did not have cultural cohesiveness and comprised numerous ethnic groups each with its own language, while East Pakistan was unified culturally and had just one language.

The main difference between the politics in East Pakistan and West Pakistan from 1947–1971 was the socio-economic positions of the constituents. In West Pakistan, politics was more of a hobby and pastime for wealthy and influential social elites that had been awarded and rewarded by the British for their loyalty to the Empire. Politics in East Pakistan attracted the educated middle class and permeated down to the grassroots level of society. As a result, the leadership in West Pakistan was made up of aristocratic wealthy landlords and property owners, whereas people of East Pakistan (Bengalis) were led by highly educated professionals, i.e. lawyers, professors and retired officials. This was showcased in the second constituent assembly of Pakistan (1956–1958), out of 40 members from West Pakistan, 28 were property owners, whereas 20 lawyers and 9 retired officials represented East Pakistan. None of the Bengali elected officials aka members of the national assembly were aristocratic landlords or property owners.[30]

[30] Mushtaq Ahmad, *Government and Politics in Pakistan*, 1st edition, (Karachi: Pakistan Publishing House, 1959), 115.

1   India before Partition

2   India and Pakistan after Partition

In February 1948, shortly after Pakistan had gained independence, the newly installed government, to the dismay of its citizens in the eastern wing, declared Urdu the official language of the West and the East—despite Bengali-speaking people of East Pakistan being a majority linguistic group in both wings of the country. Since Urdu was only spoken in two cities—Lahore and Karachi, both in West Pakistan—the justification of Urdu as the nation's 'most commonly spoken language' or 'Islamic language' created an outcry in the eastern wing. Staying true to their region's respective linguistic traditions, the people of West Pakistan in the province of Punjab spoke Punjabi, the people in Sindh spoke Sindhi, the people in Balochistan spoke Balochi and those in NWFP spoke Pashto. Further, Bengali was the native language of more than half of the population of Pakistan. East Pakistan was home to around 55 per cent of the population, the majority of which was Bengali-speaking Hindus and Muslims.[31]

On 23 May 1948, the constituent assembly of Pakistan adopted a resolution presented by the government that proclaimed Karachi in West Pakistan as the capital of Pakistan.[32] This decision did not consider the sentiments of the people of East Pakistan who had numerical majority. The following year, the constituent assembly of Pakistan initiated preparatory work on the formulation of a constitution. The main recommendations of the first interim report of the committee, presented to the assembly on 28 September 1950, were as follows: The federal legislature would consist of the house of units (elected by the provincial legislature) and the house of people (elected by voters) and these two houses would have equal powers. The report also included

---

[31] The majority of Bengalis (Hindus and Muslims) in East Pakistan spoke Sanskrit-based Bengali.

[32] Keesing's research report (9), *Pakistan from 1947 to the Creation of Bangladesh* (New York: Charles Scribner's Sons, 1973), 14.

a number of questionable points, which the people of East Pakistan viewed with suspicion.

By 1951, the population of East Pakistan far exceeded that of West Pakistan, with Bengalis outnumbering their western counterparts by about 8.2 million.[33] The geographic divide between Pakistan's two wings was exacerbated by cultural, economic and linguistic disparities. This resulted in significant gaps and fragmentation at the political level, with no single party or organisation representing both wings' interests cohesively. East Pakistani politicians were beginning to believe that their West Pakistani counterparts were preventing their region's prosperity and treating them as a colony. The leaders in West Pakistan made active efforts to block the political participation of the East— including through actions by civilian and military leaders at the national level in order to displace duly elected Bengali governments whose concerns were incompatible with those of the dominant western elites. In effect, what were considered 'fundamental and rightful claims' in the eastern wing were perceived in the western wing as existential threats to 'core values'.[34]

The uprisings in Bengal against the British rule resulted in the latter ceasing to allocate funds to Bengal for the development of resources, which was the primary cause for the underdevelopment of infrastructure in Bengal before the partition of India. There were very few East Pakistani Bengalis in the British civil service. As far as the armed forces were concerned, Bengalis were deliberately excluded as the advent of the 1857 upheaval belonged to Bengalis in the British Indian Army. The British wanted to punish them

---

[33] Christophe Jaffrelot and Gillian Beaumont, *A History of Pakistan and its Origins* (London: Anthem Press, 2002), 20. In 1951, the population of East Pakistan was 41.9 million and the population of West Pakistan was 33.7 million.

[34] Richard Sisson and Leo E. Rose, *War and Secession: Pakistan, India, and the Creation of Bangladesh* (Berkeley: University of California Press, 1990), 9.

for their role in what they referred to as 'Sepoy Mutiny', which the South Asian nationalists christened as the first war of Independence. The British introduced the concept of martial races, changed their recruitment policy and began to recruit soldiers from areas that had helped them suppress the Mutiny—namely Punjab and the North-West Frontier.[35] This trend continued after Independence and the Pakistani rulers did not make any special efforts to attract recruitment from under-represented areas like East Pakistan.[36]

The Government of Pakistan remained the largest employer in the country after Independence. Since the Hindus and the Bengali-speaking Muslims of the eastern wing were not proficient in Urdu (declared as the national language in 1948), they experienced significant cultural hardship from 1948 onwards. Under the new federal language requirement, they faced increasing discrimination and had difficulty securing employment. They were in essence discouraged from applying for desirable government jobs. For example, although East Pakistan comprised more than 55 per cent of the country's population as well as supplied a significant part of Pakistan's foreign exchange through its export of jute, it was apparent that easterners were under-represented in all federal government positions, including uniformed forces, judiciary and civil services.

In 1956, the Pakistan Army had 894 officers in grades of major through lieutenant general and only 14 (1.6 per cent) were from East Pakistan. The total ranks of naval officers were 593 and only 40 (7.3 per cent) were from East Pakistan. The air force had 640 officers and 40 (6.3 per cent) were from East Pakistan. In 1965, out of 6,000 army officers, 300 were from East Pakistan. The officers in the navy and

---

[35] James Heitzman et al., *Bangladesh: A Country Study* (Washington: Federal Research Division, Library of Congress, 1989), 11.

[36] P.R. Chari and Pervaiz Iqbal Cheema, *The Simla Agreement 1972: Its Wasted Promise* (New Delhi: Manohar Publishers & Distributors, 2001), 95.

air force were 800 and 1,200 respectively. The percentage of East Pakistanis in the navy and air force had improved but remained a distinct minority; also, most of them were in technical or administrative positions and not in command positions. In 1969, Yahya Khan implemented a major policy change in recruitment and promotions. The recruitment of Bengalis was to be doubled and new centres were established in East Pakistan for greater visibility and publicity of the recruitment process. East Pakistan's participation, as a result, was expected to improve but it was too little too late, given the fast-approaching Bangladesh debacle.[37]

The infrastructure development, conducted during British rule in what became West Pakistan after the Partition, continued, while the underdevelopment of the eastern wing persisted. The majority province of East Pakistan, in essence, felt as if the minority in the West treated it unequally.[38] The Government of Pakistan built considerable infrastructure in West Pakistan, including roads, schools, universities and hospitals, while the East remained vastly underdeveloped. All the major government offices were occupied by West Pakistanis—even in Dhaka.

East Pakistan was also receiving much less than its fair share of development funds. During the Partition, in 1947, Muslim businesspersons from Bombay began relocating to the new capital of Karachi in the western wing. The condition worsened when Pakistan failed to follow India's devaluation of its currency in line with the sterling in 1949, thereby effectively cutting off the east wing from its traditional economy—the jute mill industry of West Bengal in India. To make matters worse, on 27 March 1955— through an ordinance by the governor general—East Bengal,

[37] James Heitzman et al., *Bangladesh: A Country Study* (Washington: Federal Research Division, Library of Congress, 1989), 207–08.
[38] Katherine Frank, *Indira: The Life of Indira Nehru Gandhi* (London: HarperCollins, 2001), 330.

at the behest of the central government, was renamed East Pakistan, in spite of ferocious opposition by the population of the eastern wing. These successive moves by the central government indicated time and again to the Bengalis that their culture and heritage were not acceptable and that they were subservient to elites in the West who formed the ruling coterie. Continuing with these trends, on 14 June 1960, the Islamabad Capital Development Authority was created in West Pakistan. Resources from both wings (east and west) of the country were expended in developing the new capital, Islamabad, in West Pakistan's Punjab Province. On 14 August 1967, Islamabad became the new capital of Pakistan.

The population and the politicians of East Pakistan felt continued subjugation and political as well as economic exploitation at the hands of the government dominated by the western wing. By 1959, economists in the provincial planning department in Dhaka reported that, on an average, East Pakistanis were 20 per cent financially worse off than their less numerous compatriots in the West. By 1968, this disparity had widened to 38 per cent.[39] In 1959–1960, the per capita income in West Pakistan was 32 per cent higher than in the East and by 1969–1970, the per capita income in the West was 61 per cent higher than in the East.[40] The year 1968 was particularly bad for East Pakistan due to the destruction of over one million tons of rice by floods as well as a significant decline in the province's per capita income.

The majority of Pakistan's population that lived in the overcrowded east wing felt not only exploited economically by the west wing but also oppressed politically and militarily, much the same way most South Asians had felt under the

---

[39] G.W. Choudhury, *The Last Days of United Pakistan* (Bloomington: Indiana University Press, 1974), 62.
[40] Ibid., 15.

British imperial rule.[41] These disparities were highlighted and projected when, on 18 March 1969, *The Financial Times* published an article claiming that East Pakistan was more impoverished and overcrowded than almost any other region of a developing nation in the world. It was under the leadership of Sheikh Mujibur Rahman, a former student leader who had also been active in the Pakistan movement of Independence, that East Pakistan formally announced its political grievances in the form of six points.

### SUMMARY

At the time of Independence, both Nehru and Jinnah assured the citizens of their new nations respectively that religion, cast and creed were not the business of the State and that all citizens had equal rights. This notion eroded with time and the resulting atrocities were witnessed in the form of religious persecution in India and the marginalisation of Bengalis in Pakistan. Another remarkable fact is that throughout history, minorities have typically sought independence from their majorities; East Pakistan is the only exception to this rule as East Pakistan (aka East Bengal or Bangladesh) was a majority that sought independence from its minority (West Pakistan).

[41] Stanley A. Wolpert, *Bhutto of Pakistan: His Life and Times* (New York: Oxford University Press, 1993), 135.

# 3

## Mujib's Rise to Power; Bhutto's Rise to Power

*Power is the ultimate aphrodisiac.*

—Henry Kissinger[1]

### ANTI-REGIME SENTIMENT IN PAKISTAN

By 1954, Pakistan's constituent assembly had been wrestling for seven years with writing a constitution and searching for ways to reconcile fundamental regional and tribal differences within its complex and divided body politic. The elusive constitution would have to be acceptable both to representatives of some 55 per cent of Pakistan's Bengali population, who lived in East, and to 28 per cent in the West's largest province, Punjab, which also provided almost 85 per cent of the nation's recruits for the army and the higher civil bureaucracy.

Moreover, Sindhis, Pathans and Balochis clamoured for special provincial provisions of their own. Seven years had not been long enough to reconcile the many differences among all these discrete cohorts, nor did the preceding seven-year interlude—from the Muslim League's adoption in March 1940 of its famous Lahore (Pakistan) Resolution to the traumatic birth of the Dominion of Pakistan in mid-August 1947—suffice Jinnah and his advisors to

[1] https://www.goodreads.com/quotes/59866-power-is-the-ultimate-aphrodisiac
(accessed 20 October 2019).

formulate clear guidelines for the constitutional character of the nation they sponsored.[2]

It is ironical that first the Muslim League and later the Awami League were both formed in Dhaka, the Bengali capital of East Pakistan, and not in any other city or province of what would become Pakistan. The Awami League was formed in Dhaka in East Bengal on 4 June 1949 in reaction to the claims by the Muslim League that it was the only legitimate political party in Pakistan. At the time, Mujib's election as joint secretary of the Awami League took place while he was imprisoned in Dhaka by the government for his political activities and opposition to government policies.

From 8 to 11 March 1954, provincial elections were held for the East Bengal (East Pakistan) legislative assembly. The pan-Bengali nationalist United Front Alliance (led by the Awami League) swept the elections—out of a total of 309 seats, the Muslim League won only 10 seats, while the United Front Alliance (made up of the Awami League, Krishak Sramik Party and Nizam-i-Islam) acquired 228 out of 237 Muslim seats.[3] A part of this success was attributed to the Awami League's pre-election activities. In a run-up to these elections, the Awami League produced and distributed pamphlets containing details of discrimination against Bengalis by the central government of Pakistan, which was dominated by West Pakistanis. The pamphlets were an attempt to highlight as accurately as possible the growing discontent and resentment brewing in the eastern wing.

The defeat of the Muslim League in the East Bengal elections led to a demand for the disbanding of the central government and a dissolution of the constituent assembly by

---

[2] Stanley A. Wolpert, *Bhutto of Pakistan: His Life and Times* (New York: Oxford University Press, 1993), 43.

[3] Salahuddin Ahmed, *Bangladesh: Past and Present* (New Delhi: APH Publishing, 2004), 140.

the politicians of East Pakistan.[4] These demands, however, were initially ignored and later rejected by the central government as it comprised of politicians and bureaucracy from West Pakistan. Real problems started popping up from 1958 onwards when Pakistan came under a military rule and democracy was sent packing. Under this new regime, Bengalis progressively felt alienated and marginalised. The growing instability and lack of trust between East Pakistan and West Pakistan created fertile ground for new political alternatives. Zulfikar Ali Bhutto and Sheikh Mujibur Rahman wasted no time in capitalising on these gulfs. This chapter highlights the growing nationalism and the political tensions, as well as Bhutto's and Mujib's respective rise to power.

During Ayub Khan's era (1958–1969), the political, economic, social and cultural conflict between East Pakistan and West Pakistan intensified to a point where their differences became irreconcilable.[5] Despite these cultural and linguistic dichotomies, the people of East Pakistan and West Pakistan shared a mutual anti-regime sentiment, which continued brewing and peaked in 1969. In essence, the eastern and western regions of Pakistan were united on only one front—removing the military from power and returning it to barracks. The Bengali communities in East Pakistan found support under the Awami League, which 'completely identified' with their cultural and regional interests.[6] In contrast, the communities in West Pakistan found support under Bhutto's newly established Pakistan People's Party (PPP). In Pakistan, neither of the successive governments—either that of Ayub Khan's or General Yahya

---

[4] Keesing's research report (9), *Pakistan from 1947 to the Creation of Bangladesh* (New York: Charles Scribner's Sons, 1973), 32.

[5] Ashok Kapur, *Pakistan in Crisis* (London: Routledge, 1991), 52.

[6] Sharif Al Mujahid, 'Pakistan: First General Elections,' *Asian Survey* (Volume 11, No. 2, 1971), 159–71, www.jstor.org/stable/2642715 (accessed 2 January 2019).

Khan's—had satisfied a popular interest or taken serious heed of the compounding discontent.

## Bhutto and Mujib's Ascent

Despite fundamental differences in their visions for the country, Bhutto and Mujib shared some distinct similarities in terms of their parties' political platform and in their style of politics and leadership.

First, both Mujib and Bhutto were young, magnetic and enthusiastic political leaders—a stark contrast to many of the older bureaucrats in Ayub's government. Both were potent orators and took full advantage of mass media to trumpet their platforms. Though this primarily included radio and the emergent television, they also relied on traditional forms of print media. For example, in 1946, Mujib successfully started and ran a newspaper, *Millat*. The purpose of the paper was to circulate politically relevant information and other (propagandist) ideas amongst the members and workers of the Muslim League. Similarly, Bhutto's representation of Pakistan as its foreign minister provided him ample opportunity to rise and shine on the world stage and also concurrently make a lasting impression on the people of Pakistan. Through such feats, Bhutto and Mujib were able to communicate a renewed, innovative and brighter vision of the future to their respective constituencies.

Second, Bhutto and Mujib each expressed their discontent with military governments of Ayub Khan and Yahya Khan, and stressed the need for justice and fairness in Pakistan. While building their political platforms and paving a way to power, both Bhutto and Mujib emphasised on the economic challenges to the nation, the 'over-concentration of wealth in too few hands'.[7] Bhutto's and Mujib's

[7] L.F. Rushbrook Williams, *The East Pakistan Tragedy* (London: T. Stacey, 1972), 42.

respective political parties advocated for resolving the economic inequities between the eastern and the western regions, with each leader offering a unique programme for reasonable distribution of capital and profit provincially.[8] Bhutto was the youngest minister in Ayub Khan's federal cabinet and Mujib joined Fazlul Huq's cabinet of the United Front coalition government in East Pakistan as its youngest minister.[9]

Lastly, like Bhutto, Mujib was an avid admirer of Muhammad Ali Jinnah, the founding father of Pakistan, and stated, 'The day Jinnah died, [conspiratorial] politics surfaced in the country.'[10] Jinnah's vision for Pakistan had been based on the principle of 'one nation, one culture and one language'.[11] In 1948, after the death of Jinnah, Mujib was of the opinion that since Pakistan had no Opposition party, the government had left the path of democracy and was on a clear road to dictatorship. Under Ayub Khan, executive power was in the hands of governors, who were personally nominated by Ayub, with little regional autonomy for the eastern and the western wings. Both Mujib's Awami League and Bhutto's PPP were, in essence, direct products of the failures and overall ineffectiveness of Ayub's government. Also, Awami League and PPP were well received amongst the people of East and West Pakistan respectively, since both promised merit, fairness, accountability and security for their constituents, and also pledged not to make any law repugnant to the injunctions of the Quran and the Sunnah.[12]

[8] Sharif Al Mujahid, 'Pakistan: First General Elections,' *Asian Survey* (Volume 11, No. 2, 1971), 159–71, www.jstor.org/stable/2642715 (accessed 2 January 2019).

[9] *International Journal of Scientific and Research Publications* (Volume 4, Issue 5, May 2014), 3 (last accessed 2 May 2019).

[10] Mujibur Sheikh Rahman, *The Unfinished Memoirs* (Karachi: Oxford University Press, 2012), 82.

[11] Christophe Jaffrelot and Gillian Beaumont, *A History of Pakistan and its Origins* (London: Anthem Press, 2002), 1.

[12] Sharif Al Mujahid, 'Pakistan: First General Elections,' *Asian Survey* (Volume 11, No. 2, 1971), 159–71, www.jstor.org/stable/2642715 (accessed 2 January 2019).

## The Journey from Sheikh Mujib to Bangabandhu

*No man in the entire history of the modern world,*
*except Mao, for different reasons has hypnotised his*
*people as Mujib did.*

—Yatindra Bhatnagar[13]

East Pakistanis (Bengalis) ceaselessly and rightfully complained that East Pakistan was continually dominated and discriminated by the central government of West Pakistan.[14] In retaliation, Mujib, along with a few friends, launched a movement to demand the inclusion of Bengali as an official national language in Pakistan. He declared 11 March 1948 as Bengali Language Demand Day. The movement was cut short when Mujib was arrested the same day for his political activities. Despite repeated arrests, his relentless pursuits and advocacy for Bengalis' rights laid the foundation for a nationalistic movement advocating an independent Bangladesh.

In 1949, the East Pakistan Awami Muslim League was formed and Sheikh Mujibur Rahman served as its first joint secretary. An advocate of socialism, he became known for his opposition to the ethnic and institutional discrimination of Bengalis in the new State of Pakistan. The same year, Mujib organised a 'Resistance Day' in Dhaka to protest against the brutality and violence unleashed by Pakistani national authorities towards some student protesters during the peaceful Bengali language demand protests.[15] This resulted in Mujib's third arrest and incarceration since the 1947 partition of the Indian subcontinent. While in prison, Mujib banded together with fellow political prisoners and

---

[13] Yatindra Bhatnagar, *Mujib: The Architect of Bangladesh* (New Delhi: R.K. Printers, 1971), 16.

[14] Ashok Kapur, *Pakistan in Crisis* (London: Routledge, 1991), 102.

[15] Mujibur Sheikh Rahman, *The Unfinished Memoirs* (Karachi: Oxford University Press, 2012), 117.

appealed and petitioned for the rights of political prisoners. When the appeal and petition failed, he and his fellow prisoners went on a hunger strike, resulting in the death of some and permanent disability of a number of others, partly due to their ill-treatment by prison authorities. During this episode of imprisonment, a civil surgeon asked Mujib why he was spending time in prison, to which he responded that he wanted to achieve power. The civil surgeon inquired as to what Mujib would do after 'getting power'. He responded that he would simply 'do something' for his people and the country.

In 1951, Mujib went to Karachi to meet Prime Minister Khawaja Nazimuddin. The meeting, which was scheduled for 20 minutes, lasted over one hour, during which Mujib emphasised that democracy could not function without a valid Opposition and that as the only Opposition party in the country, Awami League should be allowed to operate. He also requested for the release of political prisoners in East Pakistan and emphasised the importance of having two official languages in East Pakistan—Urdu and Bengali. Bengali students formed a considerable support base of Mujib's Awami League. Concerned over their careers and their economic prospects upon graduation, students in East Pakistan saw the marginalisation of their people as a threat to their future. They also saw the rejection of their native language by the central authorities as an intolerable offence against their culture.

As a result of their unfettered support for Mujib and the Awami League, some Bengali students were killed in police shootings in February 1952 during anti-Urdu language riots.[16] The victims would later go on to be commemorated as the first martyrs of the Bengali independence movement, and their martyrdom is still celebrated in Bangladesh

---

[16] Richard Sisson and Leo E. Rose, *War and Secession: Pakistan, India, and the Creation of Bangladesh* (Oakland: University of California Press, 1991), 9.

every year. It was here that the future East-West conflict was provoked and the Bengali-Pakistani enmity was officially initiated. Henceforth, the mutual distrust between East Pakistan and West Pakistan continued, eventually culminating in a bloody civil war and the creation of an independent Bangladesh.

Sheikh Mujibur Rahman epitomised the sentiments of his people and was at the forefront of Bengali nationalism in the 1950s, participating in a diverse array of political affairs within Pakistan and abroad. In one instance, in September 1952, Mujib attended a peace conference in Peking, China, as part of a 30-member delegation representing Pakistan. The conference included delegates from Southeast Asia and Pacific Rim. Mujib saw the event as a worthwhile opportunity to publicise Bengali nationalism. He delivered his speech exclusively in Bengali—a bold, provocative move that irked the other attendees, especially those from West Pakistan. Because of his absolute loyalty to the Bengali cause, Mujib was elected as the general secretary of the Awami League in 1953 and then as a member of the provincial assembly of Bangladesh in 1954. Following these appointments, Mujib joined Fazlul Huq's cabinet of the United Front and became the youngest minister.[17]

On 7 May 1954, the Pakistan constituent assembly approved a formula according to which the official languages of the Islamic Republic of Pakistan would be Urdu and Bengali, with other provincial languages to be declared by the head of the State upon a recommendation by provincial legislatures.[18] In May 1954, the United Front coalition held

---

[17] *International Journal of Scientific and Research Publications* (Volume 4, Issue 5, May 2014), 3. The United Front was a coalition of political parties in East Pakistan that contested the 1954 East Bengal legislative elections and consisted of the Awami Muslim League, the Krishak Praja Party, the Ganatantri Dal (Democratic Party) and Nizam-e-Islam.

[18] Keesing's research report (9), *Pakistan from 1947 to the Creation of Bangladesh* (New York: Charles Scribner's Sons, 1973), 33.

its oath-taking ceremony at the governor's house in East Pakistan. Shortly afterwards, news reached the newly sworn ministers that there had been a violent breakout between Bengali and non-Bengali mill workers at Adamjee Jute Mill in Narayanganj near Dhaka (East Pakistan). It was alleged that 400 people, including innocent women and children, had been killed mercilessly in the conflict and that more than 1,000 had been injured. These riots spiralled out of control and the Pakistani army was sent in to restore order.[19]

Mujib strongly believed that these riots were part of a broader national conspiracy by the central government to destabilise the United Front government in East Pakistan at the behest of the interests of West Pakistan. In the aftermath of the riots, the elected United Front government was sent packing and the central government in Karachi (western wing) took over the Government of East Pakistan. The elected chief minister of the United Front government, Fazlul Haq, was placed under house arrest. Mujib, who at the time was both a minister in the provincial government in East Pakistan and a general secretary of the Awami League, was also arrested and thrown behind bars. He was imprisoned for 14 months, released and then re-arrested in February of 1962.

In the latter part of the 1950s, Pakistan remained under military rule. On 8 October 1958, President Iskander Mirza imposed martial law throughout the country, appointing General Ayub Khan, the chief commander of the Pakistani army, as the martial law administrator. On 27 October 1958, General Ayub overthrew Iskander Mirza's government in a bloodless coup. This was the beginning of the end for a united Pakistan, through the continued alienation and disillusionment of the people of East Pakistan. In a democracy, through a combination of ballot and protests,

---

[19] Mujibur Sheikh Rahman, *The Unfinished Memoirs* (Karachi: Oxford University Press, 2012), 269.

they had been able to voice their concerns; but, with military rule, this lid to let off steam was closed.

## Bhutto and the Ayub Khan Era (the 1960s)

> If things do not change, there will be nothing left to change. Either power must pass to the people or everything will perish.
>
> —Z.A. Bhutto[20]

President Ayub Khan, who eventually assumed the rank of field marshal, ruled Pakistan until early 1969 under a system of basic democracies, with cabinet minister Bhutto by his side. Sir Morrice James, the then British high commissioner to Pakistan, wrote the following about Ayub's and Bhutto's once close personal and professional relationship: 'It must have looked to Ayub as if he had found an ideal representative of a new and untarnished generation of political leaders to help him and, if all went well, perhaps even become his successor.'[21] Within a few years, however, Ayub would discover the true colours of the man whom he and others in his inner circle had viewed as loyal and trustworthy—a 'confidant, friend and valued lieutenant'.[22]

## The 1965 Indo-Pak War and Kashmir

The 1965 Indo-Pak War was the second formal war between the two newly independent nations of India and Pakistan, and it concerned the statuses of the states of Jammu and Kashmir. The 1947 Indo-Pak War over the same issue had ended in UN mediation, with Kashmir joining the Republic

[20] https://en.wikiquote.org/wiki/Zulfikar_Ali_Bhutto (accessed 20 October 2019).
[21] Inder Malhotra, *Dynasties of India and Beyond: Pakistan, Sri Lanka and Bangladesh* (New Delhi: HarperCollins, 2003), 253.
[22] Ibid.

of India, to the disapproval of the Pakistani government. In 1963, after several failed attempts of negotiations between the Indian and the Pakistani governments over Kashmir, Foreign Minister Bhutto declared his personal frustration, stating, 'Let it be known beyond doubt that Kashmir is to Pakistan what Berlin is to the West, and that without a fair and proper settlement of this issue, the people of Pakistan will not consider the crusade for Pakistan complete.'[23]

Tensions notably intensified in early 1965 when Pakistan and Indian forces clashed over disputed territory (Kashmir) along the border between the two nations.[24] In August 1965, the Pakistani army invaded the Indian territory of Kashmir but was unsuccessful in its attempts to overtake Kashmir by force. Following Pakistan's invasion, the Indian government rapidly internationalised the issue and appealed to the UN to end the conflict peacefully. The UN's intervention was effective. Amongst other sanctions, UN member states, such as the US and the United Kingdom (UK), cut off their arms' supplies to the Indian and Pakistani armed forces.[25] The war ended in a stalemate in September 1965. Above all, it was the 1965 war that 'dug Ayub Khan's political grave' and paved the path for Bhutto's rise to power.[26] During this time, Bhutto's popularity amongst the Pakistani community had been rising rapidly and his relationship with Ayub Khan dissipated just as quickly.

Only a small force (army) was stationed in East Pakistan, whose main job was to assist the law-enforcing

---

[23] Salmaan Taseer, *Bhutto: A Political Biography* (London: Ithaca Press, 1979), 58–59.

[24] United States Government Office of the Historian, 'The India-Pakistan War of 1965', https://history.state.gov/milestones/1961-1968/india-pakistan-war (accessed 3 February 2017).

[25] Ibid.

[26] Inder Malhotra, *Indira Gandhi: A Personal and Political Biography* (London: Hodder & Stoughton, 1989), 255.

agencies to maintain internal security, and in times of war, conduct holding operations for as long as possible. In order to relieve pressure on East Pakistan, an attack would be launched from West Pakistan. This gave birth to the notion that the defence of East Pakistan lay in offence from West Pakistan. This was highlighted in the 1965 Indo-Pak War. India did not attack East Pakistan in the 1965 war (as India fully recognised the fact that the alienation and disaffection of East Pakistanis then was not conducive to an Indian intervention); however, the inability of Pakistani rulers to provide adequate security to East Pakistanis raised many awkward questions and concerns including why should the Pakistani rulers jeopardise the security of 50 million Pakistanis (in East Pakistan) for the sake of a few million non-Pakistani Kashmiris? [27]

The ongoing affection for Kashmiris' struggle for self-determination and self-governance in West Pakistan is because of geographic continuity between Kashmir and West Pakistan. Also, since 1947, Kashmiris have migrated, settled and flourished in all provinces and cities of West Pakistan and, therefore, politicians of West Pakistan have remained committed to the cause of Kashmir. These connections and concerns never existed in East Pakistan and consequently, while the population of West Pakistan considers Kashmir and Kashmiris as part of West Pakistan, no such affinity ever existed in the Bengalis for the Kashmiris. [28]

---

[27] P.R. Chari and Pervaiz Iqbal Cheema, *The Simla Agreement 1972: Its Wasted Promise* (New Delhi: Manohar Publishers & Distributors, 2001), 96.

[28] Ibid., 116.

## Bhutto's Rising Popularity and Dissolving Relationship with Ayub Khan

> Bhutto's rise was meteoric. His intelligence, ability and
> capacity for hard work [set] him apart.
> —Salman Taseer[29]

Bhutto's most effective political skills by far were demonstrated in the field of foreign policy. As foreign minister, Bhutto had been public about his contempt for India. He had played a fundamental role in influencing Ayub Khan's government to act against India in the 1965 war. Bhutto stated, 'I wrote to Ayub Khan saying that if we wanted to pursue a policy of confrontation with India, time was running out. We had to act now or it would be too late.'[30] Days before the war began, Bhutto had also made a public statement on television saying, 'The heroic struggle of the people of Jammu and Kashmir is a part of the glorious essay against colonial domination... This endeavor will not be for Pakistan, nor will it be for Jammu and Kashmir... It cannot and it shall not fail.'[31]

Unlike Bhutto, however, Ayub Khan had been immensely sceptical about the idea of another major confrontation with India. During the climax of the war, Ayub resorted to 'plead[ing] with the United States Ambassador' for US intervention to stop the conflict, and he appeared ready to accept whatever help was offered to him.[32] From Ayub's viewpoint, the only two options left for Pakistan were 'an honorable draw or defeat'. [33] Thus, on 23 September 1965, Ayub Khan's government accepted a UN resolution

[29] Salmaan Taseer, *Bhutto: A Political Biography* (London: Ithaca Press, 1979), 41.
[30] Ibid., 60.
[31] Ibid., 62.
[32] Ibid.
[33] Inder Malhotra, *Indira Gandhi: A Personal and Political Biography* (London: Hodder & Stoughton, 1989), 55.

ordering the immediate cessation of Indo-Pak hostilities—'a first step towards a peaceful settlement of the outstanding differences between the two countries on Kashmir and other related matters.'[34] Men in Ayub's inner circle told him that he had been wrong to accept Bhutto's 'irrational advice' on foreign policy.[35]

## The Tashkent Declaration

As foreign minister, Bhutto defended the Tashkent Declaration, a peace agreement between India and Pakistan signed on 10 January 1966 and considered by many as nothing short of a 'masterpiece of ambiguity'. In February 1966, Bhutto defended the Tashkent Declaration, affirming: 'The Tashkent Declaration provides yet another framework within which the pursuit of a just and honourable solution of the Kashmir dispute will be continued.'[36] One month later, Bhutto reiterated his support for Tashkent Declaration in the national assembly but this time he was much more forceful: 'The Tashkent Declaration has been the subject of a great deal of comment at home and abroad... The Tashkent Declaration forecloses no possibility, blocks no avenues, the achievement of our legitimate aims and the vindication of our just rights.'[37] At the same time, however, Bhutto told the Pakistani people that he would have continued the war with India for 'a thousand years' if necessary and that it was only because of a 'phone call from Ayub that he, as the foreign minister, had accepted the UN ceasefire'.[38] Bhutto's ultimate goal was to prop himself up as the loyal patriot

[34] Salmaan Taseer, *Bhutto: A Political Biography* (London: Ithaca Press, 1979), 62.

[35] Inder Malhotra, *Indira Gandhi: A Personal and Political Biography* (London: Hodder & Stoughton, 1989), 255.

[36] Salmaan Taseer, *Bhutto: A Political Biography* (London: Ithaca Press, 1979), 70.

[37] Ibid., 71.

[38] Inder Malhotra, *Indira Gandhi: A Personal and Political Biography* (London: Hodder & Stoughton, 1989), 255.

and defender of Pakistan while painting a picture of Ayub as a villain and traitor. Amongst other issues, the signing of the Tashkent Declaration by the Indian government was vastly criticised in India because it did not include any clause regarding a 'no-war pact' with Pakistan, thus leaving open the possibility that Kashmir may become a battleground between India and Pakistan again in the future.

Bhutto's relationship with Ayub Khan was forever blemished following their differences during the 1965 Indo-Pak War. In 1966, Bhutto departed for Europe on a personal trip at Ayub Khan's insistence, but rumours soon arose that he had left politics because of political differences and 'ill health'. In an address to the Pakistani community at Conway Hall in London, Bhutto responded to the rumours, stating, 'I am not supposed to be in good health, but I can assure you, no matter how poor my health, it is good enough for Indira Gandhi.'[39]

Bhutto, once Ayub Khan's loyal foreign minister, had now revolted against the very man whom Ayub had once considered the 'eventual heir apparent to the political leadership of Pakistan',[40] In the same address at Conway Hall, Bhutto stated, 'I was advised it would not be a good thing for me to meet and address Pakistanis in England... I have not spoken in the country [Pakistan] for good reasons, and I don't think that I would like to speak here also for a good reason on internal matters.'[41] The tone in which Bhutto spoke made clear his true intentions, which were to express public criticism of the Ayub Khan government and its stance on the foreign policy situation with India. In the same speech, Bhutto had referred to the 1965 Indo-Pak War as a 'glorious period in our history...[when] the nation

[39] Salmaan Taseer, *Bhutto: A Political Biography* (London: Ithaca Press, 1979), 77.
[40] Inder Malhotra, *Indira Gandhi: A Personal and Political Biography* (London: Hodder & Stoughton, 1989), 253.
[41] Salmaan Taseer, *Bhutto: A Political Biography* (London: Ithaca Press, 1979) 77.

unitedly stood as a rock against the onslaught of [the] predator. The Indians said that by evening, Lahore shall fall, and my reply was, "No Indian mother had given birth to an Indian who could take Lahore".[42]

In August 1966, one of Bhutto's loyal defenders, Lord Bertrand Russell, wrote a piece to *The Economist* in reply to political condemnations of Bhutto:

> *The fate of national leaders who respond to the needs of their people is increasingly clear unless they find the means to resist the pressures applied to them, in which case journals such as* The Economist *attach unpleasant labels to them. Mr. Bhutto is a national leader of his country in the tradition of Jinnah, and the storm of prolonged applause he receives is not restricted to London.*[43]

President Ayub Khan's weaknesses in the second Indo-Pak war, combined with his overall political insecurities, not only paved the way for his resignation but also brought Bhutto into political limelight. From 1967 onwards, growing resentment in Pakistan against Ayub Khan's regime culminated into widespread violent demonstrations and riots.[44] An attempt was made on President Ayub's life in November 1968 and several leaders of the Opposition movement, including Bhutto, were subsequently arrested and imprisoned for their activities. Mujib was also in police custody. Political workers were able to paralyse the country through sustained demonstrations even in the absence of their leadership.[45] Domestic unrest, therefore, became indigenous and self-propagating.

---

[42] Salmaan Taseer, *Bhutto: A Political Biography* (London: Ithaca Press, 1979), 78.
[43] Ibid., 78.
[44] Fatima Bhutto, *Songs of Blood and Sword: A Daughter's Memoir* (New York: Nation Books, 2010), 96–97.
[45] Lawrence Ziring, *Pakistan in the Twentieth Century: A Political History* (Karachi: Oxford University Press, 1997), 313.

## MUJIB AND EAST PAKISTAN (THE 1960S)

*I believe that capital is a tool of the oppressor. As long*
*as capitalism is the mainspring of the economic order,*
*people all over the world will continue to be oppressed.*
— Sheikh Mujibur Rahman [46]

### Six-Point Movement (1966)

In 1964, Mujib was elected as the general secretary of
the Awami League, and an all-party action committee
led by Mujib was formed to deal with communal riots
between the East and the West. Hence, the Awami League
began its constitutional struggle under his leadership. For
East Pakistanis, a combination of economic deprivation,
political disaffection and anger at being left undefended by
the Pakistan Army during the 1965 war had taken its toll
and nurtured questions about the merits of continuing the
provincial union with West Pakistan.[47]

Originally, Mujib had planned to announce the six
points in early February 1966 at a joint conference of the
Opposition political parties in Lahore in West Pakistan.
He sought the support of politicians in West Pakistan on
his six points and, in exchange, offered the Awami League
support in bringing down Ayub Khan's government. Mujib
was not permitted to do so by the other participants,
including the president of the Awami League at the
time, Nawabzada Nasrullah Khan. The politicians of
West Pakistan found the plan too 'inflammatory' to be
made public. Mujib took offence to the obstruction of
his plan and announced his six points the following day,

[46] Mujibur Sheikh Rahman, *The Unfinished Memoirs* (Karachi: Oxford University Press, 2012), 237.
[47] Farzana Shaikh, 'ZULFIKAR ALI BHUTTO: In Pursuit of an Asian Pakistan' in Ramachandra Guha edited, *Makers of Modern Asia* (Cambridge: Harvard University Press, 2014), 285.

5 February 1966, at a news conference in Lahore. He began his speech on an acrimonious note: 'Does it not put you to shame that every bit of reasonable demand of East Pakistan has got to be secured from you at tremendous cost and after bitter struggle as if snatched from unwilling foreign rulers as reluctant concessions?'[48]

The six points:

1. Pakistan would have a federal structure of government based on the spirit of the Lahore Resolution of 1940, with a Parliament elected on the basis of universal adult franchise.
2. The central government would have authority only in defence and foreign affairs, and all the other subjects would be handled by the federating units of the state of Pakistan.
3. There would be two freely convertible currencies for Pakistan's two wings or two separate reserve banks for the two regions of the country.
4. The power of taxation and revenue collection would be vested in the federating units.
5. There would be two separate accounts for foreign exchange reserves for the two wings of Pakistan (East and West).
6. East Pakistan would have a separate militia or paramilitary force as a measure of its security.

The six-point plan was part of Mujib's broader strategies, which were to increase tensions and division between East Pakistan and West Pakistan and destabilise Ayub's government. Amongst other enticements, the six-point plan promised the Bengali middle class many political benefits if they loosened their links with West Pakistan.[49]

[48] Anthony Mascarenhas, *The Rape of Bangladesh* (Delhi: Vikas Publications, 1971), 6.
[49] Shahid Javed Burki, *Pakistan Under Bhutto: 1971–1977,* Second edition (London: Macmillan, 1988), 59.

Just as the former British high commissioner to Pakistan Sir Morrice James (1961-1965) had given his observations about Bhutto, Archer Blood—who was the US consul general to Dhaka—gave his observation about Mujib:

> In private meetings, he is charming, calm and confident... On the rostrum, he is a fiery orator who can mesmerise hundreds of thousands in pouring rain. As a party leader, he is tough and authoritative, often arrogant. Mujib has something of a messianic complex, which has been reinforced by the heady experience of mass adulation. He talks of my people, my lands, my forests, my river. It seems clear that he views himself as the personification of Bengali aspiration.[50]

## Agartala Conspiracy Case (1968)

> People can be won over by good manners, love and sympathy, and not by force, hatred or oppressive means.
>
> —Sheikh Mujibur Rahman[51]

'The East Pakistan leader Sheikh Mujibur Rahman was arrested repeatedly between 1956 and 1970, culminating in his being accused of high treason in the Agartala Conspiracy Case.'[52]

Towards the end of 1968, there was major upheaval and perpetual political crisis in the western wing, while demands for democracy and autonomy intensified in the eastern wing. Not surprisingly, none of the six points was accepted by President Ayub's government, who labelled these as a threat to the unity of Pakistan.

[50] B.Z. Khasru, *The Bangladesh Military Coup and the CIA Link* (New Delhi: Rupa Publications, 2014), 85.

[51] Mujibur Sheikh Rahman, *The Unfinished Memoirs* (Karachi: Oxford University Press, 2012), 200.

[52] J.N. Dixit, *India-Pakistan in War and Peace* (London: Routledge, 2002), 157–58.

On 6 January 1968, Ayub's regime shocked the entire Pakistani nation when it declared that 28 out of a total of 35 criminals had been arrested on the charge of conspiring to secede East Pakistan from Pakistan proper.[53] Ayub's regime alleged that the accused—which included Sheikh Mujibur Rahman—had secretly conspired with the high commission of India in Dhaka and visited the town of Agartala in India near the border with East Pakistan to discuss plans for secession with Indian officers. The case, henceforth, became known in Pakistan as the Agartala Conspiracy Case— colloquially known as the 'Bengali conspiracy' to bring about the separation of East Pakistan with the help of India and Indira Gandhi's Congress party. During the June 1968 trial, Mujib and the other alleged co-conspirators—all of whom pleaded 'not guilty'—were accused of 'plotting to deprive Pakistan of its sovereignty over a part of its territory by an armed revolt with weapons, ammunition and funds provided by India'[54].

Trouble started when the name of Mujib was announced as an accomplice in the conspiracy. It created doubts and suspicion amongst people because Mujib's name was included about 15 days after the scheme was unearthed. Moreover, at the time, he was behind bars and people questioned how could he participate in the conspiracy if he were in prison. The Pakistani government did not offer any convincing explanation of these suspicions, which grew stronger with the passage of time.[55]

The national encyclopaedia of Bangladesh has described the Agartala case as a case 'framed by the Pakistan government in 1968 during the Ayub regime, against Sheikh

---

[53] Salahuddin Ahmed, *Bangladesh: Past and Present* (New Delhi: APH Publishing, 2004), 161.
[54] Ibid., 162.
[55] Safdar Mahmood, *The Deliberate Debacle,* 1st edition (Lahore: Sh. Muhammad Ashraf, 1976), 48–49.

Mujibur Rahman, some in-service and ex-service army personnel and high government officials'.[56] At the time of its initiation, the Agartala case only intensified Bengali nationalism, turning Mujib into a 'hero overnight' in the eastern wing.[57] The case further strengthened opposition to the Ayub regime, provoking a massive mobilisation effort against the central government in West Pakistan.[58] In the face of the rising opposition movement, the central government felt it was at risk of losing its hold on power. Following the Agartala case's initiation, the dire situation in the country only worsened, reaching its pinnacle in 1969 with the resignation of President Ayub Khan.

Faced with a mass opposition movement, Ayub's government was ultimately compelled to withdraw the Agartala Conspiracy Case on 22 February 1969.[59] This was followed by the honourable release of Mujib and his other co-accused conspirators, including a naval officer, three senior civil servants and a number of junior military personnel.[60] Following these events, the Central Students' Action Council of the Awami League arranged a reception in honour of Mujib on 23 February 1969 at a racecourse in Dhaka, where over one million loyal attendees flocked and conferred Mujib with the epic title of 'Bangabandhu'— friend of Bengal.

Since Ayub's regime failed to quell the uprisings and create stability in the nation, on 26 March 1969, the

---

[56] Government of Bangladesh, National Encyclopedia of Bangladesh, 'Agartala Conspiracy Case', http://en.banglapedia.org/index.php?title=Agartala_Conspiracy_Case (accessed 9 January 2017).

[57] Salahuddin Ahmed, *Bangladesh: Past and Present* (New Delhi: APH Publishing, 2004), 162.

[58] Ashok Kapur, *Pakistan in Crisis* (London: Routledge, 1991), 84.

[59] Government of Bangladesh, National Encyclopedia of Bangladesh, 'Agartala Conspiracy Case,' http://en.banglapedia.org/index.php?title=Agartala_Conspiracy_Case (accessed 9 January 2017).

[60] Salahuddin Ahmed, *Bangladesh: Past and Present* (New Delhi: APH Publishing, 2004), 161.

commander-in-chief of the Pakistani armed forces, General Yahya Khan, put martial law into effect, bestowing upon himself the title of chief martial law administrator. This ultimately resulted in the overthrowing of Ayub's government. Four days after putting martial law into effect, General Yahya Khan revoked the Constitution of 1962 and declared himself the new (third) president of Pakistan.

There was certainly a significant difference in Ayub's martial law and Yahya's martial law. When Ayub imposed army rule, politicians and political institutions had already lost their credibility. People were tired of politicians whose corrupt practices, intrigues and exploitation had turned the Parliament into a mockery. On the contrary, when Yahya Khan took over, army rule had already been condemned by the whole nation and the struggle to restore a parliamentary form of government had assumed the character of an organised movement. Yahya's assumption of power was thus resisted and disliked. It caused great disappointment and trepidation in the country, as most of the people thought that it would not only adversely affect the army discipline, but also delay the growth of democratic institutions.[61]

## SUMMARY

Bhutto and Mujib both knew that this change in the power structure, along with the growing instability between Pakistan's two wings, was a profitable political opportunity. Neither politician wasted any time—Z.A. Bhutto swooped in on West Pakistan, while Sheikh Mujibur Rahman pounced in on East Pakistan.

[61] Safdar Mahmood, *The Deliberate Debacle* (Pakistan: Sh. Muhammad Ashraf, 1976), 55.

# 4

## PAKISTAN'S AND INDIA'S GENERAL ELECTIONS: THE LEAD-UP TO WAR

*[Society] is a sensitive organism; remove or destroy
the unifying element, and it breaks into a thousand
pieces; men still live together, but the cement which
bound them into one is gone. And there is much in
man that is selfish and disruptive; he lives largely
by his instincts and emotions, and when the highest
of these instincts loses its object, he is left only
with those more animal ones by which to live. Live
he does, at a lower level, harnessing his powers to
attain his baser ends, conspiring and combining
with some, the better to accomplish his purpose
against others. This happens in any society when its
ideals are shattered... once the faith is shaken and
destroyed...*

—R.E. Smith[1]

By all accounts, the 1970s were the crux of political
mayhem, transformation, turmoil and tragedy in the Indian
subcontinent. From 1970 onwards, politics in India and
Pakistan was a struggle between competing visions of
democracy. East Pakistan and West Pakistan were embroiled
in a vehement debate over Zulfikar Ali Bhutto's vision of
Islamic socialism and Sheikh Mujibur Rahman's vision of

---

[1] R.E. Smith, *The failure of the Roman Republic* (New York and London:
Cambridge University Press, 1955), 163–64.

Bengali nationalism and eastern autonomy.[2] Mujib and Bhutto were fiery orators in highly capricious situations. Each had garnered passionate and committed followers in hundreds of thousands who were willing to make any sacrifice for their leader.[3] The fate of the State of Pakistan depended entirely upon the upcoming general elections, where it would be decided, at last, exactly what the position of Bengalis was in Pakistani society.

## INDIA AND INDIRA

> 'Satisfied' is a word I use only in reference to my country, and I'll never be satisfied for my country. For this reason, I go on taking difficult paths, and between a paved road and a footpath that goes up the mountain, I choose the footpath.
>
> —Indira Gandhi[4]

### Remaking of the Congress Party and Centralisation of Power (1966–1971)

Opinion polls in India consistently name Indira as the best prime minister the country has ever had. Indeed, in a recent poll, nearly a third of the respondents voted for her—a number that placed her well ahead of her predecessors as well as her successors. Such expressions of popular opinion confound her critics.[5] Indira Gandhi in death seems as puzzling and paradoxical as she was when she

---

[2] Ashok Kapur, *Pakistan in Crisis* (London: Routledge, 1991), 98.

[3] Lawrence Ziring, *Pakistan in the Twentieth Century: A Political History* (Karachi: Oxford University Press, 1997), 335.

[4] Oriana Fallaci, *Interview with History* (Boston: Houghton Mifflin, 1977), 181.

[5] Srinath Raghavan, 'Indira Gandhi: India and the World in Transition' in Ramachandra Guha edited, *Makers of Modern Asia* (Cambridge: Harvard University Press, 2014), 215.

was alive.[6] Her elevation as the prime minister was by no means a smooth affair. In the event, the bosses of the Congress party—a group of five regional heavyweights, collectively known as the syndicate—masterminded Indira's candidature. Ironically, it was her political weakness and ideological imprecision that led them to believe that she would be a pliable prime minister. Her ability to borrow the lustre of her father Jawaharlal Nehru was also seen as an advantageous proposition.[7]

Prime Minister Indira Gandhi in 1967 found herself managing an India on the brink of starvation; the economy was in its worst condition given the impact of the recent war with China in 1962 and Pakistan in 1965, and the failure of two consecutive monsoons. A few weeks into her premiership, Indira wrote the following in a letter to a friend:

> The state of affairs is quite extraordinary here… When I am depressed, which is often, I feel I must quit. At other times, that I must fight it out even if the results are negligible… Congress as a party is dormant and inactive… As I see it, we are at the beginning of a new dark age. The food situation is precarious, industries are closing. There is no direction, no policy on any matter… As a child, I wanted to be like Joan of Arc—I may yet be burnt at the stake.[8]

Later, she would add, 'The problem is not in the problems I have; it's in the idiots around me.'[9] Shortly after her election victory, Gandhi began reforming the Congress party from within, doing whatever was necessary to consolidate power into her own hands. Within the next 18 months, the Congress

---

[6] Ibid., 216.
[7] Ibid., 220.
[8] Ibid., 223.
[9] Oriana Fallaci, *Interview with History* (Boston: Houghton Mifflin, 1977), 156.

party underwent a 'complete organisational makeover',[10] with Gandhi seizing control from some of the most senior members of the party as well as eliminating established power blocs. The result was vehement opposition towards Gandhi from members within Congress, culminating in the party's split into 'anti-Gandhi' Indian National Congress (Organisation)—or Congress (O)—and Indira's Congress (R) or Indian National Congress (Requisitionists), in late 1969.[11]

Gandhi demonstrated her prolific political ability when she responded to these and other internal divides within the Congress party by widening the gulf instead of repairing and uniting existing relations. Her electoral strategy was to develop a strong alliance between progressive elements within Congress and the Communist Party of India.[12] Indira rallied a new faction of the party with her populist and left-leaning position on the economy; at the same time, fixating and strengthening her hold on power. As Srinath Raghavan explains:

> On the one hand, [Indira] decided to force a showdown with the party elders and cut them to size... On the other hand, she projected a more left-wing stance on policy matters. This was essential to developing alliances with progressive elements within the Congress and with the Communist Party of India. [13]

---

[10] Srinath Raghavan, 'Indira Gandhi: India and the World in Transition' in Ramachandra Guha edited, *Makers of Modern Asia* (Cambridge: Harvard University Press, 2014), 223.

[11] A detailed discussion on Congress party's split is beyond the scope of this book.

[12] Srinath Raghavan, 'Indira Gandhi: India and the World in Transition' in Ramachandra Guha edited, *Makers of Modern Asia* (Cambridge: Harvard University Press, 2014), 223.

[13] Ibid.

## Indira's Socialist and Populist Programmes as Prime Minister

During Gandhi's leadership, the Congress party's campaign and political platform were organised around socialist issues such as poverty, inequality and social disparity. Leading up to the 1971 election, Gandhi strategically introduced a series of sweeping reforms and policy changes that she anticipated would be popular amongst the lower and middle classes of Indian society. This certainly augmented her public image. Indira nationalised 14 leading commercial banks in India on 19 July 1969, leaving out foreign-owned banks. The outcome of bank nationalisation was electric, with the entire population admiring the prime minister's actions. In cities, joyous crowds danced in the streets as they were enthused by the fact that the rich monopolising the nation's wealth and resources were being put in their place by Indira's government.[14]

Indira, through a presidential proclamation, abolished the privy purses and privileges of princes in India in September of 1970 and nationalised the general insurance in May 1971.[15] She also legislated for restrictions on large businesses so as to further legitimise her 'left-wing' (socialist) credentials. All these bold initiatives were unprecedented and, therefore, the outcome of such undertakings was risky and unpredictable. These strategies ultimately culminated in a decisive electoral victory for her party in 1971. Gandhi won by a margin that 'exceeded that of her father's best performance', and Congress (R) returned to power with an astounding 352 out of 518 seats, as shown in Table 4.1.[16]

---

[14] Inder Malhotra, *Indira Gandhi: A Personal and Political Biography* (London: Hodder & Stoughton, 1989), 73.

[15] Ibid., 130.

[16] Srinath Raghavan, 'Indira Gandhi: India and the World in Transition' in Ramachandra Guha edited, *Makers of Modern Asia* (Cambridge: Harvard University Press, 2014), 224.

TABLE 4.1: Results of the Indian General Election (5th Lok Sabha), 1971

| National Party | Seats Won (out of 518) | Percentage of Votes Polled |
|---|---|---|
| Bharatiya Jana Sangh | 22 | 7.35% |
| Communist Party of India | 23 | 4.73% |
| Communist Party of India (Marxist) | 25 | 5.12% |
| Indian National Congress (R) | 352 | 43.68% |
| Indian National Congress (O) | 16 | 10.43% |
| Praja Socialist Party | 2 | 1.04% |
| Samyukta Socialist Party | 3 | 2.43% |
| Swatantra Party | 8 | 3.07% |

Source: Government of India, 'Statistical Report on General Elections, 1971 to the Fifth Lok Sabha, Volume I (National and State Abstracts and Detailed Results),' Election Commission of India, New Delhi, http://eci. nic.in/eci_main/StatisticalReports/LS_1971/Vol_I_LS71.pdf (accessed 29 December 2016).

Indira Gandhi's calculated moves culminated in the electoral victory of her party indicating that she knew precisely what she wanted—for the Congress party, for India and for herself as a politician—and she wasted no time in following through with these visions once in power. Even in the face of widespread regional protests opposing her reforms and slogans such as 'Indira *hatao*' (remove Indira), Indira Gandhi persevered and reacted with nothing but determination towards achieving her goals; she responded to her opponents fearlessly with the phrase '*garibi hatao*' (remove poverty), which instantly resonated with the masses and electrified the electorate.[17]

[17] Srinath Raghavan, 'Indira Gandhi: India and the World in Transition' in Ramachandra Guha edited, *Makers of Modern Asia* (Cambridge: Harvard University Press, 2014), 224.
As Raghavan explains, this slogan against Indira was adopted by the self-styled 'Grand Alliance', a hastily cobbled-together coalition comprising the Congress (O), the right-wing Jana Sangh, the pro-business Swatantra, the socialists and a smattering of regional parties who opposed Indira's left-leaning reforms.

Her masterful manoeuvring of events, which led to the surrender of the Pakistan Army in East Pakistan on 16 December 1971 and the creation of an independent Bangladesh, gave her the adulation of the masses in India and also the nickname 'Durga', meaning Goddess of War. Indira was now at the pinnacle of her power and glory. *The Economist*'s description of her as the 'Empress of India' seemed apt.[18] By 1972, Indira Gandhi had established her hold over the Congress party, mesmerised the people of India and proved her prowess and leadership acumen to the rest of the world.

Throughout 1972, the Indian government strengthened its control over the economy. In May, the coking coal industry was nationalised; in August, the government took over the management of the Indian Iron and Steel Company without paying compensation to the original owners. The general insurance companies came under State control in September followed by shipping, gold and copper. In October of that year, 46 textile mills were transferred to the State-owned textile corporation. Wartime food riots and the need to feed refugees had emptied out grain supplies and a drought failed to replenish them. To alleviate the high price and to further revitalise her radical image, the following April, Indira transferred the wholesale trade in wheat and rice to public agencies.[19]

During her first tenure, India became the sixth member of the Nuclear Club, the most exclusive in history, when it conducted in May 1974 an underground nuclear experiment. Six years later, on 18 July 1980—mainly as a result of her earlier support—India successfully blasted

[18] Inder Malhotra, *Indira Gandhi: A Personal and Political Biography* (London: Hodder & Stoughton, 1989), 141.

[19] Leslie Derfler, *The Fall and Rise of Political Leaders: Olof Palme, Olusegun Obasanjo, and Indira Gandhi*, 1st edition (New York: Palgrave Macmillan, 2011), 162.

off its first satellite launching vehicle, SLV-3, placing in orbit an indigenously designed and built 35-kilogram satellite Rohini-I. In collaboration with France, scientists of the Indian Space Research Organisation successfully put a communication satellite in its final geostationary position. In 1984, India's first spaceman joined the crew of Soviet's Salyut 7 space station.[20] During her 11 years in power until 1977, Indira had not only sustained but also strengthened her father's policy of maintaining close and friendly relations with the Soviet Union.[21]

In March 1977, Indira and her party were ousted from power in a general election. The accusations against her were high-handed, dynastic and authoritarian policies during the 21-month Emergency rule from 1975 to 1977.[22] She ferociously and successfully fought back legal battles in courtrooms and political battles in public meetings. The new government's ineffectiveness and internal bickering made the Indian public realise that Indira's rule, while authoritarian, delivered on promises and yielded results. Also, the ceaseless vendetta of the new government against Indira helped her gain public sympathy. The new government's incompetence coupled with its vendetta against Indira brought her closer to the electorate and her mass appeal multiplied to the extent that on 6 January 1980, during the first hour of counting of votes, it was clear that the woman who was supposed to have been 'thrown into the dustbin of history' after her fall from power and colossal losses in the 1977 general elections was India's chosen leader once again. The banner headline of The Times of India 'IT'S INDIRA ALL THE

---

[20] Inder Malhotra, *Indira Gandhi: A Personal and Political Biography* (London: Hodder & Stoughton, 1989), 262.

[21] Ibid., 218.

[22] Kathryn Jacques, *Bangladesh, India and Pakistan* (New York: St Martin's Press Inc, 2000), 34.

WAY' said it all.[23] At times, it seemed they were running not so much against a diminutive 62-year-old political candidate, but a myth; a legend in a sari and pair of dusty sandals.[24]

Upon becoming the prime minister a second time, Indira retained the defence portfolio. She increased the outlay for defence research and development, and accelerated projects of local defence production, devoting special attention to missilery and nuclear propulsion of ships and submarines.[25] On 22 February 1982, Indira organised a ministerial conference of 122 developing nations in New Delhi to press for a proper 'restructuring of the international economy'. During the three-day conference, she regretted deterioration in global economy, deplored the 'protectionism of the Western countries', which amounted to 'victimisation of developing nations' and called for a world conference on food security, energy and finance.[26]

In March 1983, Indira conducted the seventh Non-Aligned Movement (NAM) summit in New Delhi as its chair and host. She managed the NAM summit with remarkable agility, reconciling conflicting opinions and patiently evolving consensus on all contentious issues.[27] In her time, India became the third-largest reservoir of highly skilled technical workers in the world, in addition to the fifth military power, the sixth member of the Nuclear Club, the seventh to join the race for space and the tenth industrial power.[28]

[23] Inder Malhotra, *Indira Gandhi: A Personal and Political Biography* (London: Hodder & Stoughton, 1989), 213.

[24] Pupul Jayakar, *Indira Gandhi: An Intimate Biography* (New York: Pantheon Books, 1992), Part VII.

[25] Inder Malhotra, *Indira Gandhi: A Personal and Political Biography* (London: Hodder & Stoughton, 1989), 263.

[26] Ibid., 265.

[27] Ibid., 281.

[28] Ibid., 307.

## ELECTIONS IN A UNITED PAKISTAN

On 1 January 1970, the ban on political activities in Pakistan was lifted to allow political parties to campaign for the general elections, which were to be held by the end of the year. On 30 March 1970, President Yahya issued a Legal Framework Order (LFO), breaking up the One Unit of West Pakistan[29] and reconstituting the original four provinces, i.e. Punjab, Balochistan, Sindh and NWFP. The four western provinces were to have their own legislative assemblies, along with East Pakistan. A national assembly was to be constituted that would be divided between East Pakistan and the four western provinces, the former receiving a larger proportion of seats as a consequence of its greater population.[30] LFO articulated five principles as the basis of the upcoming elections in Pakistan:[31]

1. Pakistan must be based on Islamic ideology.
2. Pakistan was to have a democratic constitution providing for free elections. Pakistan's territorial integrity must be upheld in the Constitution.
3. Disparity (between East and West Pakistan) must be eliminated in a specific period of time.
4. Maximum autonomy must be granted (to provinces) in the Constitution with adequate powers for the federal government to discharge its responsibilities, including the preserving of the country's integrity.
5. The Constitution was to be framed (by the newly

---

[29] The One Unit policy was announced by Prime Minister Muhammad Ali Bogra on 22 November 1954. On 5 October 1955, Iskander Mirza (acting governor general of Pakistan) passed an order unifying all of West Pakistan in what became known as the 'One Unit Scheme'.

[30] Lawrence Ziring, *Pakistan at the Crosscurrent of History* (New Delhi: Manas Publications, 2005), 115.

[31] Safdar Mahmood, *The Deliberate Debacle* (Pakistan: Sh. Muhammad Ashraf, 1976), 59–60.

elected national assembly) within 120 days.
The president (Yahya Khan) had the right to
authenticate or reject it.

The abrogation of the 1962 Constitution by President Yahya
was not without cost as the absence of a constitutional
structure and the attempt to create one from election
results provided Mujib and Bhutto with ample opportunity
to advance their separate and highly ambitious political
programmes.[32]

On 14 August 1970—Pakistan's Independence Day—the
students at the University of Dhaka had flaunted a new
map exhibiting the creation of Bangladesh, and the flag of
the potentially emerging country was prominently paraded
at a meeting to celebrate Independence Day. There were
reports not only from Pakistan's intelligence services but
also from some foreign countries that money and arms from
India were being sent to East Pakistan both for the success
of the Awami League in the elections and for the eventual
confrontation with the Pakistan Army. Further intrigues
were highlighted by G.W. Choudhury, the communications
minister, who hailed from East Pakistan and was at the
epicentre of it all:

> When Mujib's party was debating Yahya's scheme of
> power under the LFO of 1970, Mujib was reported to
> have said to his inner cabinet that his sole aim was to
> establish Bangladesh. Yahya was presented with a tape-
> recorded account of these talks of Mujib with his close
> associates. Mujib was unmistakably heard saying: 'My aim
> is to establish Bangladesh; I will tear the LFO into pieces
> as soon as the elections are over. Who could challenge
> me once the elections are over?' He also hinted to his

[32] Lawrence Ziring, *Pakistan in the Twentieth Century: A Political History*
(Karachi, Oxford, New York, Delhi: Oxford University Press, 1997), 335–36.

*colleagues about help from 'outside sources', presumably from India. When Yahya listened to this 'political music' played by his intelligence services, he was bewildered. He could instantly recognise Mujib's voice and the substance of his talk.*[33]

Yahya and Mujib both seemed to have more than one plan. As preparations got underway to hold the elections and revitalise the nation's economic life, a disaster of unprecedented magnitude struck East Pakistan. On 12 November 1970, a tidal wave over 30 feet high lashed by cyclonic winds of 120 miles per hour wrecked five of East Pakistan's coastal districts. It was called the worst natural catastrophe in modern history. Casualties were estimated to be between 200,000 and 500,000, and the property damage was colossal throughout the region. There was an immediate need for assistance from people across all disciplines. Bengalis even looked to their countrymen in West Pakistan for aid. President Yahya was visiting China and did not visit the devastated areas until the better half of a week had passed. By that time, international relief efforts were well underway.

Mujib bemoaned:

*West Pakistan has a bumper wheat crop, but the first shipment of food grain to reach us is from abroad... that the textile merchants have not given a yard of cloth for our shrouds. We have a large army but it is left to the British Marines to bury our dead. The feeling now pervades... every village, home and slum that we must rule ourselves. We must make decisions that matter. We will no longer suffer arbitrary rule by bureaucrats, capitalists and feudal interests of West Pakistan.*[34]

---

[33] G.W. Choudhury, *The Last Days of United Pakistan* (Bloomington: Indiana University Press, 1974), 98–99.

[34] James Heitzman et al., *Bangladesh: A Country Study* (Washington: Federal Research Division, Library of Congress, 1989), 29.

Reports filtering out of East Pakistan contrasted these external efforts with the seeming indifference of Pakistani government. The episode was sufficient proof to the Bengalis that their brethren in the western wing of the country cared little for their plight, let alone for their well-being. Bengali bitterness hence waxed into outspoken hatred.[35]

Mujib held three secret meetings with Yahya at the president's house in Dhaka in November and in early December 1970, during which Mujib made a solemn promise that he would show the draft constitution before presenting it to the national assembly for discussion and approval. He was reported to have assured Yahya that his six-point programme did not imply a division of the country and that Yahya's five points, as laid out in the LFO, and his own six points would be incorporated in the future constitution. G.W. Choudhury states:

> The whole Yahya-Mujib dialogue during the three secret meetings was, as usual, taped and I heard the tape-recorded version of the talks. Nobody listening to the tape-recorded version could blame Yahya. However, I also obtained a copy of the preliminary draft constitution prepared by the experts of the Awami League, in which there was no hope for united Pakistan. The division of the country was not formally proposed, but a rigid and comprehensive interpretation of the Six-Point Programme was in the draft. If the six points were incorporated in toto, there could hardly be a federal union.[36]

During the election campaign, Mujib's task was simple and easy compared to that of other political leaders. His only manifesto was the exploitation of Bengal by the West

[35] Lawrence Ziring, *Bangladesh From Mujib to Ershad: An Interpretive Study* (Karachi: Oxford University Press, 1992), 56.

[36] G.W. Choudhury, *The Last Days of United Pakistan* (Bloomington: Indiana University Press, 1974), 101–02.

Pakistanis; his promise was that of a '*sonar* (golden) Bengal'. This was a most popular appeal to a poverty-stricken populace of 75 million. Just as the Muslims of undivided India were convinced that a separate State of their own would give them a land of opportunities, so were the Bengalis in rural areas, for whom Mujib held tremendous appeal, as they considered the idea of a 'golden Bengal'. The only condition was to give him and his party votes in the elections.[37]

Before the general elections in December 1970, Mujib's public statements gave mixed messages. On one occasion, he stated that he was campaigning for full regional autonomy of East Pakistan and, at the same time, declared that if a democratic process was impeded, he would lead his people to fight for independence 'so that we can live as free people'. On yet another occasion, in Dhaka, during his address to a public gathering, Mujib retorted: 'Why East Pakistan having a majority of the country's population would want to secede. Let them (West Pakistani's) secede if they want to.'[38]

Leading up to the 1970 general elections, Bhutto had emerged as the leading politician and a well-liked figure in the western wing; however, a prevalent issue he faced was with One Unit. As mentioned earlier, One Unit was a geopolitical programme launched by the Government of Pakistan in November 1954. The programme was enacted to resolve the difficulty of administrating the two unequal polities of Pakistan and, as a result, this programme merged the four provinces of West Pakistan (Punjab, Sindh, Balochistan and NWFP) into a single province. One Unit was still popular with the Punjabis but was bitterly opposed by the smaller provinces of West Pakistan.

---

[37] G.W. Choudhury, *The Last Days of United Pakistan* (Bloomington: Indiana University Press, 1974), 118.
[38] Safdar Mahmood, *The Deliberate Debacle* (Pakistan: Sh. Muhammad Ashraf, 1976), 66–67.

In Punjab, Bhutto delivered inflammatory speeches on confrontations with India, on a thousand-year war with India and on Ayub's alleged sacrifices of the national interest at the Tashkent conference of 1966, but such emotional issues did not have much appeal in Balochistan or the NWFP or even in Bhutto's home province of Sindh. Bhutto had to speak of land reforms and Islamic socialism with the goal of gaining the support of the newly awakened have-not groups, particularly in industrial cities, while also being vigilant not to push the big property owners or business people too far.[39]

Pakistan's first general election in its 23-year history commenced on 7 December 1970. Approximately 56 million people cast ballots for the national assembly in a peaceful and orderly atmosphere. The ritual was repeated on 17 December for the provincial legislative assemblies of East Pakistan, Sindh, Balochistan, Punjab and NWFP.[40] Zulfikar Ali Bhutto's campaign in West Pakistan and Sheikh Mujibur Rahman's efforts in East Pakistan paid off ostentatiously. Each of their political campaigns had scored masses of new supporters and followers who were fed up of the way Pakistan had been run under military leaders General Yahya Khan and Ayub Khan. The electorate decided and gave a clear verdict that it was time for a change.

Zulfikar Ali Bhutto's PPP secured a majority vote in West Pakistan but ultimately fell short against Sheikh Mujib's Awami League and their staggering victory in the East. The Awami League shocked the country with its unprecedented landslide victory in the general elections, winning 160 of the total 162 seats allotted to East Pakistan in the national

[39] G.W. Choudhury, *The Last Days of United Pakistan* (Bloomington: Indiana University Press, 1974), 122.

[40] Lawrence Ziring, *Bangladesh From Mujib to Ershad: An Interpretive Study* (Karachi: Oxford University Press, 1992), 58.

assembly, and 288 of the 300 seats in the provincial legislature. This outcome gave the Awami League a clear majority in the national assembly and entitled Sheikh Mujib to become prime minister of Pakistan under a majority government.[41]

Bhutto's PPP won 81 national assembly seats out of the 138 seats allotted to the western wing in the national assembly, and 144 of the 300 in the provincial assemblies in the western provinces, a victory which, although impressive in its own right, was fervently overshadowed by the Awami League's spectacular success. However, Bhutto was prepared to go to extraordinary lengths to get what he wanted and this election was no exception. The overall sagacity and political prowess of this Sindhi politician from West Pakistan was nothing short of extraordinary—it was a strength that was in fact far greater than the election results had suggested.

Unlike the Awami League, Bhutto and his PPP had managed to win over the influential and politically valuable Punjabi communities, as shown in Table 4.2. The PPP achieved 62 out of the total 83 seats in the province of Punjab. The PPP used their victory in Punjab as an opportunity to stand up against and challenge the Awami League, with Bhutto proudly propping himself up as the 'real' representative of West Pakistan. Bhutto also made it clear that he was not willing to accept defeat so easily when he declared: 'Punjab and Sindh are the bastions of power in Pakistan. Majority alone does not count in national politics.'[42] Bhutto and the PPP wanted to show the Bengalis that they were outmanoeuvred.

[41] Inder Malhotra, *Indira Gandhi: A Personal and Political Biography* (London: Hodder & Stoughton, 1989), 132.
[42] Christophe Jaffrelot and Gillian Beaumont, *A History of Pakistan and its Origins* (London: Anthem Press, 2002), 25.

TABLE 4.2: Results of the Pakistan National Assembly Elections, 1970

| | Punjab | Sindh | NWFP | Balochistan | West Pakistan | East Pakistan | Total Out of 300 Seats |
|---|---|---|---|---|---|---|---|
| Awami League | - | - | - | - | - | 160 | 160 |
| Pakistan People's Party | 62 | 18 | 1 | - | 81 | - | 81 |

Source: Shahid Javed Burki, *Pakistan Under Bhutto, 1971–1977*, 2nd edition (London: Macmillan, 1988), 57.

In the 1971 elections, out of the total of 300 national assembly seats, the Awami League and PPP won 241 seats and other political parties shared success in the remaining 59 constituencies, with the Pakistan Muslim League— the political organisation, which, under the leadership of Jinnah, had created Pakistan in 1947—securing only 18 seats.[43] This rejection of the Muslim League and its policies at a national level in 1971 was similar to the results of the provincial elections in East Bengal (East Pakistan) in 1954. In the years following the Partition, the Muslim League was perceived as a political party, which bureaucrats and dictators embraced and used as a ploy to justify and prolong their rule in Pakistan.

As soon as the results of the elections were announced, Yahya sent compliments to Mujib and Bhutto. He was eager to begin talks with them and invited them both to Islamabad. Mujib, however, declined to discuss or negotiate the post-election scenario with Yahya in the capital city in West Pakistan. This significant move was interpreted in some quarters as Mujib's lack of interest in becoming the prime minister of a united Pakistan; a more realistic interpretation was that Mujib wanted to assert that going forward, all crucial decisions were to be made in Dhaka (East Pakistan) and not in Islamabad (West Pakistan). The Awami League in its own way helped the government to misrepresent the picture. Sheikh Mujibur Rahman's refusal to visit West Pakistan after the elections enabled the government to name him anti-West Pakistani and a 'separatist'.[44]

On 3 January 1971, in one of his first post-election speeches, Sheikh Mujib declared that the national elections had constituted a referendum on the six-point programme.

[43] P.R. Chari and Pervaiz Iqbal Cheema, *The Simla Agreement 1972: Its Wasted Promise* (New Delhi: Manohar Publishers & Distributors, 2001), 92.
[44] Anthony Mascarenhas, *The Rape of Bangladesh* (Delhi: Vikas Publications, 1971), 116.

All Awami League members elected to the provincial and national assembly were required to join him in making a solemn pledge to devote their energies and resources in order to realise the Awami League programmes for provincial autonomy: 'to save [their] people from the exploitation of the vested interests and from the scourge of nature... He welcomed the political awakening in the West but refrained from calling upon Bhutto's People's Party for cooperation and assistance, instead calling upon the "awakening masses" of West Pakistan to join their Bengali brethren in an effort to realise common aspirations.'[45]

Yahya, therefore, had to go to Dhaka, where he arrived on 12 January 1972. He expected that Mujib would show him a draft of the Constitution prepared by the Awami League, as he had pledged during their secret meetings, including the one on the eve of the elections. The first one-on-one meeting between Yahya and Mujib took place on 12 January and lasted over three hours. G.W. Choudhury mentions in his book:

> I received and answered a summons from the President's House to see Yahya. I found him bitter and frustrated. He told me, 'Mujib has let me down. Those who warned me against him were right; I was wrong in trusting this person.' Mujib had refused to show him the draft of the constitution he had promised before the election. He made it clear to Yahya that as a leader of the majority party, he and he alone was responsible for the new constitution. Yahya's job was to summon the assembly immediately. Mujib threatened Yahya with dire consequences if he failed to do so.[46]

---

[45] Richard Sisson and Leo E. Rose, *War and Secession: Pakistan, India, and the Creation of Bangladesh* (Berkeley: University of California Press, 1990), 58.

[46] G.W. Choudhury, *The Last Days of United Pakistan* (Bloomington: Indiana University Press, 1974), 149.

It was in this unhappy state that Yahya went to Bhutto's hometown, Larkana, in West Pakistan, to have a discussion with him. After this meeting, Bhutto was regarded by Mujib and his party as an 'agent' of the hawkish elements of the junta who, according to him, had still not accepted the idea of any genuine transfer of power. Another complicating factor in the Mujib-Bhutto understanding was their divergent attitude towards India. Mujib was in favour of friendly relations with New Delhi, while Bhutto's anti-India rhetoric had endeared him to multitudes in West Pakistan.[47] Following the elections, in January 1971, Bhutto expressed his resentment with Yahya for having announced that 'Mujib will be the next prime minister' without consulting other political leaders. Yahya's response was justified when he pronounced that it was Mujib's electoral majority that gave him the mandate for prime ministership.[48] Yahya also told Bhutto that it was in his and the PPP's best interest to work out an understanding between him and Mujib. In response, Bhutto told Yahya that Mujib was 'a clever bastard' who wanted to convene the national assembly session as soon as possible so that he could 'bulldoze' his constitution and other plans for the government. Bhutto further declared that a national assembly meeting in Dhaka would be a 'slaughterhouse'.[49]

Mujib's stance became more and more confrontational. In his post-election speeches, from January to March 1971, there was no indication that there would be any adjustment to his six points, contrary to the pledge he made throughout 1969 and 1970 (during the three secret consultations in Dhaka with Yahya) when he promised that he would modify the extreme aspects of his six points. Mujib's agreement of

[47] Ibid., 154.
[48] Richard Sisson and Leo E. Rose, *War and Secession: Pakistan, India, and the Creation of Bangladesh* (Berkeley: University of California Press, 1990), 67.
[49] Ibid., 67–80.

showing flexibility and compromise on the six points is highlighted by G.W. Choudhury: 'I carefully examined the substance of Yahya-Mujib and Mujib-Ahsan (Vice Admiral Syed Mohammad Ahsan, who was the governor of East Pakistan from 1 September 1969–7 March 1971) talks in 1969–1970 and can vouch that Mujib repeatedly assured that he would modify his six points once the elections were over.'[50] In spite of his earlier pledge, Mujib, after his spectacular electoral success, declared that the six-point plan was 'the property of people of East Pakistan (Bangladesh)' and that would not be compromised.

Bhutto's speeches were no less uncompromising and provocative. In one of his earlier speeches, Bhutto declared, 'No constitution could be framed, nor could any government at the center be run, without my party's cooperation.' Both Mujib and Bhutto had realised their political strength, following and mass appeal proven by their recent electoral success. Mujib emerged as the sole leader of Bengalis. Who, after such an incomparable victory, could challenge him? Bhutto knew his strength—he had won the votes of the *jawans* (soldiers) and the inhabitants of the 'recruiting areas' for the Pakistan Army.[51]

To complicate matters, an Indian airlines flight from Srinagar to Jammu (Kashmir) was hijacked by two young Kashmiri 'freedom fighters' on 30 January 1971 and forced to land in Lahore (West Pakistan). Bhutto visited the hijackers, admired their heroism and supported their request for asylum. He declared that this heroic act was a sign that no power on earth could stop the Kashmiri struggle and that his PPP would offer assistance and backing to the hijackers and Kashmiri National Liberation Front. Mujib, in contrast, expressed his disgust of the hijacking

[50] G.W. Choudhury, *The Last Days of United Pakistan* (Bloomington: Indiana University Press, 1974), 92.
[51] Ibid., 145–47.

86

and urged the government to take 'effective measures to prevent interested quarters from exploiting the situation for their nefarious ends'. It was, he said, an attempt to distort the process of the transfer of power.[52] India as a reaction banned all Pakistani flights over its territory. The hijacking and its aftermath further heightened tension between India and Pakistan.

Towards the end of January 1971, Bhutto led a team of PPP delegates to Dhaka for talks with the Awami League on a power-sharing agreement. Mujib and the Awami League were adamant in their stance to frame a new (revised) constitution for Pakistan on the basis of the six points, something that worried Yahya, Bhutto and the politicians of West Pakistan as they had envisioned a different future for Pakistan. It was generally believed in East Pakistan that the Yahya regime and Bhutto were not going to allow Mujibur Rahman to form the national government and draft a new constitution according to the aspirations of the people of East Pakistan based on the six points.

On 15 February 1971, Mujib urged Yahya to accept the verdict of the majority and threatened that, 'in 1968–1969 when we were in prison, workers and peasants had brought down Ayub regime. Now that we are outside the prison, they should know what could happen'.[53] In response, Bhutto retorted, 'We can not go there (Dhaka) only to endorse the Constitution prepared by a party and to return humiliated. If we are not heard and even reasonable proposals put by us are not considered, I don't see the purpose to go there.'[54] Such proclamations added fuel to the fire on both sides. Bhutto's

[52] Richard Sisson and Leo E. Rose, *War and Secession: Pakistan, India, and the Creation of Bangladesh* (Berkeley: University of California Press, 1990), 76.
[53] Safdar Mahmood, *The Deliberate Debacle* (Pakistan: Sh. Muhammad Ashraf, 1976), 102.
[54] Ibid.

party also hardened its stance and in a show of solidarity all elected PPP members of national and provincial assemblies handed over their resignations to Bhutto.

While Mujib and his party were concerned with convening the national assembly, Bhutto was more interested in assuring the position that he and his party would have in the new government. He was less inclined to discuss the details of the six points; rather, he was 'prepared to accept them'—albeit under a few provisions. In exchange for accepting Mujib's six points, Bhutto demanded 'four of the ten cabinet positions' in Mujib's government for his party, along with 'either the deputy prime ministership or the presidency for himself'. Much to Bhutto's astonishment and displeasure, Mujib's response to Bhutto's demands was that 'the cabinet would be decided by the majority party—and that [Bhutto] could not be guaranteed a position in the ministry'. Mujib also allegedly told Bhutto that the presidency 'had already been promised to someone else'.[55]

Following this encounter, Mujib reportedly told his other party leaders that he was incensed at 'Bhutto's arrogance'[56] and his overall lack of respect for the Awami League. Mujib was under the impression that Bhutto had come to him to 'discuss constitutional issues'. However, as the events of the meeting indicated, all Bhutto was interested in was securing job openings for himself and his party members. Bhutto's overall reaction to the meetings in Dhaka was hopeful, even though many of his fellow party members perceived the discussions as 'pointless'.[57]

[55] Richard Sisson and Leo E. Rose, *War and Secession: Pakistan, India, and the Creation of Bangladesh* (Berkeley: University of California Press, 1990), 70.
[56] Ibid., 70.
[57] Ibid., 71.

Bangabandhu Sheikh Mujibur Rahman and Zulfikar Ali Bhutto in December 1971

Source: *The Daily Star,* 'In their words: Bhutto and Mujib, 23 December 1971', 15 November 2014, http://www.thedailystar.net/in-their-words-bhutto-and-mujib-december-1971-50468

The entire ordeal of the general election and its aftermath only enhanced Mujib's popularity in East Pakistan. Mujib's quest for political autonomy intensified after the results of the election were announced and Bhutto, after enthusiastically accepting the role of the 'sole representative of the people of West Pakistan', began brainstorming a strategy to block East Pakistan's movement towards independence.[58] Bhutto's relations with the army, though not perfect, were optimal considering the circumstances of his opponent, Mujib, who was deeply mistrusted by the generals for his secessionist posturing. In next to no time, Bhutto assumed the role of the representative of the western wing of Pakistan. He even refused to allow the national assembly to meet in Dhaka

[58] Shahid Javed Burki, *Pakistan Under Bhutto: 1971–1977*, 2nd edition (London: Macmillan, 1988), 58.

until there was an agreement between him and Mujib on the future constitution and power structure in Pakistan. From this deadlock was born the most indomitable nationalist movement in Pakistan's modern history.

## BHUTTO'S GROWING CONTEMPT FOR THE AWAMI LEAGUE

In February 1971, President Yahya summoned the first national assembly session in Dhaka on 3 March. Bhutto immediately raised his flag of rebellion and declared that unless there was an understanding between Mujib and himself on the future constituent assembly, they would not be allowed to meet. He also threatened 'a revolution from the Khyber to Karachi'.[59] By the last week of February, Bhutto went on record to say that there was no room left for negotiations with the Awami League and that he was adopting the path of non-cooperation.[60] Bhutto announced his decision not to participate in this meeting unless the Awami League modified its position on the six-point programme. Bhutto also threatened to boycott the national assembly and to oppose the government if Mujib was invited by President Yahya Khan to form the next government—forcefully demanding the PPP's inclusion in any power-sharing agreement.

Bhutto made a public declaration regarding the current political crisis between the Awami League and the central government. In his speech on 28 February 1971, Bhutto threatened personal and public harm if he were denied control of the situation.[61] Bhutto explained to the press that

[59] G.W. Choudhury, *The Last Days of United Pakistan* (Bloomington: Indiana University Press, 1974), 155.

[60] J.N. Dixit, *India-Pakistan in War and Peace* (London: Routledge, 2002), 164.

[61] Richard Sisson and Leo E. Rose, *War and Secession: Pakistan, India, and the Creation of Bangladesh* (Berkeley: University of California Press, 1990), 88.

whatever was going on at the national level had nothing to do with him or the Pakistan People's Party. Bhutto also emphasised the intensity of the brewing tensions with India. Resorting to his tried and tested socialist rhetoric, Bhutto stated, 'My primary duty is with the people, the peasants, and the working class. My place today is in villages and I call upon my party men to go to the people, to give them leadership, to stand by them and to be a source of strength in case there is an attempt by the predatory aggressor.'[62] Bhutto knew how to play up words and issues in a way that propped him up as the victim; however, while Bhutto painted himself as a victim to the public, to his internal party members, he was intolerant and unforgiving. He threatened to break the legs of any member of his party who would dare go to Dhaka for the constituent assembly session before Mujib agreed to PPP's demands, warning them that they had better get a 'one-way ticket'.[63]

Meanwhile, Mujib and the Awami League continued to reject Bhutto's demands for power-sharing and remained concrete in their principled stand and rightful claim to form the government. Mujib was mindful of the fact that the only way forward for Yahya Khan's government was to rightfully hand over power to the Awami League (and thus restore the sessions of the national assembly). He informed Yahya and his regime that he was 'ready for practical political compromises', despite Bhutto's acts of sabotage. On 24 February 1971, Mujib issued a lengthy press statement declaring that he was 'willing to have detailed and constructive discussions with the leaders of West Pakistan and with Yahya Khan' so as to resolve all of the problems provoking the current debate.[64] Mujib additionally reassured his fellow Awami League members that, 'the six

[62] Ibid., 80.
[63] Ibid., 89.
[64] J.N. Dixit, *India-Pakistan in War and Peace* (London: Routledge, 2002), 164.

points would not be susceptible to adjustment' under any means—promising to use 'whatever strategy necessary' to implement the Awami League's original political stand and election manifesto.[65] As evidenced from his actions and overall resilience with the central government in Pakistan, Mujib was devoted to the Bengali cause and was willing to pay any price to make good on his election manifesto and promises he had made to the people of East Pakistan.

On 27 February 1971, the Awami League parliamentary party approved the Awami League's draft constitution incorporating the six points.[66] Mujib assured that the six points would not be imposed on West Pakistan, which meant two different constitutions for the two wings of one country. Bhutto's response was, 'one document containing two different constitutions for East and West Pakistan would be an oddity'. Bhutto also made suggestions to resolve the crisis and hinted at the postponement of the national assembly session or removal of the 120-day limit for framing the Constitution as enshrined in Yahya's LFO. Speaking about the six points, 'he narrowed down his disagreement to foreign trade and foreign aid which could not be entrusted to the Provincial Governments'[67].

The Awami League held a simple but clear position regarding talks of their political programme—'No compromise on principles, but accommodation in their application.'[68] Mujib and the Awami League were genuinely concerned about Bhutto's involvement in the constitutional negotiations. The Awami League's doubts were confirmed when, on 1 March 1971, President Yahya Khan made

[65] Richard Sisson and Leo E. Rose, *War and Secession: Pakistan, India, and the Creation of Bangladesh* (Berkeley: University of California Press, 1990), 78.

[66] Safdar Mahmood, *The Deliberate Debacle* (Pakistan: Sh. Muhammad Ashraf, 1976),104–06.

[67] Ibid.,107.

[68] Richard Sisson and Leo E. Rose, *War and Secession: Pakistan, India, and the Creation of Bangladesh* (Berkeley: University of California Press, 1990), 56.

a surprise statement declaring the postponement of the national assembly session scheduled for 3 March 1971. He stated, 'For a healthy and viable constitution, it is necessary that both East and West Pakistan have an adequate sense of participation in the process of constitution making... Majority party from West Pakistan had declared its intention not to attend national assembly session on 3rd March. In addition, the general situation of tension created by India has further complicated the whole position. I have therefore decided to postpone the summoning of the national assembly to a later date.'[69] The explanation given by Yahya was considered ambiguous, elusive and defensive.

The news of the postponement, two days before national assembly proceedings were to commence, shocked all the members of the national assembly and ignited the passions of the people of East Pakistan. This news resulted in mass uprisings across East Pakistan, with students raising a Bengali flag of Independence at Dhaka University. As mass protests erupted across East Pakistan, Mujib announced a civil disobedience movement against the national government and all its offices and activities in an attempt to press for the convening of the national assembly. Mujib's call for non-cooperation was also taken for a call to arms, and a campaign of murder, arson and looting seized East Pakistan. A campaign of revenge was unleashed against the population perceived to be in support of the West Pakistan government. The East Pakistan minority community (Biharis) was also targeted and were butchered in large numbers.[70] There were some small but potentially dreadful skirmishes with the army, which was out in full force.

---

[69] Safdar Mahmood, *The Deliberate Debacle* (Pakistan: Sh. Muhammad Ashraf, 1976), 106.
[70] Lawrence Ziring, *Bangladesh From Mujib to Ershad: An Interpretive Study* (Karachi: Oxford University Press, 1992), 64.

Upon hearing the news of the postponement of the assembly session, the US Consul General to Dhaka, Archer Blood, raced up to the roof of the Adamjee Court building. 'We could see Bengalis pouring out of office buildings all around that neighbourhood. Angry as hornets.' They were disappointed and agitated since they were being robbed of their democratic victory. Although the crowds stayed peaceful, many people were carrying clubs or lathis (long wooden staffs, a weapon of choice for police in the subcontinent). He told the US State Department, 'I've seen the beginning of the breakup of Pakistan.' Scott Butcher, the young political officer, remembered a wave of civil disobedience, with incensed crowds in the streets and a number of clashes with the Pakistani authorities. The next day, Bengalis launched a general strike and at Mujib's word, normal life came to a halt. Bengali youth roved the city, shouting, *Joy Bangla!*—Victory to Bengal. Butcher was impressed by the military's restraint, which he found remarkable, 'They were being spat upon, harassed and hassled by locals, but behaving quite well under the circumstances.'[71]

Between 3 and 25 March 1971, the central government's writ did not run in East Pakistan and on 6 March, the Awami League declared it was establishing a parallel administration. Yahya broadcast an angry speech to the nation on 6 March, accusing the 'forces of disorder' of engaging in looting, arson and killing. The postponement of the assembly session had created an explosive situation from 1 March onwards. The government's helplessness was evident and having no other choice, on 6 March, Yahya decided to summon the national assembly session to Dhaka on 25 March without any conditions. But with the politicians still deadlocked, Yahya threatened the worst, 'It is

---

[71] Gary Jonathan Bass, *The Blood Telegram: Nixon, Kissinger, and a Forgotten Genocide* (New York: Alfred A Knopf, 2013), 28–29.

the duty of the Pakistan armed forces to ensure the integrity, solidarity, and security of Pakistan, and in this, they have never failed.'[72] It was assumed that after the announcement of a date for convening the national assembly, law and order situation would improve and riots, looting, arson and killing would stop, but it continued.

On 7 March 1971, Mujib delivered a landmark speech at Ramna Racecourse in Dhaka to an audience of over one million. He stated, 'The struggle now is the struggle for our emancipation; the struggle now is the struggle for our independence. *Joy Bangla!* Since we have given blood, we will give more blood. God willing, the people of this country will be liberated... Turn every house into a fort. Face (the enemy) with whatever you have.'[73] Mujib did not declare Independence on 7 March, but laid down four conditions to be met before he could consider participating in the session of the national assembly: immediate withdrawal of martial law; the army's return to barracks; a judicial inquiry into the loss of life caused by the army's action; and instant transfer of power before the assembly met or could frame a constitution.[74] In response to Mujib's demands, Bhutto declared, 'If power were to be transferred to the people before any constitutional settlement as demanded by Sheikh Mujibur Rahman, it should be transferred to the majority party in East Pakistan and the majority party in West Pakistan.'[75] On 10 March 1971, Bhutto sent a telegram to Mujib stating, 'Pakistan must be saved at any cost. I am willing to come to Dhaka to device a common solution to end the crisis so that assembly can proceed with the framing

[72] Ibid.
[73] Sayedur Rahman et al., 'Evaluation of Charismatic Leader of Bangabandhu: Sheikh Mujibur Rahman', *International Journal of Scientific and Research Publications* (Volume 4, No. 5, 2014), 3.
[74] G.W. Choudhury, *The Last Days of United Pakistan* (Bloomington: Indiana University Press, 1974), 158.
[75] Ibid.

of the constitution.'[76] This offer was not taken seriously, given the existing distrust.

Yahya arrived in Dhaka on 15 March and the same day Mujib issued a highly inflammatory and provocative statement, 'The heroic struggle of the people marches forward... The people of Bangladesh, civil servants, office and factory workers, peasants and students have demonstrated in no uncertain terms that they would die rather than surrender...The spirit of freedom in Bangladesh cannot be extinguished...The struggle shall, therefore, continue with renewed vigor until our goal of emancipation is realised.'[77] Mujib arrived at the president's house at 11:00 a.m. on 16 March for his first meeting with Yahya. His car bore a black flag to mourn the death of those killed during the preceding two weeks and also bore a symbol of Bangladesh. During this meeting, Mujib put forward his four points relating to the immediate lifting of martial law and the transfer of power.[78]

On 19 March 1971, eager to reduce tensions between the government and the Awami League, Yahya Khan arranged an impromptu meeting with Mujib. During the meeting Yahya told Mujib that Bhutto had been 'made aware' that an agreement between the Awami League and the West 'had been reached' and Bhutto was 'expected to attend scheduled deliberations for the interim constitution and the formation of the cabinet'.[79] In response, Mujib bluntly informed Yahya that 'if [Bhutto] were to be involved in anything', then the Awami League 'no longer wanted a cabinet at the national

---

[76] Safdar Mahmood, *The Deliberate Debacle* (Pakistan: Sh. Muhammad Ashraf, 1976),116.

[77] G.W. Choudhury, *The Last Days of United Pakistan* (Bloomington: Indiana University Press, 1974),162.

[78] Ibid., 164.

[79] Richard Sisson and Leo E. Rose, *War and Secession: Pakistan, India, and the Creation of Bangladesh* (Oakland: University of California Press, 1991), 120.

level'.[80] Mujib further conveyed the unequivocal distrust that he and the Awami League members felt for Bhutto, and how they believed that Bhutto and the PPP had a hidden strategy to stop the Awami League's plans from manifesting in the government.

Yahya and Mujib also discussed the formation of an interim government. It was after this meeting that Mujib informed a senior military officer that he and Yahya had tentatively agreed on establishing a national government composed of 11 ministers. Six of these, including the prime minister, would come from East Pakistan, and five—three from Bhutto's PPP and two from the National Awami Party (Wali Khan)—would be from West Pakistan.[81]

Bhutto arrived in Dhaka on 21 March 1971 and received an ostentatious display of acrimony by the Bengalis all the way from the airport to his hotel room. Upon his arrival, Bhutto met with Yahya who informed him that Mujib had insisted on the immediate lifting of martial law, the convening of the national assembly, creation of two constitutional committees—one for East Pakistan and the other for West Pakistan—the adoption of the six-point programme affirming East Pakistan's autonomy, and another autonomy manifesto that would be developed to serve the interests of several provinces of West Pakistan.[82]

On 22 March 1971, Yahya, Mujib and Bhutto met to deliberate and negotiate plans for the resumption of the national assembly session. It was the first time these three were face-to-face since the December elections.[83] Mujib was not happy to see Bhutto, especially since he had told Yahya about the Awami League's distrust of Bhutto and

[80] Ibid.
[81] Ibid., 116.
[82] Lawrence Ziring, *Pakistan in the Twentieth Century: A Political History* (Karachi: Oxford University Press, 1997), 350.
[83] Richard Sisson and Leo E. Rose, *War and Secession: Pakistan, India, and the Creation of Bangladesh* (Oakland: University of California Press, 1991), 122.

his PPP. Bhutto was concerned, as he did not expect Mujib and the Awami League to shift from their position, given their spectacular election success. 'It is reported that during the encounter, neither Mujib nor Bhutto would look at one another for more than a few seconds at a time, and that they both sat half turned away from each other.'[84] Yahya intervened and admonished their childish behaviour after which the two leaders agreed to leave the room for a private talk.

Bhutto later recalled the encounter between him and Mujib as conversational, explaining how Mujib had 'argued strongly for [Bhutto's] acceptance of the constitutional proposals' while also expressing that he 'recognised the PPP as the dominant party in the West and that the leaders of the other parties were good for nothing'. Bhutto also reported that Mujib told him 'not to trust the military'.[85] According to the Awami League's recollection of the same meeting, however, it was Bhutto who had told Mujib that the military could not be trusted; Bhutto also told Mujib that he was a 'fool' to believe that the military would 'hand over power to anyone, let alone "a Bengali"'.[86] It is reasonable to assume that neither of these men was looking out for anyone but their own political agendas.

Following the 22 March meeting, Yahya reassured leaders in West Pakistan that progress was being made, but that Mujib was proving difficult—Yahya relayed that Mujib had been easily agitated and 'unpredictable, agreeing to certain things and then coming back to ask for something different or more'.[87] The following passage extracted from G.W. Choudhury's *The Last Days of United Pakistan*

[84] Ibid.
[85] Ibid.
[86] Richard Sisson and Leo E. Rose, *War and Secession: Pakistan, India, and the Creation of Bangladesh* (Berkeley: University of California Press, 1990), Ibid., 122.
[87] Ibid.,129.

describes the events of 23 March in the years 1940, 1947 and 1971:

> March 23 has for long been a celebrated day for the
> Muslims of Indian subcontinent. It was on this day in
> 1940 that Quaid-i-Azam Mohammad Ali Jinnah, the
> founder of the future state of Pakistan, proclaimed to the
> world that the ultimate goal of Muslim nationalists in
> India was a separate state of their own. On the creation
> of Pakistan in 1947, March 23 was declared a 'national
> day' and is still observed with solemnity and dignity, just
> as January 26 is observed as Republic Day in India. But in
> Dhaka on March 23, 1971, it was considered 'Resistance
> Day'. No Pakistani flag was allowed to be hoisted, even
> on public buildings, let alone private houses; the two
> lonely flags that were hoisted were those at the president's
> house, where Yahya was staying, and at the Provincial
> Government's residence; and of course, it was also flown in
> the cantonment areas in Dhaka. Not only was the Pakistani
> flag not hoisted, it was burned and insulted while the flag
> of Bangladesh was displayed everywhere.[88]

The army command was apprehensive over a meeting of ex-servicemen that was addressed by two retired Bengali army officers, Maj. Gen. M.U. Majid and Col. M.A.G. Osmani, who advocated support of the Bangladesh liberation movement and led a procession to Dhanmandi in Dhaka for Mujib's blessing. Similarly, the Joy Bangla Brigade, a student militia, staged a parade at Paltan Maidan, where leaders of the Awami League-affiliated student organisations saluted and raised the Bangladesh flag before proceeding to Dhanmandi for Mujib's blessings.

On 23 March 1971, the Awami League delegation arrived at the president's house for negotiations. The car

---

[88] G.W. Choudhury, *The Last Days of United Pakistan* (Bloomington: Indiana University Press, 1974), 171.

that brought them bore a Bangladesh flag and those present to receive the delegation felt this to be a deliberate insult at a time when a political solution was deemed possible.[89] During the discussion between Awami League delegation and government representatives, a member of the Awami League team stated that Mujib had instructed him to change 'Federation of Pakistan' to 'Confederation of Pakistan'. One distinguished member of the government team reacted by leaping out of his chair and exclaiming that 'a confederation was, in essence, an agreement between two sovereign states, and that such an arrangement had not even been intimated, much less discussed, before'. He further elaborated that the word 'union'—if the Awami League was so intent upon using the Constitution of India as a model—was acceptable, but that 'confederation' was synonymous with the break-up of Pakistan and therefore not negotiable.[90]

No meetings took place between Mujib and Yahya after 22 March. There was a final meeting between Yahya's team and the Awami League delegation on 24 March at 6:00 p.m. In the meantime, all of the West Pakistani leaders that did not belong to Bhutto's party had meetings with Mujib and tried to persuade him to avoid confrontation, but to no avail. Bhutto and his team also had meetings with Yahya on 24 March.[91]

The disagreement between President Yahya, Bhutto and Mujib delayed the transfer of power to the Awami League and Mujibur Rahman. A cascade of events resulted in rebellion in East Pakistan and the imposition of a military solution by the Pakistani government, and consequently the infamous 'Operation Searchlight' when the armed forces of Pakistan marched into the cities of East Pakistan to

---

[89] Richard Sisson and Leo E. Rose, *War and Secession: Pakistan, India, and the Creation of Bangladesh* (Oakland: University of California Press, 1991), 123.

[90] Ibid., 127.

[91] G.W. Choudhury, *The Last Days of United Pakistan* (Bloomington: Indiana University Press, 1974), 178.

initiate their crackdown and suppress the tide of Bengali nationalism. The objectives of Operation Searchlight were to neutralise the political power of the Awami League and to re-establish public order:[92]

1. The top leadership of the party had to be captured.
2. Priority was to neutralise its more radical elements, in particular, student leaders, organisations and various cultural organisations that advocated a Bengali renaissance.
3. Several residential halls at the University of Dhaka were to be searched for arms that were believed to have been collected in support of rebellion and student leaders were to be arrested.
4. In case of armed resistance, troops were to respond with force.

Mujib was arrested and flown under military custody to a jail cell in West Pakistan. Within hours, student leaders, university teachers, writers, poets and other prominent Bengali intellectuals were arrested, and anyone protesting on the streets was shot.

It was about this time that the army displayed its might in other directions. Bhutto was in Dhaka and had an appointment with Mujib for the evening of 25 March. He was tied up with many engagements and telephoned Mujib at about 6:00 p.m. suggesting they postpone their meeting to the following day since he wanted to meet Yahya first. Mujib told him that he had no objection to a postponement, but how did Bhutto expect to see the president when he had already left for Karachi? According to the evidence given by some student leaders, Bhutto was taken aback. He tried to get through to the president's house but was told that

---

[92] Richard Sisson and Leo E. Rose, *War and Secession: Pakistan, India, and the Creation of Bangladesh* (Oakland: University of California Press, 1991), 157.

the president was 'having dinner at the Eastern Command Headquarters' and would not be able to see him. Bhutto, it seems, got the message. He was to get a more pertinent one the following day. Before putting him on a plane bound for Karachi, his military escort took him on a brief tour of the city, where the army was still in action.[93]

As the military began its crackdown, Mujib made a statement to his supporters by telegraph at midnight on 26 March 1971:

*Today Bangladesh is a sovereign and independent country. On Thursday night, West Pakistani armed forces suddenly attacked the police barracks at Razarbagh and the EPR headquarters at Pilkhana in Dhaka. Many innocent and unarmed have been killed in Dhaka city and other places of Bangladesh. Violent clashes between EPR and police on the one hand and the armed forces of Pakistan on the other are going on. The Bengalis are fighting the enemy with great courage for an independent Bangladesh. May Allah aid us in our fight for freedom. Joy Bangla!*[94]

The very next morning, Major Ziaur Rahman made a radio broadcast to the Bengali people on behalf of their leader, Mujib. Major Zia also declared an 'independent, sovereign Republic of Bangladesh'.[95] The final chapter of Bengali Liberation War thus began.

*This is Swadhin Bangla Betar Kendra. I, Major Ziaur Rahman, at the direction of Bangabandhu Mujibur Rahman,*

[93] Anthony Mascarenhas, *The Rape of Bangladesh* (Delhi: Vikas Publications, 1971), 116.

[94] Sayedur Rahman et al., 'Evaluation of Charismatic Leader of Bangabandhu: Sheikh Mujibur Rahman', *International Journal of Scientific and Research Publications* (Volume 4, No. 5, 2014),

[95] Mashuqur Rahman and Mahbubur Rahman Jalal, 'Swadhin Bangla Betar Kendro and Bangladesh's Declaration of Independence', *The Daily Star*, 25 November 2014, https://www.thedailystar.net/swadhin-bangla-betar-kendro-and-bangladeshs-declaration-of-independence-52001 (accessed 5 February 2017).

*hereby declare that the Independent People's Republic of Bangladesh has been established. At his direction, I have taken the command as the temporary Head of the Republic. In the name of Sheikh Mujibur Rahman, I call upon all Bengalis to rise against the attack by the West Pakistani Army. We shall fight to the last to free our motherland. Victory is, by the Grace of Allah, ours. Joy Bangla.*

Mujib and the Awami League were adamant in their stance to frame a new, revised constitution for Pakistan based on the six points, something that worried Yahya, Bhutto and the politicians in the West because they were convinced that the six-point plan was a secession plan. Yahya's insistence on a constitutional agreement and power-sharing formula between Bhutto and Mujib (before the first session of the newly elected Parliament) was considered logical in the West, as it would pre-empt and prevent a secessionist eventuality. In East Pakistan, the belief was that such an agreement would be yet another attempt to usurp the legitimate right of the East (Bengalis) to form a central government without the need for coalition and alliances. While the PPP was aggressive and confrontational, the Awami League was reactive and ameliorative, but firm nonetheless.

It is ironic that Bhutto supposedly represented a single wing of the country yet possessed a national programme, while Mujib claimed to represent a national majority, but had a programme that addressed the grievances and demands of a single region. Being reactive, the Awami League increasingly turned confrontational, and as the six points came under attack, it tried harder to develop a more intense internal commitment to the points in order to resist outside efforts to abort them.[96]

---

[96] Richard Sisson and Leo E. Rose, *War and Secession: Pakistan, India, and the Creation of Bangladesh* (Berkeley: University of California Press, 1990), 61.

As Mujib was given to hyperboles about 'revolution' and 'succession', Bhutto was also rousing the emotions of his audiences when he declared his willingness to martyr himself to a holy cause. Bhutto's larger-than-life rhetoric matched Mujib's and his constituents were just as emotionally charged as those addressed by Mujib. The problem in this ostentation was the dearth of logic and national purpose. Each politician masterfully outperformed the other and little attention was given to the potential of a break-up of Pakistan and it's aftershocks.[97]

## Summary

Irrespective of which narrative is the most credible, it is clear that the atmosphere was of utter disdain and there was distrust between Yahya's government, Mujib and Bhutto. Emotions were running high and all three characters in this game suspected medieval palatial intrigues against them and their plans. One thing that was indeed common between Bhutto and Mujib was their mutual distrust of Yahya and his government. Neither side was ready to look at the situation from the other's perspective, hence their paranoia and insecurities became more and more entrenched.

[97] Lawrence Ziring, *Pakistan in the Twentieth Century: A Political History* (Karachi: Oxford University Press, 1997), 336.

# 5

## BENGALI LIBERATION MOVEMENT LEADING TO THIRD INDO-PAK WAR

*Le secret des grandes fortunes sans cause apparente est
un crime oublié, parce qu'il a été proprement fait.
The secret of a great success for which you are at a loss
to account is a crime that has never been found out,
because it was properly executed.*

—Honoré de Balzac[1]

From Shiekh Mujibur Rahman and Zulfikar Ali Bhutto's
point of view, the poor management of the political
situation in the aftermath of the national elections
of 1970 by the Pakistani national government served
as the tipping point. The circumstances that brought
each man to political power could not have been more
favourable. Following the results of the general election,
politics in Pakistan was characterised by the dissolution
of basic democratic principles, such as a representative
government and respect for human rights. Pakistan faced
its biggest social and political shake-up in 1971 under
the Bengali Liberation War—the climax of the religious,
ethnic and linguistic instabilities in the region along with
stark economic disparities and dissatisfaction with the
ruling regime. Prime Minister Indira Gandhi's government

---

[1] https://www.goodreads.com/quotes/327664-le-secret-des-grandes-fortunes-sans-cause-apparente-est-un (accessed 12 June 2019).

formally supported the Bengali nationalist movement, in part, because India had much to gain from a divided, destabilised and hence, weaker Pakistani nation state.[2]

The assembly, which was elected through the first national elections in Pakistan in December 1970, did not meet. President Yahya announced that Mujib's trial would begin on 11 August 1971. The trial was held on camera, and the government did not break its silence on the proceedings until 28 September when it announced in a press release that the prosecution had begun presenting its case on 7 September and that 20 witnesses had been called to testify. The trial was to last through the escalation of the crisis between India and Pakistan in the fall, and the results had not been made public by the time war was declared on 3 December 1971.[3]

The Pakistan government banned the Awami League, which was the political party of the eastern wing that had secured a clear majority. The government also disqualified 76 of its 160 elected members in East Pakistan, labelling them as traitors. The Awami League was consequently reduced from 160 to just 84 in the house of 313—similar to Bhutto's PPP, which had won 81 seats in Punjab and Sindh. But General Yahya was living in a fool's paradise; he amended his legal framework order in September 1971 to facilitate the election commission (EC) and organise by-elections to fill East Pakistan's 'vacant seats'. By that time, it was inconceivable for the Government of Pakistan to function or have control in East Pakistan.[4]

---

[2] Mark Dummett, 'Bangladesh war: The article that changed history', BBC, 16 December 2011, http://www.bbc.com/news/world-asia-16207201 (accessed 12 June 2019).

[3] Richard Sisson and Leo E. Rose, *War and Secession: Pakistan, India, and the Creation of Bangladesh* (Oakland: University of California Press, 1991), 172.

[4] Tahir Mehdi, 'Revisiting 1971: What if they elected traitors?', *Dawn*, 17 December 2012, http://www.dawn.com/news/771987 (accessed 12 June 2019).

Religious parties spotted an opportunity within this forsaken situation. Six of them, led by the Jamaat-e-Islami—a religious and political organisation—decided to field candidates to fill these seats, knowing that no one would oppose their nominees. So, on 11 November, the EC found 63 candidates and as predicted, none were contested. The PPP initially criticised the by-elections, but later found the loot sale (guaranteed victory) too tempting and joined in on contesting the election for the vacant seats. Sixty-three seats were decided and the EC announced to hold polls on the remaining constituencies from 7 to 20 December 1971. On 3 December 1971, war broke out on the western front and the EC announced the postponement of the by-elections.[5]

According to G.W. Choudhury, even before Mujib surrendered to the Pakistani army in March, there was a secret deal mediated through the US officials guaranteeing Mujib's safety and security, whereas the Pakistan Army was out to eliminate other top Awami League members. Strangely, the army treated Mujib and his family congenially.[6] During Mujib's nine-month incarceration in West Pakistan, guerrilla war broke out between Pakistani government forces and Bengali nationalists aided by India.

Negotiations towards a constitutional settlement and transfer of power in Pakistan (before the Bangladesh Liberation War) in 1971 began with four sets of domestic participants, three major and one minor—the Awami League, the Pakistan People's Party, the government and the smaller political parties. The process ended in polarisation between coalitions and the outbreak of civil war. The following factors were critical in this transformation:

1. Curse of knowledge of past injustice leading to mistrust of their counterparts and misperceptions

---

[5] Ibid.
[6] G.W. Choudhury, *The Last Days of United Pakistan* (Bloomington: Indiana University Press, 1974), 196.

about the meaning and rationale of actions that others took in pursuing their avowed intentions.

2. Partakers took positions that were vague and at times contradictory, thus exacerbating the existing inclination to question and suspect one another.

3. Each participant was fearful that its core interests could not be protected under any arrangement in the transfer of power.

The process of polarisation was encouraged by the military regime's inability to preserve its neutrality in the negotiations. With time, divisive elements, both natural and calculated, resulted in popular pressure within the constituency of each group and served to reduce the flexibility of its leadership. The most constraining forces, however, were the stereotyping and distrust drawn from past political conflicts; the former serving to distort images of old figures in new situations, and the latter resulting in the contortion of their resolves and intents.[7]

On March 31, the Indian Parliament passed a resolution in support of the 'people of Bengal'. In Delhi, open interference in the internal affairs of Pakistan went hand in hand with feverish activity by the Research and Analysis Wing (RAW) agents operating in Calcutta. They played a central role in helping the Awami League leaders who had escaped the army's dragnet to establish a government-in-exile in Calcutta on April 17.[8]

On 17 April 1971, the Mujibnagar government, constituted in the Meherpur district of Bangladesh to conduct the Bangladesh War of Liberation, formally proclaimed Bengali independence and named Sheikh Mujib

---

[7] Richard Sisson and Leo E. Rose, *War and Secession: Pakistan, India, and the Creation of Bangladesh* (Oakland: University of California Press, 1991), 266–67.

[8] Dilip Hiro, *The Longest August: The Unflinching Rivalry Between India and Pakistan* (New York: Nation Books, 2015), 201.

as its president.[9] Soon after the civil war broke out, refugees from East Pakistan were flowing into India in massive numbers; at its peak, 150,000 people a day flowed in, totalling 10 million over the next nine months. India was covertly supporting the liberation movement by training and equipping the guerilla fighters.[10]

Like her Pakistani rival, Bhutto, Prime Minister Indira Gandhi made valuable use of socialist language to appeal to the masses, describing the war with Pakistan as a 'bigger war against poverty'.[11] One month after the refugees began pouring in West Bengal (India), Indira visited the refugee camps there and saw the realities of war first-hand, although unprepared for the atrocities that confronted her. In an emotional speech to the Indian public and the broader global community about the war in East Pakistan, Indira described how she was 'haunted by the tormented faces in the overcrowded refugee camps'.[12] Moreover, Indira Gandhi's 'initial and instinctive reaction was to give immediate recognition to a free Bangladesh and to back the liberation struggle and the resistance movement with full military support'.[13]

To deal with the influx of refugees, Indira created a separate government department under the charge of the secretary of rehabilitation. Indira further took up the East Pakistan crisis with the UN, filing an appeal with the Economic and Social Council (ECOSOC) as well as the UN High Commission for Refugees (UNHCR).[14] Indira Gandhi's government decided on a policy approach to

[9] James Heitzman et al., *Bangladesh: A Country Study* (Washington: Federal Research Division, Library of Congress, 1989), 31.

[10] Katherine Frank, *Indira: The Life of Indira Nehru Gandhi* (London: HarperCollins, 2001), 331.

[11] Ibid., 343.

[12] Ibid., 331.

[13] J.N. Dixit, *India-Pakistan in War and Peace* (London: Routledge, 2002), 174–75.

[14] Ibid.

the situation in Pakistan and comprised the following key elements as noted by J.N. Dixit in *India-Pakistan in War & Peace*:[15]

- The East Pakistan crisis could be resolved only if Pakistan respected the results of the general elections and assured the fulfilment of the legitimate political and constitutional aspirations of the people of Pakistan, especially East Pakistan.
- To achieve this objective, the military regime should immediately release Sheikh Mujibur Rahman from custody, enabling him to return to Dacca, and should recommence political negotiations with him.
- Pakistan should ensure the return of all East Pakistan refugees to their homes, undertaking to guarantee their safety, honour and economic well-being.
- Pakistan should immediately stop the military crackdown on the people of East Pakistan, and Pakistani troops should return to their barracks.
- The international community should pressurise Pakistan to resolve the East Pakistan crisis by peaceful means; this advice and pressure should be generated through bilateral diplomatic channels and the United Nations.
- The United Nations and its specialised agencies should initiate immediate steps to give relief and rehabilitation assistance to millions of East Pakistani refugees in India and those who had become shelterless within East Pakistan due to the military crackdown.

In early June, secretary-general of UN U. Thant proposed to the Indian representative at the UN that the UNHCR 'establish a presence' in the refugee camps in India and in

[15] Ibid., 175–77.

the 'reception centers' in East Pakistan that had been set up on the border to 'facilitate the reentry' of refugees. The Indian response was 'categorically negative' on the grounds that no refugee could return to East Pakistan, whatever the policy position of the Government of Pakistan, until a 'climate of security' was achieved through the establishment of an Awami League-led government.[16]

On 9 August 1971, Indira signed the Soviet-Indian friendship treaty which comprised of the Treaty of Peace, Friendship and Cooperation between the two countries. Amongst other provisions of this treaty, its strategic significance included consultations and remedial measures if either country was attacked.[17] This treaty at a time when war was imminent between India and Pakistan showcased Indira's political prowess and sagacity.

New Delhi reacted even more negatively to the secretary-general's suggestion of a mutual withdrawal of Indian and Pakistani military forces from their respective borders and the posting of a team of UN observers on each side of the border. In a letter dated 20 October to the president of Pakistan and the prime minister of India, U. Thant offered 'his good offices' in mediating the dispute and called for a mutual withdrawal of forces from the border by both sides. President Yahya Khan welcomed the initiative and responded favourably, but Mrs Gandhi replied in a 1,000-word letter that, in effect, accused the international community, and by implication the secretary-general, of trying to save the military regime in Pakistan: 'This is what must be kept in mind instead of the present attempt to save the military regime. To sidetrack this main problem and to

[16] Richard Sisson and Leo E. Rose, *War and Secession: Pakistan, India, and the Creation of Bangladesh* (Oakland: University of California Press, 1991), 189.

[17] Henry Kissinger, *The White House Years* (Boston: Little, Brown and Co., 1979), 866.

convert it into an Indo-Pakistani dispute can only aggravate tensions.' U. Thant was urged to focus his attention on a political settlement in 'East Bengal which meets the declared wishes of the people.'[18]

## THE THIRD INDO-PAK WAR AND INDO-BENGALI RELATIONS

> *Once I get an idea in my head, no one in the world can make me change my mind... a person like me doesn't have fear first and regrets afterwards.*
>
> —Indira Gandhi[19]

Indira had no intention of allowing the leadership in Pakistan to resolve or recuperate from its political and military dilemmas. To intensify the crisis, she rejected all offers and initiatives by Pakistani leadership without offering an amicable alternative. She was also well aware that if the discussion between Awami League and Pakistani leadership started it may lead to some sort of compromise and Indira was not willing to risk it.[20]

Henry Kissinger in his book *The White House Years* explains the response to meditation by the US government:[21]

> *Our first overture was to Yahya, with encouraging results. On 11 October 1971, he accepted our proposal of a mutual pullback of troops from the borders. He now gave us a timetable for a political solution. He would convene a new National Assembly before the end of the*

---

[18] Richard Sisson and Leo E. Rose, *War and Secession: Pakistan, India, and the Creation of Bangladesh* (Oakland: University of California Press, 1991), 189–190.

[19] Oriana Fallaci, *Interview with History* (Boston: Houghton Mifflin, 1977), 176–79.

[20] Henry Kissinger, *The White House Years* (Boston: Little, Brown and Co., 1979), 871.

[21] Ibid., 876.

*year and submit a constitution to it. Shortly after the
National Assembly met he would turn over power to a
civilian government. Provincial assemblies would meet
in both West and East Pakistan. East Pakistan would
have a majority in the civilian national government
(in effect guaranteeing an outcome compatible with
Bengali aspirations). He promised again that Mujib's
death sentence would not be carried out; the civilian
government could deal with his future within three
months. On October 16 our charge in Islamabad met with
Bhutto, who agreed that the leading positions in a new
government should go to East Pakistan; Mujib could play
an active role. There was now little doubt left that East
Pakistan would be able to decide its future once Yahya had
stepped down.*

*The results in India were less auspicious. On October
12 [Ambassador] Keating saw Swaran Singh and was
given the familiar catalogue of Indian grievances: The
United States was not using its influence with Islamabad
adequately; the efforts to start a dialogue with the
Bangladesh exiles were a subterfuge to bypass Mujib. A
mutual troop withdrawal, the Foreign Minister indicated,
was unacceptable, but a unilateral Pakistani withdrawal
from the frontier would be useful and India might
reconsider if the Pakistanis in fact withdrew. Singh did
not explain how Pakistan could withdraw troops while
the Indian army was massed at its frontier and infiltrating
thousands of guerillas.*

The Third Indo-Pak War took place between November and
December 1971. It had its roots in the Bengali nationalist
movement in East Pakistan when millions of East Pakistani
Bengalis began pouring into India in an effort to escape the
acrimonious conflict between Bengali nationalist guerillas
and the Pakistani military. Indira Gandhi embarked upon

a diplomatic offensive and visited many capitals of the world, ostensibly with the objective of communicating to the powerful nations the enormous burden placed on India by the presence of a massive number of refugees and to ensure the necessary aid from them. The real objective of the diplomatic onslaught was two-fold—to stress that unless a settlement was secured quickly, India would be compelled to intervene militarily and to assess how the world would react if India invaded Pakistan.[22]

This excerpt extracted from Gary J. Bass's novel *The Blood Telegram* is an effectual account of the Bangladesh Liberation War: [23]

*India secretly had its army and security forces use bases on Indian soil to support Bengali guerrillas in their fight against the Pakistani state. India devoted enormous resources to covertly sponsoring the Bengali insurgency inside East Pakistan, providing the guerrillas with arms, training, camps, and safe passage back and forth across a porous border. Indian officials, from Gandhi on down, evaded or lied with verve, denying that they were maintaining the insurgency. But in fact, as India's own secret records prove, this massive clandestine enterprise was approved at the highest levels, involving India's intelligence services, border security forces, and army.*

*In the event, Pakistan rashly struck the first blow of a full-scale conventional war, with a surprise air attack in December 1971 that brought fierce combat in both West and East Pakistan. But while Indians today generally remember the war as outright Pakistani aggression, India's actual path to war shows a great degree of Indian responsibility as well. India knew it had a fearsome*

[22] P.R. Chari and Pervaiz Iqbal Cheema, *The Simla Agreement 1972: Its Wasted Promise* (New Delhi: Manohar Publishers & Distributors, 2001), 106.

[23] Gary Jonathan Bass, *The Blood Telegram: Nixon, Kissinger, and a Forgotten Genocide* (New York: Alfred A. Knopf, 2013), xviii.

*military advantage, and Gandhi's government used that*
*ruthlessly. According to senior Indian generals, Gandhi*
*wanted her forces to go to war not long after the start of*
*Pakistan's crackdown, and had to be persuaded to wait*
*for cooler fighting weather and more time to train. While*
*the Indian military waited for winter, the Indian-backed*
*insurgency bled the Pakistan army, leaving it demoralised*
*and stretched thin. India's support for the Bengali rebels*
*led to border clashes with Pakistani troops, and, as winter*
*approached, to several substantial Indian incursions onto*
*Pakistani territory... Still, Pakistan's air attack was a final*
*act of folly for the military dictatorship. The war, fought*
*in just two weeks, ended with a resounding Indian victory,*
*and created the fledgling state of Bangladesh.*

On the night of 21 November 1971, discontinuing their earlier routine of returning to Indian soil after pinprick attacks in East Pakistan, India's forces stayed put. Two days later, Yahya Khan declared a state of Emergency in all of Pakistan and called on Pakistanis to prepare for war with India. By 25 November, several Indian Army divisions attacked some border regions of East Pakistan, using armour and artillery fire. Unable to circumvent, deter or respond to India's activities in the East, on 3 December 1971, Pakistan launched air attacks on several Indian airfields inside India, including Ambala in Haryana, Amritsar in Punjab and Udhampur in Jammu and Kashmir. However, the attacks did not yield the intended results.[24]

When Indira Gandhi was informed of this move, she remarked, 'Thank God, they've attacked us.' Observers considered India's 11-day-old military moves in East Pakistan as part of the nationalist Bengalis' ongoing armed struggle. At midnight, Indira Gandhi declared war on Pakistan.

---

[24] Global Security, 'Indo-Pakistani War of 1971', http://www.globalsecurity.org/org/overview/index.html (accessed 9 February 2017).

On 4 December, India launched an integrated ground, sea and air invasion of East Pakistan of such might that it won the moniker of a 'blitzkrieg without tanks'. Accompanied by Mukti Bahini[25] fighters, Indian troops penetrated the East Pakistani frontier and advanced on Dhaka from the north, east and west. General Niazi, commander-in-chief of the Pakistani forces in East Pakistan, tried to slow down the enemy's advance by blowing up bridges. Aided by Mukti Bahini guerrillas already inside East Pakistan, the invading forces cut off communication between the capital and other important cities. By capturing vital railheads, they immobilised the defenders. Indians responded to Pakistan's air and ground assaults on their soil with attacks on targets in West Pakistan.[26]

Yahya Khan's military government responded to India's policy stance with accusations that Indira Gandhi and the Indian government were trying to dismantle the Pakistani nation state. The war was yet another example of Yahya Khan's high-handedness and lack of comprehension of the gravity of the situation. Yahya Khan also appointed a Bengali politician, Nurul Amin, as the prime minister, with Bhutto as the deputy prime minister and foreign minister on 6 December 1971. In the 1970 elections, Amin was elected to the national assembly as one of the only two non-Awami League members from East Pakistan. Amin would have never been acceptable to the Awami League or the majority in the East, but this smokescreen was to demonstrate to the people in West Pakistan and the world that a Bengali was appointed to the highest office in the country by Yahya

---

[25] Mukti Bahini, translated as 'freedom fighters' or 'liberation army', also known as the Bangladesh Forces, was the guerrilla resistance movement formed by the Bangladeshi military, paramilitary and civilians during the War of Liberation that transformed East Pakistan into Bangladesh in 1971.

[26] Dilip Hiro, *The Longest August: The Unflinching Rivalry Between India and Pakistan* (New York: Nation Books, 2015), 209–10.

Khan's government in recognition of East Pakistan's election victory.

Bhutto arrived in New York on 10 December 1971 and spoke at the Security Council on 12, 13 and 15 December. On 15 December 1971, annoyed by Soviet Union's repeated vetoes in the UN, facilitating India's offensive in East Pakistan, Bhutto delivered an emotional speech declaring that this was his last address to the UN Security Council[27]:

*We were hoping that the Security Council, mindful of its responsibilities for the maintenance of world peace and justice, would act according to principles and bring an end to a naked, brutal aggression against my people... For four days we have been deliberating here. For four days the Security Council has procrastinated. Why? Because the object was for Dacca to fall. That was the object. It was quite clear to me from the beginning. All right, so what if Dacca falls? Cities and countries have fallen before. They have come under foreign occupation... If India talks about the will of the people of East Pakistan and claims that it had to attack Pakistan in order to impose the will of the people of East Pakistan, then what has it done about Kashmir? East Pakistan is an integral part of Pakistan. Kashmir is a disputed territory. Why does India then not permit it to exercise its will... The refugee problem was used as a pretext, an ugly, crude pretext, a shameful pretext to invade my country, to invade Pakistan... Muslim Bengal was a part of Pakistan of its free will, not through money. We did not buy it as Alaska was purchased... I find it disgraceful to my person and to my country to remain here a moment longer than is necessary. I am not boycotting. Impose any decision, have a treaty worse than the Treaty of Versailles, legalise aggression, legalise occupation, legalise everything that has been illegal upto 15 December 1971.*

[27] https://www.bhutto.org/1970-1971_speech46.php (accessed 18 March 2019).

*I will not be a party to it. We will fight; we will go back and fight. My country beckons me. Why should I waste my time here in the Security Council? I will not be a party to the ignominious surrender of a part of my country. You can take your Security Council. Here you are. I am going.'*

As Belokrenitsky and Moskalenko explain, 'Bhutto's bravado, mixed with the tears of bitterness and hard feelings, was meant to affect both the international and domestic audience.'[28] Instead of acknowledging the exploitation of Bengalis since 1947 and the ineptness of Yahya Khan's government in amicably resolving the situation, Bhutto prompted to lay the entire blame on India, alleging Indira Gandhi's deviousness in formulating the succession of East Pakistan.

In the UN, Bhutto masterfully pleaded Pakistan's case and grievances. His tactics worked; his strategy was persuasive and won the support of the US administration as well as UN member states that believed in preserving the prevailing borders of a State. As a result, the majority of member states voted for an immediate ceasefire in the Indo-Pak war.[29] Shortly after the negotiations, US president Nixon dispatched a US navy task force into the Bay of Bengal. The Nixon administration later explained this decision as a tactic to apply pressure on India to end the war, though the move seemed like an attempt by the US to protect and prevent Pakistan from disintegrating further.[30]

India's formal declaration of war on 3 December brought on a spate of resolutions in the UN Security Council—a total of 24 over a 2-week period submitted by member states and combinations of members. Poland presented a resolution which was provocative and potentially embarrassing for the Government of India. This resolution, like the earlier Soviet

---

[28] V.Y. Belokrenitsky and V.N. Moscalenko, A *Political History of Pakistan, 1947–2007* (Oxford: Oxford University Press, 2013), 207.

[29] Ibid., 206–09.

[30] Ibid.

resolutions, called for the transfer of power in East Pakistan to the representatives elected in December 1970, i.e. the Awami league; and this was, of course, Indian policy. But unlike Soviet resolutions, 'the Polish proposal also called for an immediate cease-fire and troop withdrawals by both sides, as well as the renunciation of claims to any territories acquired by force during the war. These provisions aroused considerable distress in New Delhi'[31]. In the Security Council proceedings on 15 December, 'Bhutto denounced the failure of the United Nations to act promptly, tore up a copy of the Polish resolution, and stormed out of the session, halting all consideration of the subject.'[32] Two days later, Dhaka fell; the Pakistani army in the East capitulated and the war was concluded.

The commander-in-chief of the Pakistani forces in East Pakistan, General Niazi, signed the Pakistani Instrument of Surrender in Dhaka's racecourse the following afternoon, on 16 December 1971. He gave up his entire army—93,000 of Pakistan's soldiers, supporters and civilian officials—at the ornate administrative office of the Ramna Racecourse, the formerly exclusive club of the British officers stationed in Dhaka. It was at this very venue on 6 March 1971 that Sheikh Mujibur Rahman had declared in his historic speech—'This time the struggle is for our freedom'. And on 16 December 1971, surrounded by a large group of uniformed officers and civilian bureaucrats, the bearded Lieutenant General Jagjit Singh Aurora, wearing a starched striped turban, countersigned the instrument of surrender signed by clean-shaven General Niazi, who was sporting a beret.[33] It was the most ignominious defeat in the nation's history,

---

[31] Richard Sisson and Leo E. Rose, *War and Secession: Pakistan, India, and the Creation of Bangladesh* (Oakland: University of California Press, 1991), 218–19.

[32] Ibid., 220.

[33] Dilip Hiro, *The Longest August: The Unflinching Rivalry Between India and Pakistan* (New York: Nation Books, 2015), 215.

and probably of the contemporary world history. 'The first morning of cease-fire...officers who had been comrades at the same staff college...stood looking at one another wondering who to blame. The Indian troops – dusty in buses, jeeps, or trucks – took the garlands and embraces, the cries of "Joy Bangla" from leaping near hysterical Bengalis.'[34] In the aftermath, Bhutto's People's Party organised mass meetings and protests as word of the Dhaka debacle cast its shadow across West Pakistan. The cry of 'Death to Yahya Khan' alternated with 'Long life to Bhutto!'[35]

Text of the Pakistani Instrument of Surrender:[36]

*The Pakistani Eastern Command agrees to surrender all Pakistan Armed Forces in Bangladesh to Lieutenant-General Jagjit Singh Aurora, General Officer Commanding in Chief of the Indian and Bangladesh forces in the Eastern Theatre.*

*This surrender includes all Pakistan land, air and naval forces as also all para-military forces and civil armed forces.*

*These forces will lay down their arms and surrender at the place where they are currently located to the nearest regular troops under the command of Lieutenant-General Jagjit Singh Aurora.*

*The Pakistan Eastern Command shall come under the orders of Lieutenant-General Jagjit Singh Aurora as soon as this instrument has been signed. Disobedience of orders will be regarded as a breach of the surrender terms and will be dealt with in accordance with the accepted laws and usages of war.*

---

[34] Stanley A. Wolpert, *Bhutto of Pakistan: His Life and Times* (New York: Oxford University Press, 1993), 169.

[35] Ibid., 170.

[36] Col. S.P. Salunke, *Pakistani POW's in India* (New Delhi: Vikas Publishing, 1977), Appendix C.

*The decision of Lieutenant-General Jagjit Singh Aurora shall be final, should any doubt arise as to the meaning or interpretation of the surrender terms.*

*Lieutenant-General Jagjit Singh Aurora gives a solemn assurance that personnel who surrender shall be treated with dignity and respect that soldiers are entitled to in accordance with provisions of the Geneva Convention and guarantees the safety and well-being of all Pakistan military and para-military forces who surrender.*

*Protection will be provided to foreign nationals, ethnic minorities and personnel of the West Pakistan [region] by the forces under the command of Lieutenant-General Jagjit Singh Aurora.*

The estimate of deaths by violence in East Pakistan from 26 March to 16 December 1971 has varied wildly—from 26,000 to 3 million. According to the records of Pakistan's Eastern Command, witnessed by the Hamoodur Rahman Judicial Inquiry Commission set up by the Government of Pakistan to enquire into the 1971 debacle, the military killed 26,000 people in action, though the commission noted that the officers always provided a minimum count. The excessively inflated figure of 5 million—5 times the estimate for the unparalleled communal butchery in Punjab during 1947—was first announced by Sheikh Mujibur Rahman in his interview with British TV host David Frost, in January 1972 (after his return to Dhaka as a free man). The figure given by Indian officials to Richard Sisson and Leo E. Rose, authors of *War and Secession: Pakistan, India, and the Creation of Bangladesh*, was 100,000. A Bengali-speaking research scholar at Oxford University, Sarmila Bose, in her study published as *Dead Reckoning: Memories of the 1971 Bangladesh War* estimated a total of 50,000 to 100,000 dead, which included the worst of the alleged atrocities. Her research included interviewing participants in Pakistan and

Bangladesh—mainly retired Pakistani officers, survivors of the brutalities and their relatives in Bangladesh as well as members of the non-Bengali and non-Muslim minorities.[37]

## Bengal-India Relations

Bangladesh and Pakistan began their unconnected lives in very dissimilar contexts. In Bangladesh, blood had been spilt, large sections of the population were dislocated and much infrastructure was destroyed in the nine-month civil war. The new Pakistan (former West Pakistan) was virtually untouched, at least physically. Despite these different initial circumstances, each began its separate existence as a democracy trying to move on from 14 years of military rule in united Pakistan.[38]

In stark contrast to the situation with Zulfikar Ali Bhutto and Pakistan, Sheikh Mujibur Rahman and the newly established Bengali nation state held close ties with India. On 16 December 1971, Indira Gandhi made a statement in the Parliament formally announcing the Pakistani army's surrender in Bangladesh: 'I have an announcement to make. The West Pakistan forces have unconditionally surrendered in Bangladesh. The instrument of surrender was signed in Dhaka at 16:31 hours Indian Standard Time today...on behalf of the Pakistan Eastern Command... [The] Indian and Bangladesh forces in the Eastern Theatre accepted the surrender. Dhaka is now the free capital of a free country.'[39]

Indira further declared that India's goals in the region had been met and that the Indian Army's objectives were

[37] Dilip Hiro, *The Longest August: The Unflinching Rivalry Between India and Pakistan* (New York: Nation Books, 2015), 216–17.

[38] William B. Milam, *Bangladesh and Pakistan Flirting with Failure in South Asia* (New York: Columbia University, 2009), 29.

[39] Government of India, 'Statement of the Prime Minister of India Mrs. Indira Gandhi in Parliament on the Pakistan Army's surrender in Bangladesh', https://www.hcidhaka.gov.in/pages.php?id=1255 (accessed 20 January 2017).

limited 'to assist[ing] the gallant people of Bangladesh and their Mukti Bahini, to liberat[ing] their country from a reign of terror, and to resist[ing] aggression on our own land. Indian armed forces will not remain in Bangladesh any longer than is necessary'[40]. The landmark speech was Indira's recognition of Sheikh Mujibur Rahman as the leader and 'father' of the newly sovereign Bengali nation: 'We hope and trust that the Father of this new nation, Sheikh Mujibur Rahman, will take his rightful place among his own people and lead Bangladesh to peace, progress and prosperity. The time has come when they can together look forward to a meaningful future in their Sonar Bangla. They have our good wishes.'[41]

According to Henry Kissinger in his book *The White House Years,* the US government was convinced that Indira Gandhi wanted to take this opportunity to forcibly take over territory in West Pakistan including Pakistan-controlled Kashmir and settle these intractable territorial problems with Pakistan forever in favour of India.

> *Next day Mrs. Gandhi offered an unconditional cease-fire in the West. There is no doubt in my mind that it was a reluctant decision resulting from Soviet pressure, which in turn grew out of American insistence... It was also Chou Enlai's judgement as he later told Bhutto, that we had saved West Pakistan. The crisis was over. We had avoided the worst – which is sometimes the maximum statesmen can achieve.*[42]

India's strategic alliances couldn't have been more straightforward. As indicated in Indira's speech, the Indian government welcomed a new, third nation state into the

[40] Ibid.
[41] Ibid.
[42] Henry Kissinger, *The White House Years* (Boston: Little, Brown and Co., 1979), 912.

formerly bipartite subcontinent where politics had oscillated between India and Pakistan; in place of Pakistan, India now faced a friendly and weak Bangladesh across the negotiating table.[43]

Bangladesh declared its independence on 16 December 1971. It began its independent life somewhat lacking in the way of natural, human and financial resources compared to the new State of Pakistan. Bangladeshis set out on their nationalistic journey with a sense of euphoria resulting from liberation, which allowed their leaders to organise the government and write a constitution in a remarkably short time frame. Despite its extreme poverty and illiteracy, the dislocation caused by the war and the total absence of a culture of democratic governance, Bangladesh was relatively fertile soil for democracy. Its homogenous population and open-minded culture, as well as its tradition of grassroots mobilisation, were conducive to democratic growth, bestowing on Bangladesh a more advantageous beginning than many newly independent, developing countries.[44]

## Mujib's Release

While a prisoner of General Yahya Khan in 1971 during the Bangladesh independence struggle, Mujib had an even closer brush with death. Recounted by Anthony Mascarenhas in his book *Bangladesh: A Legacy of Blood*, Mujib was tried by a military court and found guilty of treason and sedition:

> *On 15 December 1971, the day before the Pakistan army surrendered to the Indian troops in Dhaka, General Yahya Khan had ordered Mujib's execution. A military team*

---

[43] Ishtiaq Hossain, 'Bangladesh-India Relations: Issues and Problems', *Asian Survey* (Volume 21, No. 11, 1981), 1,115–28.

[44] William B. Milam, *Bangladesh and Pakistan Flirting with Failure in South Asia* (New York: Columbia University, 2009), 30.

*went from Rawalpindi to Mianwali, where Sheikh Mujib*
*was being held in jail. The team went about its task in a*
*methodical manner. A shallow grave was dug in the cement*
*floor of the room adjoining the Bangladesh leader's cell. He*
*was told that this was being done as an air raid precaution.*
*But Mujib knew what it was for and prepared himself for*
*the worst. The jailer, taking pity on Mujib and knowing*
*that Yahya Khan was about to abdicate, smuggled him*
*to his personal quarters where he kept him for two days.*
*The operation was helped by the confusion that attended*
*the surrender of Pakistan army. When Zulfikar Ali Bhutto*
*replaced General Yahya Khan as president, he refused to*
*revalidate the execution order when asked to do so.*[45]

In the wake of violent protests across West Pakistan, Yahya
had no choice but to resign in the aftermath of the Bangladesh
debacle. Bhutto, who led the most influential political party
in West Pakistan, replaced Yahya Khan as the president
and the first civilian chief martial law administrator on 20
December 1971.[46] One week after Bhutto took charge, he
himself had driven after sundown to a well-guarded army
bungalow near the military airport. Mujib had been flown
there the day before by helicopter from his prison cell; he
had not read the newspaper, nor listened to the radio since
his arrest in Dhaka in late March 1971.[47] In an interview
aired on Pakistan television in 2015, Raja Anar Khan, who
was an intelligence officer disguised as a convict who served
Sheikh Mujibur Rahman in the jail during his incarceration
in 1971, revealed that Mujib was totally unaware of the
developments outside the jail premises including the start

[45] Anthony Mascarenhas, *Bangladesh: A Legacy of Blood* (London: Hodder &
Stoughton, 1986), 35.

[46] B.Z. Khasru, *The Bangladesh Military Coup and the CIA Link* (New Delhi:
Rupa Publications, 2014), 1.

[47] Stanley A. Wolpert, *Bhutto of Pakistan: His Life and Times* (New York: Oxford
University Press, 1993), 173.

of the third Indo-Pak War. According to Raja Anar Khan, 'President Zulfikar Ali Bhutto came to meet Sheikh Mujibur Rahman at the Rest House on 23 December 1971.' After greeting each other, Bhutto sat on a sofa. Mujib sat by his side. Mujib started the conversation.[48]

> Mujib: 'Ap kaise?' (What brings you here?)
>     Bhutto: 'I am the President and Chief Marshal Law Administrator of Pakistan.'
>     Mujib: 'How come?'
>     Bhutto: 'East Pakistan has fallen and Pakistan surrendered to India. General Yahya Khan resigned.'
>     Mujib was outraged. He stood up and scornfully demanded. 'How can it be? How can you be the president? You are a minority leader and I am the majority leader. I have the right to those positions, not you. Take me immediately to a radio or TV station, I will denounce all these and keep East Pakistan as before. I will nullify all these and fix everything.'
>     Bhutto: 'Please calm down. This is the reality now. Sit down please.'
>     Mujib sat down. After a silence, Mujib expressed his disgust at Tajuddin Ahmed, Secretary General of Awami League and wartime Prime Minister based in India, and said that he suspected he would end up with something like this (in collaboration with India).
>     Before leaving, Bhutto asked what he could do for Mujib, the latter asked for TV, newspapers, radio, etc., which were immediately provided.
>     After Bhutto left, Mujib locked himself in his room. Raja Anar Khan and others got worried that Mujib might

---

[48] Obaid Chowdhury, 'Was Sheikh Mujib for an Unbroken Pakistan or Independent Bangladesh? Sensational Revelation about Mujib in Pakistan in 1971', *South Asia Journal*, 5 February 2019, http://southasiajournal.net/was-sheikh-mujib-for-an-unbroken-pakistan-or-independent-bangladesh-sensational-revelation-about-mujib-in-pakistan-in-1971-%EF%BB%BF/ (accessed 12 June 2019).

*do something in desperation, given his earlier outbursts*
*at the news of break up of Pakistan and Bhutto becoming*
*the new leader. Khan finally succeeded in getting the*
*door opened after repeated knocks and appeals to Mujib.*
*Mujib then fell prostrate on a prayer mat and cried out (in*
*Bangla), 'Ya Allah, why all this happened? Oh God I never*
*wanted it to be like this...'*

The following dialogue of the second meeting between Bhutto and Mujib has been recorded in Stanley Wolpert's book, *Bhutto of Pakistan: His Life & Times*[49]:

*[When] Bhutto met Mujib again on January 8, 1972,*
*Bhutto   reminded Mujib, 'defence, foreign affairs and*
*currency...'*

*'Before that, you have to allow me to go,' Mujib replied.*

*'But I don't mind Confederation, however loose it is,'*
*Bhutto insisted.*

*'No, no... I have already told you that we can wait...*
*some sort of arrangements we can make. I told you it will*
*be Confederation. This is absolutely between you and me. I*
*know that you have not told anybody.'*

*'No, why should I tell? I'll keep it absolutely*
*confidential,' Bhutto replied.*

*'You leave it to me, absolutely leave it to me. Trust me,'*
*Mujib insisted.*

*'I trust you,' Bhutto replied.*

*'I will tell these things to the millions of people of*
*Bangladesh when I first go there...that Yahya, before*
*handing over the charge to Mr. Bhutto, wanted first to*
*kill me. I will demand from there, Yahya's hanging. You*
*understand trial... I'll say, "First give a trial to this man,*
*then I'll talk to you..." you understand. I have to take in*
*confidence my people. The wounds are serious.'*

[49] Stanley A. Wolpert, *Bhutto of Pakistan: His Life and Times* (New York: Oxford University Press, 1993), 175.

'Who do you think was the bigger villain – Yahya or Peerzada?' Bhutto asked him.

'Both.'

'I know' Bhutto agreed. 'Listen, presidentship, prime ministership. Whatever you take, I am prepared to retire to the county. I swear by the Holy Quran that I'm prepared to retire.'

Mujib replied, 'I told you there is no objection. My idea was that we would live together and we will rule this country. This bastard (Yahya) started the fuss telling me this was what you had said...and...communicating to you. Then the disaster started in Bengal.'

'But now we have to put the things right.' Bhutto reminded him.

Mujib responded, 'We have to try, but you know the route. I have to go. I have to cope... You know the occupation army is there... Our army massacred...as in Indonesia...another point is there, I tell you frankly...the West Bengalees... I have to take them out from Bengal and crush... My difficulties you understand.'

'Yes, it is very difficult. I am prepared to fly to Dhaka,' Bhutto agreed.

Mujib said, 'No, no. I'll meet with my people...I want time...I'll tell you from there...You have become a hero. You will continue for the whole life.'

Bhutto responded, 'I don't want it. You should be our president' and also offered him $50,000, which Mujib suggested should be paid for the chartered flight of Mujib.

Succumbing to international pressure, the Pakistani government released Mujib from prison on 8 January 1972, and Bhutto saw off Mujib from the Islamabad airport. 'As you can see, I am very much alive and well,' Mujib told journalists in London. He spoke well of Bhutto but emphasised that he had promised no link between Bangladesh and Pakistan. 'I told him I could answer that after I returned to my people.'[50] Anthony Mascarenhas confirms in his book *Bangladesh: A Legacy of Blood* that when he met Mujib in London, Mujib was secretly harbouring a tentative deal with Zulfikar Ali Bhutto, which would have maintained a 'link' between Pakistan and its breakaway province, Bangladesh. 'I have a big scoop for you,' Mujib said to Mascarenhas in confidence. 'We are going to keep some link with Pakistan but I can't say anything more till I have talked it over with others. And for God's sake don't you write anything till I tell you.' In his book, Mascarenhas writes in reference to this, 'I got a glimpse of this unsavory deal, which was totally at variance with the Bangladeshi mood.'[51]

When the Indian government heard of Mujib's release, Indira and many of her cabinet ministers waited to receive and welcome him on the tarmac of Delhi's Palam Airport during his stopover on his way home to Bangladesh.[52] Indira and Mujib spoke to a large public audience with Indira expressing her respect and admiration of Mujib. She stated that 'although [Mujib's] body might have been imprisoned, [nothing] could imprison his spirit'[53]. Mujib loyally responded by saying that he 'had to stop in Delhi for a personal tribute [to] the best friends of my people', the Government of India 'under the leadership of [a] magnificent prime minister, Mrs. Indira Gandhi, who is not only a leader of men but also of mankind'[54]. Mujib described his trip 'a journey from darkness to light. In these nine months my

---

[50] B.Z. Khasru, *The Bangladesh Military Coup and the CIA Link* (New Delhi: Rupa Publications, 2014), 3.

[51] Anthony Mascarenhas, *Bangladesh: A Legacy of Blood* (London: Hodder & Stoughton, 1986), 5.

[52] Katherine Frank, *Indira: The Life of Indira Nehru Gandhi* (London: HarperCollins, 2001), 342.

[53] Ibid.

[54] Ibid., 343.

people have traversed centuries. When I was taken away from my people, they wept; when I was held in captivity, they fought; and now when I go back to them, they are victorious'[55].

On 10 January 1972, Sheikh Mujib arrived in Dhaka to an unprecedented welcome. He returned to a newly independent Bangladesh to assume leadership of the provisional government and entered the office with overwhelming public sympathy and support for the role he had played in getting independence for his country. As the leader of a new Bangladesh, Mujib faced a much more daunting task than just defining his country through a new constitution—that part was easy. He faced the prospect of rebuilding a country shattered physically by civil war, with a dysfunctional economy, a crippled transportation system, severe law and order problems, and a population displaced far and wide. Two days after his return, Mujib relinquished the office of president to become the prime minister. This signalled his preference and that of his party, the Awami League, for a parliamentary system of government.

On 30 January 1972, Mujib pleaded with the nation, 'Our armed struggle has ended. We will have to turn the independence movement into a struggle for building our country. The struggle for reconstruction is more difficult than struggle for freedom.'[56] Putting together a constitution was not a serious problem; the exasperating issues that had overwhelmed the leadership of united Pakistan—centralisation vs. decentralisation, federalism vs. unity state, ethnic and regional equity and balance—did not exist in Bangladesh.[57]

---

[55] S.M. Ali, *After The Dark Night: Problems of Sheikh Mujibur Rahman* (Delhi: Thomson Press Limited, 1973), 44.

[56] Ibid.,

[57] William B. Milam, *Bangladesh and Pakistan Flirting with Failure in South Asia* (New York: Columbia University, 2009), 32.

The pattern of military rule that had characterised the 'old' (united) Pakistan had been shattered by the traumatic and humiliating events of 1971. In the 'new' Pakistan that emerged on 16 December 1971, there was the potential to institutionalise democracy. But there were also serious societal, cultural and institutional barriers which made democratisation a formidable task: feudalism, regional and ethnic tensions, a noxious political culture, poverty and illiteracy, and a tradition of military rule.[58]

Bhutto had come to power in the new Pakistan with three cards to play. The first was Mujib's release, which he had already given away. The second was recognition of Bangladesh as an independent State in the subcontinent; Bhutto wanted to recognise Bangladesh and in return expected Mujib to agree to the return of Pakistani prisoners of war (POWs) who were languishing in India. The third was 28,000 Bengali soldiers and 20,000 civil servants stranded in West Pakistan, whom Mujib and Bangladesh needed urgently.[59] Bhutto knew that he was playing a much weaker hand. His political future would rely on his ability to achieve the repatriation of Pakistani POWs (held) in India.[60] He saw prospects of negotiations with Mujib diminish because of what he considered was the persecution and killing of helpless Biharis— non-Bengalis who were federalist and had migrated to East Pakistan from India in 1947 at the time of the Partition. Also, native Bengalis who had opposed East Pakistan's secession had been dubbed as collaborators and were imprisoned.[61]

[58] Ibid., 31.
[59] B.Z. Khasru, *The Bangladesh Military Coup and the CIA Link* (New Delhi: Rupa Publications, 2014), 19.
[60] Ibid., 23.
[61] Ibid., 47.

In a television interview in Dacca on 21 February 1972, Mujib professed, 'The struggle for independence began in 1948 and through movements in 1952, 1954, 1962, 1969, 1970 and at last in 1971, it culminated in the independence of Bengal through arms' struggle. Even in 1947, we could realize that Bengalis would be totally exploited by West Pakistan.'[62] Despite the glorious victory Mujib and Bengalis had achieved during the liberation war, the country, which Mujib now led, was anything but glorious. The newly independent Bangladesh was scarred by the bloodshed during the civil war as a result of which numerous men, women and children had been murdered in cold blood. The emotional suffering was, however, only one part of the chaos. There was additionally the task of building infrastructure and the economy, and the immediate goal of distributing food to the hungry population.

Another pressing challenge for Mujib and the new government was the armed fighters and bands of guerrillas roaming freely in the Bengali countryside.[63] Some of these groups had rejected Mujib's plea to surrender their weapons and obey the law and order the government was trying to establish. Many of these men had fought in the Bengali Liberation War and had legally registered in the Bangladesh Army, thus were entitled to their weapons. Some armed groups took the law into their own hands setting up territories under their own jurisdiction.[64] The only place left to look for Mujib and his government was India—by far the new country's strongest alliance in the region.

---

[62] S.M. Ali, *After The Dark Night: Problems of Sheikh Mujibur Rahman* (Delhi: Thomson Press Limited, 1973), 18.

[63] James Heitzman et al., *Bangladesh: A Country Study* (Washington: Federal Research Division, Library of Congress, 1989), 32.

[64] Ibid., 32.

Mujib demonstrated his leadership capability by seamlessly dealing with vital issues within the first 100 days of taking over as prime minister, including the membership of the Commonwealth on 18 April 1972, recognition of Bangladesh by 60 countries including 4 of the 5 permanent members of the UN. The withdrawal of Indian soldiers in March 1972 and repatriation of 10 million refugees who had fled to India as a result of the armed conflict gave the impression that Bangladesh was master of its own house.[65]

## The Friendship Treaty of 1972: Strengthening Relations Between India and Bangladesh

In March 1972, Indira's visit to Dhaka further cemented Indo-Bangla relations. Indira and Mujib together addressed a crowd of close to one million people, with Mujib once again articulating his devotion and appreciation of Indira, saying, 'I am a pauper. I have nothing to give. I have only love to give to you.'[66] The most significant outcome of Indira Gandhi's visit to Dhaka was the agreement signed on 19 March 1972. The Friendship Treaty—also known as the Indira-Mujib Treaty— was an agreement forging close bilateral relations between the Republic of India and the newly established State of Bangladesh.[67] Mujib announced that there would be no discussions with Pakistan concerning the return of POWs until Pakistan fully recognised the independence of Bangladesh. Indira promised to turn over to Bangladesh all of the Pakistani POWs.

---

[65] S.M. Ali, *After The Dark Night: Problems of Sheikh Mujibur Rahman* (Delhi: Thomson Press Limited, 1973), 10.

[66] Katherine Frank, *Indira: The Life of Indira Nehru Gandhi* (London: HarperCollins, 2001), 342.

[67] Banglapedia, 'India-Bangladesh Friendship Treaty,' http://en.banglapedia.org/index. php?title=India-Bangladesh_Friendship_Treaty (accessed 9 February 2017).

The following 12 points were incorporated in The Friendship Treaty:[68]

(i)    The contracting parties solemnly declare that there shall be lasting peace and friendship between the two countries and each side shall respect the independence, sovereignty, and territorial integrity of the other and refrain from interfering in the internal affairs of the other side;

(ii)    The contracting parties condemn colonialism and racialism of all forms, and reaffirm their determination to strive for their final and complete elimination;

(iii)    The contracting parties reaffirm their faith in the policy of non-alignment and peaceful co-existence as important factors for easing tension in the world, maintaining international peace and security and strengthening national sovereignty and independence;

(iv)    The contracting parties shall maintain regular contacts and exchange views with each other on major international problems affecting the interest of both the states;

(v)    The contracting parties shall continue to strengthen and widen their mutually advantageous and all round co-operation in the economic, scientific and technical fields, and shall develop mutual co-operation in the fields of trade, transport and communication on the basis of the principles of equality and mutual benefit;

(vi)    The contracting parties agree to make joint studies and take joint action in the field of flood control, river basin development and development of hydro-electric power and irrigation;

---

[68] Ishtiaq Hossain, 'Bangladesh-India Relations: Issues and Problems', *Asian Survey* (Volume 21, No. 11, 1981), 1,116.

(vii)  Both the parties shall promote relations in the field of arts, literature, education, culture, sports and health;

(viii)  In accordance with the ties of friendship existing between the two countries, each of the contracting parties solemnly declare that it shall not enter into or participate in any military alliance directed against the other party. Each of the parties shall refrain from any aggression against the other party and shall not allow the use of its territory for committing any act that may cause military damage to or continue to threat the security of the other contracting parties;

(ix)  Each of the contracting parties shall refrain from giving any assistance to any third party taking part in an armed conflict against the other party. In case if either party is attacked or threatened to be attacked, the contracting parties shall immediately enter into mutual consultations in order to take necessary measures to eliminate the threat and thus ensure the peace and security of their countries;

(x)  Each of the parties solemnly declares that it shall not undertake any commitment, secret or open, towards one or more states which may be incompatible with the present treaty;

(xi)  The present treaty is signed for a term of twenty-five years and shall be renewed by mutual agreement;

(xii)  Any differences interpreting any Article of the treaty shall be settled on a bilateral basis by peaceful means in a spirit of mutual respect and understanding.[69]

Despite critics of The Friendship Treaty who allege that it was Indira Gandhi who 'imposed' the treaty onto Bangladesh, according to some claims, it was Mujib himself who had independently approached Prime Minister Indira

---

[69] Banglapedia, 'India-Bangladesh Friendship Treaty,' http://en.banglapedia.org/index.php?title=India-Bangladesh_Friendship_Treaty (accessed 9 February 2017).

Gandhi to discuss the possibility of such an agreement.[70] Mujib's insistence on signing The Friendship Treaty may be explained in the following two ways: 'Firstly, Mujib wanted to show by signing the treaty that Bangladesh was truly sovereign and independent. He believed that the act of signing a treaty would demonstrate that Bangladesh was capable of managing its own affairs and making decisions on its own. Second, it is argued by many in Bangladesh that Mujib may have wanted Indian support in any future political upheavals in his country. Article 9 of the Indo-Bangladesh Friendship Treaty allowed for mutual consultations between the two signatories in order to remove a threat if either of them was attacked.'[71]

Indira and Mujib signing The Friendship Treaty on 19 March 1972.

Source: https://madinaesani.wordpress.com/2012/12/14/the-truth-about-1971-massacres-documents-from-the-u-s-national-archives/sheikh-mujib-and-indira-gandhi-signs-the-25-year-treaty-of-friendship-and-cooperation-between-bangladesh-and-india-in-dhaka/

[70] Ishtiaq Hossain, 'Bangladesh-India Relations: Issues and Problems', *Asian Survey* (Volume 21, No. 11, 1981), 1,116.
[71] Banglapedia, 'India-Bangladesh Friendship Treaty,' http://en.banglapedia.org/index.php?title=India-Bangladesh_Friendship_Treaty (accessed 9 February 2017).

## Mujib's Socialist and Populist Programmes as Prime Minister

Mujib's rule comprised of socialist and egalitarian policies. On 26 March 1972, he announced on national radio:

> *Having regard to the objective realities of our society, the old social order must be demolished in order to lay the foundations for a new society. We will build a society free from exploitation and injustice. Today on this historic day we move forward to implement the phased programme of nationalisation of the key sector of the economy to which my Government is committed. The following sectors of the economy stand nationalised with immediate effect:*
> 1) *Banks excluding the branches of foreign banks.*
> 2) *Insurance companies – life and general – excluding the branches of foreign insurance companies.*
> 3) *Jute mills.*
> 4) *Textile mills.*
> 5) *Sugar mills.*
> 6) *Major portion of inland and coastal shipping.*
> 7) *All abandoned and absentee owners' property with fixed assets valued at Rs. 1.5 million or more.*
> 8) *Bangladesh Biman and Bangladesh Shipping Corporation, which have been set up as State Corporations to undertake and develop air and ocean transportation.*
> 9) *Major portion of foreign trade has been brought under the Trading Corporation of Bangladesh with immediate effect in pursuance of the comprehensive programme of nationalisation of foreign trade.*[72]

---

[72] S.M. Ali, *After The Dark Night: Problems of Sheikh Mujibur Rahman* (Delhi: Thomson Press Limited, 1973),106–07.

Once these orders went into effect on 27 March 1972, the government took over 86 per cent of the industrial assets of Bangladesh.[73] The government also issued an ordinance to enforce the 100 bighas (1 acre = 3 bighas) land ceiling per family. Haat (weekly market) leasing system was abolished. The owners of up to 25 bighas were exempt from land tax. These were all efforts toward the eradication of feudalism and to weaken capitalism.[74]

Mujib's charisma and towering personality helped as much as hampered the functioning of the new government. His reluctance to delegate authority resulted in the increasing inability of his cabinet colleagues to exercise initiative. This resulted in a major crisis in August and September of 1972 when Mujib travelled to the UK for medical treatment; governance suffered in his absence. The prices of daily commodities showed a staggering upsurge with the price of rice rising 200 per cent. His return from the UK in mid-September resulted in the reversal of price hike and improved law and order in Bangladesh. Within a week of his return, exercising his authority, Mujib expelled 20 members of his own party and cancelled their membership of the Parliament on charges of corruption. This act got him accolades from the press and also praise from his government's critics. He next turned to the civil services and suspended officers for corruption and some for collaboration with the Pakistani army during the Bengali Liberation War. This resulted in a sense of relief, raised morals but also expectations of the people of Bangladesh.[75]

In international relations, the Awami League government gave up the age-old Pakistani policy of confrontation with

[73] Ibid., 107.

[74] S.R. Chakravarty, *Bangladesh under Mujib, Zia and Ershad* (New Delhi: Har-Anand Publications, 1995), 18.

[75] S.M. Ali, *After The Dark Night: Problems of Sheikh Mujibur Rahman* (Delhi: Thomson Press Limited, 1973), 53–55.

India. On the contrary, The India-Bangladesh Treaty of Friendship, Cooperation and Peace cleared the pathway for a peaceful co-existence.[76] The Bangladesh constituent assembly passed the Constitution for the People's Republic of Bangladesh, and this Constitution came into effect on the historic date of 16 December 1972, marking the first anniversary of Bangladesh's independence.[77] It stated that the new nation was to have a prime minister appointed by the president and approved by a single-house Parliament. The basic tenets of the Constitution came to be known as Mujibism or Mujibbad; these included the four pillars of nationalism, socialism, secularism and democracy.[78]

In 1974, the Bangladesh government nationalised the monopoly capital, and so most of the foreign trades were nationalised. By law, the government restricted the growth of private capital by limiting amounts that could be invested, i.e. no one could invest more than 35 lakh takas in one industry. Foreign investment was banned and the feudal system of leasing the markets was prohibited.[79]

Bangladesh continued to face grave economic crises—abnormal inflation, high unemployment rates and horrible famine.[80] After the industries were nationalised, workers' participation in management was safeguarded. Further, to check the growth of the private sector proportionally, ceiling restrictions were imposed and the right of nationalisation was reserved with the government. A scheme was drawn to set up a multipurpose cooperative system at the village level. The plan involved forming multipurpose cooperative societies for each

---

[76] S.R. Chakravarty, *Bangladesh under Mujib, Zia and Ershad* (New Delhi: Har-Anand Publications, 1995), 23.

[77] Ibid., 35.

[78] James Heitzman et al., *Bangladesh: A Country Study* (Washington: Federal Research Division, Library of Congress, 1989), 32.

[79] S.R. Chakravarty, *Bangladesh under Mujib, Zia and Ershad* (New Delhi: Har-Anand Publications, 1995), 47.

[80] Ibid., 58.

of the villages of Bangladesh. These cooperatives were to be de facto owners of all available lands, orchards, fisheries and other economic properties and institutions of the village. All able-bodied persons were to be enrolled as members. These cooperatives were to be built as centres of economic, political and administrative activities for each of the villages. All government help in the form of inputs such as fertilisers, capital, technical know-how, etc. were to be channelised through these cooperatives. The total income of the concerning villages was proposed to be divided by the cooperatives among the member workers, the owners of the land and the government. Mujib announced this policy on 26 March 1975 and asked people to consider it essential for survival.[81]

## SUMMARY

The 24 years of ongoing disparity (1947–1971) between the eastern and western wings of Pakistan ultimately poured out like a volcanic eruption. Important contributing factors included, but were not limited to, ignoring Bengalis' demands for the adoption of the Bengali language and, instead, imposing Urdu as the only national language, which resulted in the exclusion of Bengalis from government jobs; declaring Karachi and later Islamabad in West Pakistan as the capital of the country; renaming East Bengal, East Pakistan against the wishes of the people. The deprivation of people of East Pakistan (Bengalis) resulted in their acrimonious rebellion against the government and people of West Pakistan. Indira Gandhi's government availed the opportunity by facilitating and supporting the Bengali Liberation War.

[81] Ibid., 80.

# 6

## WELCOMING THE ENEMY: MEETINGS BETWEEN BHUTTO, MUJIB AND INDIRA

*So let us begin anew, remembering on both sides,*
*that civility is not a sign of weakness, and sincerity is*
*always subject to proof. Let us never negotiate out of*
*fear. But let us never fear to negotiate.*

—John F. Kennedy[1]

Zulfikar Ali Bhutto's outrage and disdain of the architects of Bangladesh was showcased in his comments and public speeches. He demonstrated no inclination towards acknowledging the Bengali nationalist movement and its cause. Such a resolve reflected Bhutto's striking characteristics since he was described as 'unpredictable, bizarre, carried away by whims, by strange decisions', and 'highly intelligent'.[2] In a 1972 interview, on the question of why there were such discrepancies in the reported number of casualties and refugees in East Pakistan, Bhutto nonchalantly replied, 'Since the Bengalis all look alike, who was to know?'[3] 'Every government, every country, has the right to exercise force when necessary. For instance, in the name of unity. You can't build without destroying. To build a country, Stalin was

---

[1] John F. Kennedy, 'Inaugural Address Transcript', John F. Kennedy Presidential Library and Museum, https://www.jfklibrary.org/learn/about-jfk/historic-speeches/inaugural-address (accessed 12 June 2019).

[2] Oriana Fallaci, *Interview with History* (Boston: Houghton Mifflin, 1977), 183.

[3] Ibid., 189.

obliged to use force and kill. Mao Tse-tung was obliged to use force and kill. To mention only two recent cases, without raking over the whole history of the world. Yes, there are circumstances where a bloody suppression is justifiable and justified. In March the unity of Pakistan depended on the suppression of the secessionists. But to carry it out with such brutality on the people instead of on those responsible wasn't necessary. That's not the way to convince poor people who've been told that with the Six Points there'll be no more hurricanes, no more floods, no more hunger. I spoke out against such methods more emphatically than anyone else, and when no one dared do so.'[4]

Following the chaos of the Bengali Liberation War, Bhutto made clear his feelings about Sheikh Mujibur Rahman, calling him 'a congenital liar'[5] amongst other names. Although the Awami League's spectacular electoral victory in East Pakistan had proven Mujib's political capability and skill, Bhutto did not consider Mujib or the Awami League an equal counterpart to himself and his PPP. In speaking about his attempts at diplomacy with Mujib, Bhutto stated that '[to] make Mujib understand…was a desperate undertaking — you can't expect brains from someone who doesn't have them',[6] and further added that '[Mujib] can't help telling lies… Mujib talks at random, depending on his mood and the disorders of his sick mind'[7].

Bhutto's criticism of Mujib mostly resorted to ad hominem attacks against the Bengali politician, with the former providing few reasons for the latter's political incapability other than his conviction that Mujib was 'conceited, lacking in culture, common sense, [and] everything'[8]. Bhutto made

[4] Ibid., 190.
[5] Ibid., 188.
[6] Ibid., 192.
[7] Ibid., 188.
[8] Ibid., 194.

142

no attempts to downplay or polish his lack of respect for Mujib. Rather, he declared that he 'understood from the very first moment' he met Mujib that there was 'no depth... no preparation [to him]... [he] was an agitator breathing a lot of fire and with an absolute lack of ideas.'[9]

## INDO-PAK RELATIONS AFTER THE BENGALI LIBERATION WAR

The period between 1965 and 1975 witnessed the revival of tensions and misunderstandings between the government in Jammu and Kashmir and the central government of India.[10] The complexity of Kashmir continues to plague India-Pakistan relations since 1947.[11] In December 1971, military conflict in Kashmir was confined to those areas which were of 'vital and strategic interest' to the two opposing regimes.[12] Following the chaos of 1971, both Bhutto and Indira wanted to usher in a new era of lasting peace between India and Pakistan. On 28 June 1972, a peace summit between the two countries took place at the hill station of Simla, where Indira met with her Pakistani counterpart, Zulfikar Ali Bhutto. After her skilful handling of the 1971 Indo-Pak War, it was with the Simla Agreement that Indira allegedly faltered.[13]

India's military victory over the Pakistan Army enhanced its overall influence in the region while decreasing the morale in Pakistan. As a result, the Indian government was at an advantageous position to press for policy changes in its favour. The situation put renewed pressures on Bhutto

---

[9] Ibid., 195.

[10] J.N. Dixit, *India-Pakistan in War & Peace* (London: Routledge, 2002), 78.

[11] Sumit Ganguly, 'Avoiding War in Kashmir', *Foreign Affairs* (Volume 69, No. 5, 1990), 57–73.

[12] Zubeida Mustafa, 'The Kashmir Dispute and the Simla Agreement', *Pakistan Horizon* (Volume 25, No. 3, 1972), 45.

[13] Inder Malhotra, *Indira Gandhi: A Personal and Political Biography* (London: Hodder & Stoughton, 1989), 320.

and his government to alleviate instabilities and chaos in the region. On 31 December 1971, Indira Gandhi hinted that an 'adjustment' in the old ceasefire line in Kashmir would be 'necessary for settling matters'.[14] In March 1972, in an interview with Italian journalist Oriana Fallaci, Indira Gandhi, while discussing Indo-Pak relations, described President Zulfikar Ali Bhutto as an 'unbalanced person'.[15] Bhutto was enraged by Indira's comments and summoned Fallaci to Karachi to respond to Indira and also to condemn those involved in the Bangladesh debacle. In the aftermath of the Bengali Liberation War, Bhutto said that Indira Gandhi was exaggerating the number of fatalities and displaced people in the region as part of a strategic plan to 'legalise her offensive and invade East Pakistan'.[16] Bhutto consistently dismissed Indira's political abilities, at one point declaring that Indira had 'never impressed [him]' and that the only reason Indira had acquired her position was 'by the simple fact of being Nehru's daughter'[17].

Bhutto, like many of Indira's critics in India and abroad, reduced her political successes to 'Nehru's light'[18]. One of the reasons for this perception was Indira's devotion to the politics founded by Nehru as well as his broader objectives for India: '[I have] the same objectives my father had: to give people a higher standard of living, to do away with the cancer of poverty…the evil of the feudal system, the evil of the system based on caste, the evil of economic injustice…[and] to eliminate the consequences of economic backwardness.'[19]

Bhutto assumed that Indira had constructed an advantageous and profitable public image of herself, which helped expand her

---

[14] Zubeida Mustafa, 'The Kashmir Dispute and the Simla Agreement', *Pakistan Horizon* (Volume 25, No. 3, 1972), 46.

[15] Oriana Fallaci, *Interview with History* (Boston: Houghton Mifflin, 1977), 163.

[16] Ibid., 189.

[17] Ibid., 199.

[18] Ibid., 200.

[19] Ibid., 166.

appeal to Indians from all walks of life. For example, Bhutto believed Indira had made a strategic use of 'all her saris, the red spot on her forehead, [and] her little smile'[20]. 'Indira was offended to read that Bhutto called her a mediocre woman with a mediocre intelligence, a creature devoid of initiative and imagination, a drudge without even half her father's talent, and said that the idea of meeting her, of shaking her hand, filled him with acute disgust.'[21] Bhutto summarised his perception of Indira with the following statement: 'There is nothing great in [her]. Only the country she governs is great. I would like to say that it is the throne which makes her look tall and also the name which she carries.'[22]

It would later become clear that Indira was neither to live nor lead in Jawaharlal Nehru's shadow. Indira Gandhi was informed about Bhutto's comments when pieces of the interview with Fallaci were published in New Delhi newspapers. Outraged, she requested the complete text of the interview. Prior to this, there had been talks in India and Pakistan about a peace treaty—a possible meeting between Prime Minister Gandhi and President Bhutto to resolve Indo-Pak tensions for good. But upon reading Bhutto's interview, Indira announced that no meeting would take place.

Indira Gandhi, Zulfikar Ali Bhutto and Sheikh Mujibur Rahman expressed their priorities regarding the residual problems of the 1971 conflict in television interviews to American Broadcasting Corporation, which were shown in a single programme on 14 May 1972.[23] Indira Gandhi announced that any Indo-Pak agreement would have to establish the elements of a lasting peace between the two countries. She insisted that all outstanding issues between

[20] Ibid., 200.
[21] Ibid., 186.
[22] Ibid., 199.
[23] P.R. Chari and Pervaiz Iqbal Cheema, *The Simla Agreement 1972: Its Wasted Promise* (New Delhi: Manohar Publishers & Distributors, 2001), 46.

them should be taken up together, and not piecemeal. Bhutto's answers conveyed a warning that Pakistan would become an arsenal of defence in case India tried to thrust any unequal treaty. In the same breath, he assured that he could be flexible, depending on the flexibility of 'others'. Sheikh Mujib ruled out talks with Pakistan until it recognised Bangladesh. Towards the end of May 1972, Bhutto undertook a whirlwind 13-day tour of 14 countries in west Asia and sub-Saharan Africa. This was intended to express Pakistan's appreciation for their support in the UN, explain the current situation in South Asia, strengthen bilateral relations and address a Pakistani ambassadors' conference. Later, he visited another 12 countries to garner their support for the forthcoming negotiations with India.[24]

## The Simla Meeting in 1972

> *There is something about the subcontinent, with its high mountains to the north and the ocean surrounding it on all other sides, that keeps us all together and forces us to find ways to live with each other.*
>
> —President Bhutto of Pakistan[25]

Simla was not the first meeting of the leaders of India and Pakistan. Previously, the following meetings had taken place:[26]

- Prime Ministers Liaquat Ali (Pakistan) and Jawaharlal Nehru (India) met in New Delhi between 2–8 April 1950 to sign an agreement to safeguard the rights of minorities.

---

[24] Ibid., 35

[25] S.M. Ali, *After The Dark Night: Problems of Sheikh Mujibur Rahman* (Delhi: Thomson Press Limited, 1973), 176.

[26] P.R. Chari and Pervaiz Iqbal Cheema, *The Simla Agreement 1972: Its Wasted Promise* (New Delhi: Manohar Publishers & Distributors, 2001), 15

- Prime Minister Nehru (India) visited Karachi between 26–28 April 1950 to discuss the implementation of this agreement on minorities.
- Upon the request of Sir Owen Dickson, UN mediator on Kashmir, Prime Minister Liaquat Ali (Pakistan) travelled to India on 20 July 1950.
- Prime Minister Nehru (India) met Prime Minister Mohammed Ali in Pakistan between 25–28 July 1953 and issued a joint communiqué expressing their intention to resolve all their disputes by peaceful negotiations.
- President Ayub Khan (Pakistan) discussed trade and financial matters with Prime Minister Nehru (India) during his stopover at the Delhi airport on 1 September 1959.
- Prime Minister Nehru (India) met with President Ayub Khan (Pakistan) in Karachi between 19–23 September 1960 to sign the Indus Waters Treaty.
- Prime Minister Lal Bahadur Shastri (India) met President Ayub Khan (Pakistan) in Tashkent on 10 January 1966 to restore normal relations between the two countries after the Indo-Pak conflict of 1965; this resulted in the Tashkent Agreement.

In June 1972, Prime Minister Indira Gandhi and President Zulfikar Ali Bhutto met to negotiate on differences resulting from the 1971 war and the Kashmir issue. Indira Gandhi travelled a day earlier to Simla and brought along decoration and furniture from the special suites of Rashtrapati Bhavan, the president's house, in New Delhi to ensure that the rooms for the president of Pakistan and his daughter, Benazir, were impeccably decorated.[27] The two leaders' agenda and goals

---

[27] Pupul Jayakar, *Indira Gandhi: An Intimate Biography* (New York: Pantheon Books, 1992), 187.

were polar opposite since Indira, having won the 1971 war, wanted to use this chance to settle the Kashmir dispute in favour of India. Bhutto wanted an unconditional release of 93,000 Pakistanis, including soldiers, paramilitary staff and government officials who were POWs, and 5,000 square miles of land occupied by India as a result of the recent war. Moreover, Pakistan's behaviour towards India during the Sino-Indian conflict, the growing collusion between Pakistan and China (of which Bhutto was the primary architect under Ayub), and the Indo-Pak War of 1965 made India view Pakistani policy toward India with reservation.[28]

Another complicating factor was that the new state of Bangladesh had signed a Treaty of Friendship, Peace and Cooperation with India in March 1972, delineating several crucial bilateral issues that needed to be solved urgently to stabilise political and security relations in the region. By June 1972, there were suggestions that India was willing to settle for a compromise over Kashmir and would not insist on formal recognition of the ceasefire line as an international border.[29] The Indian government stated that a treaty renouncing the use of force by Pakistan would be 'acceptable to India' as long as the status quo in Kashmir was considered 'non-negotiable'.[30] Indira was waiting at the Simla airport as Bhutto stepped out of the Russian M-8 helicopter. Despite the animosity (because of what they thought and said about each other), the two most powerful, populist South Asian leaders shook hands and managed to smile at the informal start of this summit. Bhutto had met Indira first in May 1964 when he attended Nehru's funeral and placed a wreath on the deceased leader's bier on behalf of the then president Ayub Khan. On 21 June 1972,

---

[28] J.N. Dixit, *India-Pakistan in War & Peace* (London: Routledge, 2002), 165.
[29] Zubeida Mustafa, 'The Kashmir Dispute and the Simla Agreement', *Pakistan Horizon* (Volume 25, No. 3, 1972), 46.
[30] Ibid.

President Bhutto, along with his entourage of 92 officials, journalists, friends and daughter, Benazir Bhutto, came to Simla to negotiate and resolve issues arising in the aftermath of the 1971 war with Indira Gandhi and her government.

As the discussions between Indian and Pakistani delegations proceeded, several revisions and drafts of the Simla Agreement were prepared—all to the dissatisfaction of either one party or the other. Indira wanted negotiations without the mediation of a third party (the UN). She also recommended transforming the ceasefire line in Kashmir into a permanent border between India and Pakistan. In return, she was even willing to secede all Indian occupied territory to Pakistan, except the valley of Kashmir. Given his past rhetoric and posturing, Bhutto disagreed with Indira's proposals, especially concerning Kashmir. The closest Bhutto got towards making a conclusive decision over Kashmir was when he stated, 'Let there be a line of peace, let people come and go, let us not fight over it.'[31] Unsurprisingly, the two parties engaged in nothing but inconclusive deliberations.

After the negotiations between the Indian and Pakistani teams failed, Bhutto suggested that he and Indira meet one-on-one. Indira agreed and so Bhutto and she went into a small sitting room, alone, while their attendant teams went into two different rooms—the billiard room on the one side and the reception room on the other. The two leaders would discuss and then go back for further consultations with their delegates, and then meet again.[32] In an extraordinary turn of events, the Simla Agreement was signed on 2 July 1972. It was a remarkable effort by Indira and Bhutto to finally put an end to the conflict and confrontation that had marred

[31] *The Hindu*, 'Did Bhutto outwit Indira Gandhi?' 6 February 2000, http://www.thehindu.com/2000/02/06/stories/1306067g.htm (accessed 12 June 2019).
[32] Stanley A. Wolpert, *Bhutto of Pakistan: His Life and Times* (New York: Oxford University Press, 1993), 191.

Indo-Pak relations.[33] Its main clause asserted: 'The two nation state of India and Pakistan' would 'settle their differences by peaceful means through bilateral negotiations or by any other peaceful means mutually agreed upon between them' (Article II).[34] Within 30 days of ratification by both nations, Indian troops were to be withdrawn from the 5,000 square miles of Pakistani desert land occupied by India. The Indian solution to the Kashmir problem was to transform the ceasefire line in Jammu and Kashmir (in place since 17 December 1971) into a formal 'line of control' that would be respected by both parties, without prejudice of either side's position.[35]

Benazir Bhutto's political education was also part of the Simla Agreement as her father cautioned her on the plane, 'Everyone will be looking for signs of how the meetings are progressing, so be extra careful. You must not smile and give the impression that you are enjoying yourself while our soldiers are still in Indian POW camps. You must not look grim, either, which people can interpret as a sign of pessimism... Don't look sad and don't look happy.'[36]

In the Simla Agreement, there was no mention of a Kashmir plebiscite or of the 93,000 Pakistani POWs. This was because Indira had refused to discuss them without Bangladesh at the conference table. Bhutto promised to negotiate these matters further when he met with Indira and Mujib in the near future. He had at least won the promise of full withdrawal from the portions of Sindh and Punjab, still under Indian occupation, and vowed

---

[33] 'The India-Pakistan Simla Agreement, 3 July 1972', 3 March 2008, https://www.tandfonline.com/doi/abs/10.1080/00396337208441358 (accessed 14 January 2018).

[34] Sumit Ganguly, 'Avoiding War in Kashmir', *Foreign Affairs* (Volume 69, No. 5, 1990), 62.

[35] Zubeida Mustafa, 'The Kashmir Dispute and the Simla Agreement', *Pakistan Horizon* (Volume 25, No. 3, 1972), 47.

[36] Stanley A. Wolpert, *Bhutto of Pakistan: His Life and Times* (New York: Oxford University Press, 1993), 190.

that 'Insha-Allah will succeed in finding a solution' to the POW problem soon. 'We will remain friendly and peaceful towards those who do not commit aggression against us, do not occupy our territory and do not hold our POWs.' Their incarceration remained a bitter, constantly mentioned failure of Bhutto's policies. In the Simla Agreement, there was also no mention of Pakistan's recognition of the new State of Bangladesh. The Opposition in Pakistan criticised Bhutto for East Pakistan's debacle and now for the Simla Agreement. The Opposition in Pakistan was convinced that Indira being the victor in the war would have forced Bhutto to sign a 'secret agreement' to end Pakistan's claim to Kashmir and recognise the independence of Bangladesh. In response, Bhutto spoke for over three hours in the national assembly because he felt compelled to answer virtually every disapproving word uttered in the four preceding days of debate[37]:

> *Do you think Zulfikar Ali Bhutto of Larkana is responsible for the separation of East Pakistan? That this individual who was not even involved in the politics of Pakistan until 1954...is the person who is finally, exclusively and completely responsible for the separation of Pakistan? If you want that, well I say I can take this burden on myself...I did it. Yahya Khan did not. Ayub Khan did not. The policy of exploitation did not. One thousand miles of separation did not. The fact that East Pakistan was in the majority and spoke a different language did not... It is all my fault. The crisis was in our stars... It was boiling... Nobody could stop it in 1971. It could have been stopped in 1950...over the language issue... I was nowhere on the scene... Let's face the truth, hang me by all means, but the fact remains that I am not responsible for the separation.*

[37] Ibid., 194.

Indira's critics argue that the Simla Agreement was a major error in judgment on her part.[38] It is speculated that the agreement was signed based on Bhutto's last-minute decision to convert the ceasefire line in Kashmir into a 'line of control'. It is contended that he repeatedly assured Indira that Pakistan would honour its promise regarding Kashmir and that she should sincerely 'trust him'. Indira Gandhi allegedly made an error in judgment when she accepted Bhutto's assurances. In the words of Sam Goldwyn, 'An oral agreement isn't worth the paper it is written on.'[39]

The question often asked is why did Indira Gandhi—one of Indian history's most confident and influential political leader—overlook Bhutto's political manoeuvring? Was it because she was desperately seeking peace that she overlooked Bhutto's typical manipulation of circumstances in his favour? There are many stories but none authenticated about why Indira faltered in her negotiations with Bhutto. R.N. Kao, a spymaster on Indira's team and one of her closest confidants, many years after Indira's death, stated that he, too, had been downright puzzled by the events in Simla. Kao revealed that Indira had called him shortly after the final meeting with Bhutto regarding Simla, asking, '[Kao], do you think I can trust Bhutto? People tell me that if I shake hands with him, I must count my fingers.'[40]

Since Indira and Mujib had made recognition of Bangladesh by Pakistan a prerequisite to the return of 93,000 Pakistani POWs, Bhutto was eager to talk with Mujib again and tried to phone him from Lahore to arrange an early meeting in London. But Mujib was not ready to risk antagonising his Awami League colleagues

---

[38] Inder Malhotra, *Indira Gandhi: A Personal and Political Biography* (London: Hodder & Stoughton, 1989), 320.

[39] BrainyQuote, 'Samuel Goldwyn Quotes', https://www.brainyquote.com/quotes/samuel_goldwyn_122394 (accessed 12 June 2019).

[40] Inder Malhotra, *Indira Gandhi: A Personal and Political Biography* (London: Hodder & Stoughton, 1989), 320.

by agreeing to speak with the man that all of Bangladesh despised. It would not be incorrect to say that Bhutto was as insufferable to the people of Bangladesh as Yahya Khan. Meanwhile, the Opposition leaders in Pakistan continued to denounce any proposal to 'recognise' Bangladesh. The Opposition believed that it would be perceived as rewarding 'aggression' and would tempt India to grab another piece of Pakistan in the future.

Bhutto and Mujib were faced with many similar domestic problems while heading their respective countries: unable to deliver half of what they had promised, increasingly mistrusted by their religious clergy and military, and swiftly losing the support of students and hungry workers.[41] Bhutto wished that he and Muijb could agree upon a 'confederation' of Pakistan and Bangladesh, bolstering the economy of both nations. In November 1972, Bhutto announced his decision to release all 617 Indian POWs held there since the 1971 war. It was a humane, wise and bold initiative, and cast a revealing light on both India and Bangladesh for continuing to detain Pakistani prisoners long after the war had ended. Indira and Mujib remained adamant, however; the recognition of Bangladesh preceded the prisoners' repatriation.[42]

## Bhutto's Socialist and Populist Programmes as President and Prime Minister

Bhutto undertook transformative decisions, including granting full freedom to Mujib who was imprisoned by Yahya Khan since the start of the Bengali independence movement in 1971. In January 1972, Bhutto announced a programme of nationalisation of 10 categories of major industries, including iron and steel, basic metals and chemicals, pectoral

---

[41] Stanley A. Wolpert, *Bhutto of Pakistan: His Life and Times* (New York: Oxford University Press, 1993), 202.
[42] Ibid., 207.

chemicals, heavy engineering and electrical, motor vehicles, tractors, cement and public utilities. Domestically-owned life insurance companies were also nationalised[43]

In 1972, Bhutto concluded Pakistan's 24-year membership of Britain's Commonwealth of Nations followed by Pakistan's exit from the US-dominated Southeast Asia Treaty Organization, in 1973. On 10 February 1972, Bhutto announced a new labour policy in which workers' shares in company profits would increase to 4 per cent; elected shop stewards in all factories would 'represent' workers' 'interest and point of view' in all negotiations with management; affordable housing and free education up to matric level (high school) for at least one child of every worker were to be provided by the State; and old-age pensions and group insurance for injured workers, and the extension of social security benefits to domestic servants.[44]

On 11 March 1972, Bhutto announced the land reforms, which included the ceiling of land holdings to 150 acres for irrigated land and 300 acres for non-irrigated land. The land in excess was to be taken over by the State without paying compensation and was to be transferred to tenants free of cost.[45]

A comprehensive public healthcare programme was announced in August 1972, which included employee social security and opening of new medical schools to ensure an increase in the number of physicians.[46] He subsequently nationalised educational institutions and by September 1972, 175 private colleges were placed under the management of provincial departments of education. Private schools were

[43] Shahid Javed Burki, *Pakistan Under Bhutto, 1971–1977* (London: Macmillan, 1988), 114.

[44] Stanley A. Wolpert, *Bhutto of Pakistan: His Life and Times* (New York: Oxford University Press, 1993), 179–80.

[45] Shahid Javed Burki, *Pakistan Under Bhutto, 1971–1977* (London: Macmillan, 1988), 139.

[46] Ibid., 131–33.

nationalised by October 1972 when education was made free for all up to the age of 13 and in September 1974, education was made free as well as compulsory.[47]

On 16 August 1972, Bhutto announced the nationalisation of the vegetable oil industry.[48] He inaugurated Pakistan's first nuclear power plant on 28 November 1972 and personally chaired the Pakistan Atomic Energy Commission and the Ministry of Science and Technology to which he gave the 'highest priority'.[49]

By 1973, Bhutto had given retirement to many of Pakistan's bureaucrats and higher military officials whom he suspected of having political aspirations or an inclination towards Bonapartism.[50] In May 1973, the sale of expensive and branded medicines was banned and was replaced with the production of inexpensive generic medicines.[51] Bhutto's political prowess resulted in the unanimous approval of the Constitution by the national assembly, which became effective on 14 August 1973. After completing 20 months as the president, Bhutto switched his portfolio to prime minister and addressed the people of Pakistan on 23 March 1973, during the National Day celebrations over radio and television under the new Constitution.[52] In October 1973, at the start of the Yom Kippur War, led by Egypt and Syria against Israel, Bhutto wired UN secretary-general Kurt Waldheim, urging the fulfilment of the Security Council resolutions. Bhutto discussed with chiefs of army, navy and air force on 11 October 1973 and declared, '[a] cease-fire

---

[47] Ibid., 124.
[48] Ibid., 117.
[49] Stanley A. Wolpert, *Bhutto of Pakistan: His Life and Times* (New York: Oxford University Press, 1993), 207.
[50] Ibid., 186.
[51] Shahid Javed Burki, *Pakistan Under Bhutto: 1971–1977*, 2nd edition (London: Macmillan, 1988), 134.
[52] Stanley A. Wolpert, *Bhutto of Pakistan: His Life and Times* (New York: Oxford University Press, 1993), 219.

will not do... It is essential that Arab territories held by Israel – illegally by Israel – should be vacated'. He immediately wired messages of support and sympathy to Hafez Al-Assad of Syria, Hasan-Al Bakar of Iraq, King Faisal of Saudi Arabia and King Hussein of Jordan.[53] In December 1973, Bhutto laid the foundation for an integrated steel mill at Pipri near Karachi.[54]

On 1 January 1974, as a new year 'present' to the 'People of Pakistan', Bhutto announced the immediate nationalisation of all banks (private and domestically owned).[55] In May 1974, he pushed an amendment through the Parliament that gave the central government authority to ban any political party that was 'operating in a manner prejudicial to the sovereignty or integrity of the country'. Though the amendment stipulated that the Supreme Court had to approve any such ban, this appears not to have been a hindrance, as the National Awami Party was banned soon after. After Mujib turned Bangladesh into a one-party State, in January 1975, the elites and Opposition became concerned that Bhutto may try to form a one-party State like Mujib had done in Bangladesh.[56]

*'I am addressing tonight the toiling farmers of our land,'*
*Prime Minister Bhutto said in a broadcast to the nation*
*on November 10. 'With effect from the Rabi (spring) crop*
*of 1975–76, the small landowners owning up to 12 acres*
*of irrigated land and 25 acres of un-irrigated land shall be*
*exempted from the payment of land revenue, local rates,*
*development cess, and all cesses related to land revenue.'*
*It was his most revolutionary move to date, affecting more*
*than 80 percent of Pakistan's landowners, together totaling*

[53] Ibid., 224–25.
[54] Shahid Javed Burki, *Pakistan Under Bhutto: 1971–1977*, 2nd edition (London: Macmillan, 1988), 149.
[55] Ibid., 118.
[56] William B. Milam, *Bangladesh and Pakistan Flirting with Failure in South Asia* (New York: Columbia University Press, 2009), 48.

*more than all of his earlier industrial, bank, and cotton-*
*mill nationalisations. Millions of Pakistani peasants would*
*never forget that it was their Quaid-i-Awam (leader of the*
*masses) who lifted the crushing burden of taxes from their*
*sorely bent backs. Cries of 'Jiye Bhutto' (long live Bhutto)*
*and 'Bhutto Zindabad' (long live Bhutto) echoed from*
*Larkana to Lahore, from Karachi to Rawalpindi and back,*
*as tens of thousands who heard his voice danced for joy*
*and cheered their saintly leader of the people.*[57]

In 1975, Bhutto announced the decision to build a dozen
nuclear plants to cater to Pakistan's present and future
energy needs.[58] He also began assembling weapons that
would strengthen the nation's defence more than any of his
mediocre military predecessors could imagine possible.[59]

In pursuance of providing relief to the common man, in
July 1976, Bhutto's government nationalised 4,000 agro-
industries including wheat flour, rice milling and cotton
milling.[60]

## Mujib vs. Bhutto

There were many occasions before 1971 when Bhutto
supported Mujib's call for greater Bengali autonomy and for
the rights of the Bengalis to be recognised.[61] In 1968, during
the Agartala Conspiracy Case, at one stage, Bhutto appeared

---

[57] Stanley A. Wolpert, *Bhutto of Pakistan: His Life and Times* (New York: Oxford University Press, 1993), 258.

[58] Shahid Javed Burki, *Pakistan Under Bhutto: 1971–1977*, 2nd edition (London: Macmillan, 1988), 150.

[59] Stanley A. Wolpert, *Bhutto of Pakistan: His Life and Times* (New York: Oxford University Press, 1993), 228.

[60] Shahid Javed Burki, *Pakistan Under Bhutto: 1971–1977*, 2nd edition (London: Macmillan, 1988), 159.

[61] Srinath Raghavan, 'Indira Gandhi: India and the World in Transition' in Ramachandra Guha edited, *Makers of Modern Asia* (Cambridge: Harvard University Press, 2014), 286.

in the court in Muijb's support.[62] Mujib also reciprocated on several occasions, including his decision to release the Pakistani POWs in August 1973, attending the Islamic Summit Conference in Pakistan in February 1974, and on 30 October 1974, when he met with Henry Kissinger in Dhaka. During the conversation, Kissinger asked, 'Can Pakistan overcome its current political problems?' Mujib responded, 'Force won't do. The army is from Punjab. They can't keep Balochis down. But Bhutto is a politician, and he will try to deal with it that way. I hope he will do it. I have agreed to release all the POWs because I wanted to help Bhutto. If I had not done this, the military would have come to power in Pakistan.'[63]

A review of events uncovers many similarities between Mujib and Bhutto. Bhutto was the pioneer of 'Bhuttoism' in Pakistan and Mujib was the architect of 'Mujibism' in Bangladesh. They both believed that it was their destiny to lead their people. They were contemptuous and detested each other's qualities and attributes since they both had grandiose notions of themselves. Their leadership was considered indispensable in their respective countries, and both were admired for their ability to breathe new life into their respective nations. They were masterfully able to gather a cross-section of popular support and to construct a system of government that would not only provide the needed stability, but also satisfy the multidimensional interests of their populace.[64]

*It is as if the two men were inextricably intertwined. Neither could proceed without the other, and each was impeded in his quest by the other. If the impediment were not physical,*

[62] G.W Choudhury, *The Last Days of United Pakistan* (Bloomington: Indiana University Press, 1974), 26.

[63] B.Z. Khasru, *The Bangladesh Military Coup and the CIA Link* (New Delhi: Rupa Publications, 2014), 140.

[64] Lawrence Ziring, *Bangladesh From Mujib to Ershad: An Interpretive Study* (Karachi: Oxford University Press, 1992), 94–95.

*then the record would suggest something mystical. One seemed to haunt the other. They were star-crossed actors in a high stakes game. Their roles in the political process are strikingly similar, and they appeared predestined to commit the same follies, to meet the same tragic end so soon after their greatest triumph. All their victories were illusory; each demonstrated the reality of pyrrhic success.*[65]

Both Bhutto and Mujib were unable to trust their closest colleagues or accept the viewpoint of their rivals. Both resorted to private armies to protect themselves from their critics. Despite enjoying widespread popularity, both these leaders surrounded themselves with troops who they believed would loyally follow commands and sustain their authority. Mujib's Jatiya Rakkhi Bahini (national security force) created in February 1972 was matched by the Federal Security Force created by Bhutto in March 1972.[66]

## SUMMARY

The difference between Bangladesh (East Pakistan) and Pakistan (West Pakistan) was once again demonstrated. The discordant population in West Pakistan resulted in Bhutto assuming the role of president and chief martial law administrator to govern for 20 months, whereas Mujib relinquished the position of president of Bangladesh within the first week of his arrival. Homogeneity in East Pakistan was reflected when in Bangladesh, the Constitution was adopted within the first year of its independence, whereas it took 26 years and separation of the eastern wing (Bangladesh fiasco) for the Pakistani government to adopt a constitution passed by an elected assembly.

[65] Ibid., 94.
[66] Ibid., 96.

# 7

## RESOLVING THE DIFFERENCES AND GETTING ALONG

*Being willing to change allows you to move from
a point of view to a viewing point—a higher, more
expansive place, from which you can see both sides.*

—Thomas Crum[1]

Strong domestic pressures were undeniably operating and pushing these three leaders to compromise on their basic positions after the 1971 war and liberation of Bangladesh. To reiterate: the Indian government and electorate were growing increasingly cynical about the value of holding the Pakistani POWs due to enormous expense involved and because of mounting international criticism; the relatives of the POWs were intensifying pressure upon the Pakistan government to secure their repatriation; similarly, Mujib's government in Bangladesh was eager for the return of the Bengalis stranded in Pakistan which he knew could only be coupled with the exchange of POWs.[2]

---

[1] Thomas Crum, *The Magic of Conflict: Turning a Life of Work into a Work of Art* (Toronto: Simon and Schuster, 1987), 166.

[2] P.R. Chari and Pervaiz Iqbal Cheema, *The Simla Agreement 1972: Its Wasted Promise* (New Delhi: Manohar Publishers & Distributors, 2001), 69.

## Simla Agreement 1972: Bilateral Relations Between the Governments of India and Pakistan[3]

1. The Government of India and the Government of Pakistan have opted to put an end to their conflict and instead work at fostering an amicable relationship. Their desire for peace in the subcontinent has finally outweighed their differences. The countries would now devote their resources to more important matters, such as the welfare of their people.

   Thus, the two governments have agreed on the following:

   i.   The principles and purposes of the Charter of the United Nations shall govern the relations between the two countries;

   ii.  The two countries are resolved to settle their differences by peaceful means through bilateral negotiations or by any other peaceful means mutually agreed upon between them. Pending the final settlement of any of the problems between the two countries, neither side shall unilaterally alter the situation and both shall prevent the organization, assistance or encouragement of any acts detrimental to the maintenance of peaceful and harmonious relations;

   iii. That the pre-requisite for reconciliation, good neighbourliness and durable peace between them is a commitment by both the countries to peaceful co-existence, respect for each other's territorial integrity and sovereignty and non-interference in each other's internal affairs, on the basis of equality and mutual benefit;

[3] Ibid., 204–06.

iv. That the basic issues and causes of conflict which have bedevilled the relations between the two countries for the last 25 years shall be resolved by peaceful means;

v. That they shall always respect each other's national unity, territorial integrity, political independence and sovereign equality;

vi. That in accordance with the Charter of the United Nations they will refrain from the threat or use of force against the territorial integrity or political independence of each other.

2. Both governments will take all steps within their power to prevent hostile propaganda directed against each other. Both countries will encourage the dissemination of such information as would promote the development of friendly relations between them.

3. In order progressively to restore and normalize relations between the two countries step by step, it was agreed that:

i. Steps shall be taken to resume communications, postal, telegraphic, sea, land including border posts, and air link including overflights.

ii. Appropriate steps shall be taken to promote travel facilities for the nationals of the other country.

iii. Trade and co-operation in economic and other agreed fields will be resumed as far as possible.

iv. Exchange in the fields of science and culture will be promoted.

4. In order to initiate the process of the establishment of durable peace, both the Governments agree that:
   i.   Indian and Pakistani forces shall be withdrawn to their side of the international border.
   ii.  In Jammu and Kashmir, the line of control resulting from the cease-fire of December 17, 1971 shall be respected by both sides without prejudice to the recognized position of either side. Neither side shall seek to alter it unilaterally, irrespective of mutual differences and legal interpretations. Both sides further undertake to refrain from the threat or the use of force in violation of this Line.
   iii. The withdrawals shall commence upon entry into force of this Agreement and shall be completed within a period of 30 days thereof.

5. This Agreement will be subject to ratification by both countries in accordance with their respective constitutional procedures, and will come into force with effect from the date on which the Instruments of Ratification are exchanged.

6. Both Governments agree that the respective Heads will meet again at a mutually convenient time in the future and that, in the meanwhile, the representatives of the two sides will meet to discuss further the modalities and arrangements for the establishment of durable peace and normalization of relations, including the questions of repatriation of prisoners of war and civilian internees, a final settlement of Jammu and Kashmir and the resumption of diplomatic relations.

President Zulfikar Ali Bhutto and Prime Minister Indira Gandhi signing the Simla Agreement in 1972.

Source: http://www.bhutto.org/simla-agreement.php

*The two men standing behind Bhutto both served as interim prime ministers of Pakistan in later years: Malik Ghulam Mustafa Jatoi and Malik Meraj Khalid*

Zulfikar Ali Bhutto with Indira Gandhi upon signing the famous Simla Agreement (1972).

Source: *The Friday Times*, Isa Daudpota Collection TFT issue, 29 November 2013, http://www.thefridaytimes.com/tft/zulfikar-bhutto-and-indira-gandhi-1972/

While both Gandhi and Bhutto tried to guide public opinion towards more realistic pursuits, both had to face warmongering and criticism from their Opposition parties. However, such jingoistic behaviour did not deter the leaders or the promoters of sanity and normalisation of relationships.[4] Both Bhutto and Gandhi emphatically denied the existence of any secret deal during the Simla negotiations. On his return from Simla, Bhutto asserted that there was no secret deal in a speech at Lahore airport.[5] Similarly, Indira, in response to a question, also categorically dismissed it as 'fiction'. She denied the existence of a secret deal both as prime minister and when she was out of power. In the latter case, there were no particular constraints which would have prevented her from revealing any secret deal.[6]

The UN and several world leaders tried to mediate and normalise relations between Pakistan and Bangladesh. Indonesia offered to arrange a meeting of Bhutto and Mujib in Indonesia; Bhutto welcomed, but Bangladesh ignored the request. Bhutto said an actual face-to-face meeting with Mujib would be de facto recognition of Bangladesh. Many Arab nations pressed both Pakistan and Bangladesh, but most accepted Bhutto's terms—the complete and unconditional return of the Pakistani POWs—as legitimate. The Muslim world had supported Pakistan during the 1971 war and therefore Bangladesh, in spite of having a large Muslim population, did not have cordial relations with the rest of the Islamic world.[7]

At the Simla summit, Pakistan's top priorities included getting 5,000 square miles of territory occupied by

[4] Ibid., 115.
[5] Ibid., 144.
[6] Ibid., 144.
[7] B.Z. Khasru, *The Bangladesh Military Coup and the CIA Link* (New Delhi: Rupa Publications, 2014), 109–10.

India and the repatriation of POWs. Bhutto's masterful negotiations led to return of the territory, but Indira refused to release the POWs without Mujib's approval since Mujib insisted on Pakistan's recognition of the independence of Bangladesh. After the summit, Bhutto repeatedly asked the Indian government to discuss the repatriation of POWs. In order to find a solution, the Indian prime minister's special envoy, P.N. Haksar, paid a five-day visit to Bangladesh in the first week of April 1973. The foreign minister of Bangladesh, Kamal Hussain, reciprocated with a three-day visit on 13 April 1973. At the end of their meetings, they issued a joint declaration that made a distinction between the humanitarian and political dilemmas, placing the problem of the POWs in the former category. The declaration suggested the repatriation of all POWs except 195 that were charged with war crimes.[8] On 17 April 1973, Kamal Hussain announced at a press conference in Dhaka that a tribunal consisting of the judges of the Supreme Court of Bangladesh would try these 195 POWs.[9] Bhutto rejected the competence of the authorities in Dhaka to try any of the POWs and insisted on constituting a tribunal of such calibre  that could inspire 'international confidence'.

Bhutto invited the representatives of the Government of India for negotiations on the joint declaration in the midst of this controversy. A meeting was held between representatives of Pakistan and India in New Delhi on 18 August, which resulted in a consensus on 28 August 1973.[10]

---

[8] Ghulam Mustafa and Qasim S. Gill, 'The issue of POWs, 1971 and Recognition of Bangladesh', *International Journal of Business and Social Research* (Volume 4, No. 3, 2014), 116.
[9] Ibid.
[10] Ibid.

The agreement signed between the two sides included the following conditions:

a) All POWs held in India would be repatriated to Pakistan with the exception of 195 who, according to Bangladesh, were to be tried for war crimes.

b) That Bengalis held in Pakistan would be allowed to return to Bangladesh.

c) A 'substantial number' of the so-called Biharis in Bangladesh would be repatriated to Pakistan.

The agreement and resolution of the problem of Pakistani POW's eased tensions between India, Pakistan and Bangladesh creating favourable environment to address unresolved issues. Pakistan supported the Bangladesh government's decision to grant amnesty to about 40,000 Bengalis incriminated of collaborating with Pakistan during the 1971 war. Pakistan also expressed hope that Bangladesh would drop demands for trials of 195 Pakistani POWs.[11] On Pakistan's request, the International Court of Justice removed the POWs' case from its list. A train was scheduled to depart every other day, making the repatriation of Pakistani POWs possible from the end of September 1973 to April 1974. As for the 195 POWs, it was decided to keep them in India.[12]

Since the Opposition in Pakistan blamed Bhutto for collaborating with Yahya leading to Pakistan's dismemberment, Bhutto was extra cautious about recognising the status of Bangladesh as an independent nation. In July 1973, Bhutto's government brought up the matter of recognition of Bangladesh to the Supreme Court of Pakistan. The court unanimously decided that there was

[11] Samina Fakhruddin, 'Pakistan's relation with India and Bangladesh', *Pakistan Horizon* (Volume 27, No. 2, 1974), 68.

[12] Col S.P. Salunke, *Pakistani POWs in India* (New Delhi: Vikas Publishing House, 1977), 99–100.

no legal bar for the national assembly to adopt a resolution authorising the government to accord such recognition. On 10 July 1973, the national assembly gave Bhutto the authority to recognise Bangladesh.[13]

## ISLAMIC BLOCK, ISLAMIC BANK AND ISLAMIC BOMB

Bhutto lobbied for the hosting of the Organisation of Islamic Cooperation (OIC) Summit in Pakistan and at a press conference in Karachi in 1973, he said, 'Bhutto had relayed his country's position on the Middle East – he had offered support and sympathy to the leaders of Syria and Iraq in their struggle on behalf of the indomitable Arab nation against the Israeli aggressor.[14] Moreover, Bhutto had asserted, the government and people of Pakistan have always fully supported the cause of the Arab people, and will continue to do so.'[15]

Bhutto's grand plans included uniting the Muslim countries of the world and using this collective strength to sort out the problems they faced, including the Palestine and Kashmir issues. Senior officials of the majority of the 38 Islamic countries attending the OIC conference met on 18 February 1974, and for three days the Muslim foreign ministers hammered out draft resolutions that would be considered at the upcoming Islamic Summit Conference. The Palestine Liberation Organization members also attended the conference and were led by its chairman Yaseer Arafat. Until the very eve of the formal convening, the question of the Bangladesh prime minister's attendance remained unclear.

[13] Stanley A. Wolpert, *Bhutto of Pakistan: His Life and Times* (New York: Oxford University Press, 1993), 215–16.
[14] Ibid., 224.
[15] Ibid., 225.

In late 1973, both Mujib and Bhutto felt pressured by several Muslim nations to resolve their quarrels; their peace accord would pave the way for Bangladesh to attend the Islamic Summit Conference in Lahore in early 1974. Bhutto and Mujib, however, continued with their disagreement. Bhutto wanted Mujib to agree to the release of POWs before recognising Bangladesh. Mujib wanted Pakistan to recognise Bangladesh before direct talks with Bhutto. Mujib also wanted to hold war crimes' trials and he demanded Bhutto take the Biharis who opted for Pakistan. Under pressure from several Islamic nations, Bhutto gave in and sought help from Egypt's president Anwar Sadat to act as a mediator. In December 1973, Bhutto said Bangladesh would be invited to the 1974 conference and this would be Bangladesh's de facto recognition. The official recognition would soon follow, but Mujib was not taken in by Bhutto's gesture.[16]

On 22 January 1974, Pakistan released a letter from Ugandan president Idi Amin urging Bhutto and Mujib to set a meeting. Amin wrote: 'I take the opportunity to appeal to both of you in the name of [the] Islamic brotherhood to make up your political differences so that his Excellency Sheikh Mujibur Rahman will also be able to attend...'[17] Though Pakistan had initially not invited Bangladesh to attend the summit, several heads of State from the Arab world pressured Bhutto to extend an invitation to Mujib. In an attempt to appease Mujib, on 31 January 1974, Bhutto stated, 'Mujib was a great leader who had said many things in past, which was a privilege of great people.'[18] Bangladesh was formally invited

---

[16] B.Z. Khasru, *The Bangladesh Military Coup and the CIA Link* (New Delhi: Rupa Publications, 2014), 142.

[17] Ibid., 143.

[18] Ibid., 150.

on 5 February to participate in the Islamic Summit at Lahore when Hasan-ul-Tohmay, the secretary-general of Islamic Secretariat visited Dhaka. He described the invitation as 'the first step towards the recognition of Bangladesh by Pakistan'.[19]

Mujib, however, refused to participate until Pakistan announced its formal recognition of Bangladesh. The stalemate continued until 20 February because of Mujib's uncompromising attitude towards the trials of the 195 Pakistani POWs. Just two days before the Islamic Summit, a seven-member delegation of representatives of Kuwait, Somalia, Lebanon, Algeria and Senegal was sent to Dhaka on 21 February 1974 to formally invite Mujib to attend the summit. The delegation also communicated a message from Bhutto that Pakistan's government would formally recognise the sovereignty of Bangladesh at the OIC Summit.[20] In return, the delegation visiting Bangladesh was to persuade Mujib to agree to drop the demand for the 195 POWs' trials; Mujib in return assured the delegation that his government would oblige.

On 22 February 1974, the newly established OIC held its second summit in Lahore, Pakistan. The Arab heads of State called the summit to discuss the aftermath of the 1973 Arab-Israeli war and the resulting oil embargo in the western world imposed by the organisation of petroleum-exporting countries. Additionally, the OIC Summit was a rare opportunity for Prime Minister Bhutto to cement Pakistan's relations with powerful Arab countries in the

---

[19] Ghulam Mustafa and Qasim S. Gill, 'The issue of POWs, 1971 and Recognition of Bangladesh', *International Journal of Business and Social Research* (Volume 4, No. 3, 2014), 117.

[20] P. Sukumaran Nair, *Indo-Bangladesh Relations* (New Delhi: APH Publishing Corporation, 2008), 62.

Middle East, which would be advantageous in foreign relations and international diplomacy.

On 22 February 1974, Mujib flew to Lahore to attend the Islamic Summit, bringing Bhutto and Mujib face-to-face again. Upon arriving in Lahore, Mujib was greeted by Bhutto and General Tikka Khan. Even though blamed for the Pakistani military excesses during the Bangladesh Liberation War, Mujib and the Bengali delegation knew not to upset their chance at achieving peace with Pakistan. In an attempt to ease tensions, and to improve relations with the other Muslim countries attending the summit, Mujib and Bhutto appeared on the balcony of the Shalimar Gardens, their hands joined, accompanied by other dignitaries.[21] Pakistan recognised Bangladesh on the same day.

Mujib's decision to go to Pakistan was facilitated through the mediation of Egyptian president, Anwar Sadat. Mujib admitted during the Islamic Summit that he came to Lahore because he owed his life to Sadat, who was later recognised by the conference for achieving the Pak-Bangla reconciliation. In his brief speech to the summit on 24 February, Mujib thanked all those who had helped make his attendance possible, particularly Bhutto, who reciprocated by publicly demonstrating his friendship for Mujib. They held several private discussions and told the press they expected to establish diplomatic relations soon. Bhutto also accepted Mujib's invitation to visit Dhaka.[22]

---

[21] Ahmed Salahuddin, *Bangladesh: Past and Present* (New Delhi: APH Publishing, 2004), 210.

[22] B.Z. Khasru, *The Bangladesh Military Coup and the CIA Link* (New Delhi: Rupa Publications, 2014), 148.

Mujib and Bhutto at the Organisation of Islamic Countries Summit in Lahore, Pakistan on 22 February 1974.

মুজিব ভুট্টোর সাথে গলাগলি করছেন। লাহোরে ১৯৭৪ সালের ২২ ফেব্রুয়ারী

Source: https://groups.google.com/forum/#!topic/pfc-friends/ioWQjL5c7q8

The OIC was a success and it concluded with the formation of the Islamic Solidarity Fund and set the foundation for the Islamic Commission for Economic, Cultural and Social Affairs. The heads of States, ministers and dignitaries from Muslim countries all over the world attended the OIC. The participant countries included Afghanistan, Algeria, Bahrain, Bangladesh, Chad, Egypt, Gabon, Gambia, Guinea, Guinea-Bissau, Indonesia, Iran, Jordon, Morocco, Saudi Arabia, Kuwait, Lebanon, Libya, Malaysia, Mali, Mauritania, Niger, Oman, Pakistan, Yemen, Qatar, Senegal, Somalia, Sudan, Syria, Tunisia, Turkey, Uganda, United Arab Emirates, Palestine and Iraq. The summit was a success for Pakistan and Bhutto as well who took the opportunity to display support to a segment of the political world that he knew had considerable influence over the urban population in Pakistan.

Excerpts extracted from Prime Minister Zulfikar Ali Bhutto's speech:[23]

*In the name of Allah, Most Gracious, Most Merciful.*
    *Your Majesties, Royal Highnesses, Excellencies,*
    *Dear brothers in Islam,*
    *This unique assemblage of Monarchs, Presidents and Prime Ministers has gathered at the moment in world affairs, which is as critical as it can be creative. Here is a resplendent array of statesmen and leaders, profound in their insight into the issues that will engage us at this conference. By asking me to preside at it, you have conferred an honour upon me, which in reality is a tribute to Pakistan. I am filled with both humility and pride: the humility is personal and the pride national [...] A few moments ago, in deference to the sentiments of leaders participating in this conference and as a result of the mediatory efforts of this conference, my Government has extended formal recognition to Bangladesh. We hope this mutual reconciliation, which is in the spirit of Islamic fraternity, will now [bury] a past that the peoples of both our countries would prefer to see forgotten [...] We can say with confidence that our aim is to promote justice and equilibrium. Our unity is not directed against any creed, religious or secular. It is not nourished by hate or rancour. [Its] drive and force is a passion for justice [...] I trust that we will not fritter away historic opportunities now presented to us. For long centuries, we have hoped for a turning point. That turning point has arrived. The break of a new dawn is not now forlorn hope. Poverty need no longer be our portion. Humiliation need no longer be our*

---

[23] Ministry of Information and Broadcasting, Government of Pakistan, *Report on Islamic Summit 1974 Pakistan, 22–24 February* (Karachi: Ferozsons, 1974), 37–55.

*heritage. Ignorance need no longer be the emblem of our identity.*

Excerpts extracted from the speech by Prime Minister Sheikh Mujibur Rahman:[24]

*Your Majesties, Your Highnesses, Excellencies and Brothers,*
*Indeed we are very happy that the 75 million people of Bangladesh have been able to take their place in this forum to declare their fraternal solidarity with their brethren who are assembled here and extend their support to the just cause of our Arab brethren.*

*I would like to express our appreciation to all of those, including the Secretary General, who have actively worked to arrange for us to be by the side of our brothers today, and thank all the distinguished leaders who have welcomed us today, and to our host and chairman, the Prime Minister of Pakistan, I extend our thanks. I would like to state that, in opening a new chapter in our relations on the basis of sovereignty, we have paved the way for contributing together to the promotion of peace in our subcontinent and in the World [...] The illegal occupation of Arab land must be vacated. We must regain our right over Jerusalem. We salute the brave martyrs and valiant heroes of the Ramadhan War who, by their valour and their sacrifices, destroyed many myths and created new executive conditions which all promise that the right and justice will eventually triumph [...] I would end by pledging that 75 million people of Bangladesh are fully committed to contribute in every way possible to the success of this strategy.*

*May the Almighty crown all our collective endeavors with great success. Thank you, Mr. Chairman.*

[24] Ibid., 134–36.

The diplomatic prowess and political sagacity of Bhutto resulted in him being seated between Revolutionary Chairman of the Libyan Arab Republic Colonel Muammar Gaddafi and President Anwar Sadat of Egypt on one side and King Faisal of Saudi Arabia and Prime Minister Mujib of Bangladesh on the other. This was an overwhelming transformation for Pakistan given that it was less than three years after the disastrous Bangladesh Liberation War.[25] In a veiled reference to Kashmir, Bhutto, in his inaugural address to the summit, stated, 'We do not deny that there are other vital issues which agitate Muslim minds... Your host country, for instance, has been a victim of international conspiracies and is concerned with an intense question in which, it believes, its stand is based on nothing but justice and concern for Muslim rights.'[26] Bhutto's domestic and foreign policies received an endorsement from the monarchs of the Arab world and also won the admiration of influential heads of State, including King Faisal of Saudi Arabia, Libyan leader Colonel Muammar Gaddafi and Syrian president Al Assad.[27]

As part of showcasing the country's Islamic identity, Bhutto sought the backing of rich Muslim States of the Middle East to finance the development of a nuclear weapons' programme for Pakistan. The Islamic Summit served as an opportunity to garner support and harden Bhutto's defiant stance against India. Claiming that the Muslim world was entitled to its own 'Islamic bomb', he later recalled his reasons for appealing to his Muslim partners, 'The Christian, Jewish and Hindu civilizations have this [nuclear] capability. The Communist powers also

---

[25] Stanley A. Wolpert, *Bhutto of Pakistan: His Life and Times* (New York: Oxford University Press, 1993), 232.

[26] Ministry of Information and Broadcasting, Government of Pakistan, *Report on Islamic Summit 1974 Pakistan, 22-24 February* (Karachi: Ferozsons, 1974), 40.

[27] Shahid Javed Burki, *Pakistan Under Bhutto, 1971–1977* (London: Macmillan, 1988), 179.

possess it. Only the Islamic civilization was without it, but that position was about to change.'[28]

As a capstone to the successful OIC Summit, the Pakistani government declared it would sponsor 'an international conference on the life and work of the Prophet Muhammad (PBUH)'.[29] This event was meant to cater to the Islamic sentiment in the Arab world and was seen as another opportunity to 'generate support' globally for Pakistan. The success of the OIC Summit and Bhutto's political dexterity was demonstrated in Mujib's interview published on 29 February 1974 in *The Times of London*: 'I am impressed by Mr. Bhutto's sincerity. I am overwhelmed by the love and affection shown by the people of Pakistan. Thousands of them lined the route from the airport to the venue of the Islamic Summit. They called me by my name.' In reference to Bhutto, Mujib said, 'I want to help him. He is an old friend.'[30]

The following has been extracted from the *International Journal of Business and Social Research*, summarising to a degree the negotiations between Pakistan and Bangladesh: [31]

> *After Pakistan's recognition of Bangladesh, Sheikh Mujib's attitude towards the trials of POWs changed. He reversed his earlier stand and began to minimise the importance of the trials, asserting that Bengalis were great enough to forgive those who had treated them inhumanly. Later, a*

[28] Farzana Shaikh, 'ZULFIKAR ALI BHUTTO: In Pursuit of an Asian Pakistan' in Ramachandra Guha edited, *Makers of Modern Asia* (Cambridge: Harvard University Press, 2014), 294.

[29] Shahid Javed Burki, *Pakistan Under Bhutto, 1971–1977* (London: Macmillan, 1988), 179.

[30] B.Z. Khasru, *The Bangladesh Military Coup and the CIA Link* (New Delhi: Rupa Publications, 2014), 81.

[31] Ghulam Mustafa and Qasim S. Gill, 'The issue of POWs, 1971 and Recognition of Bangladesh', *International Journal of Business and Social Research* (Volume 4, No. 3, 2014), 117.

*tripartite conference [held by] the Indian External Affairs*
*Minister Swarn Singh, Bangladesh Foreign Minister Dr*
*Kamal Hussain, and Pakistan Minister of State for Defence*
*and Foreign Affairs Aziz Ahmad was held in New Delhi on*
*April 5, 1974. The agreement was signed on April 9, 1974.*
*Bangladesh agreed to abandon the demand of the trials*
*of 195 Pakistani POWs; the Pakistan government agreed*
*to accept a limited number of the Biharis who fulfilled the*
*criteria set by the Pakistan government. In return, Pakistan*
*offered assurance on reviewing lists of potential repatriates*
*from Bangladesh.*

During his term as the chairman of the OIC, Bhutto
demonstrated agility in political discussions, further
strengthening relations with powerful Middle Eastern
heads of State, including the Shah of Iran, the King of Saudi
Arabia, Colonel Muammar Gaddafi of Libya, Hafez al
Assad of Syria and the Sheikh of Abu Dhabi.[32]

On 27 June 1974, Prime Minister Bhutto paid an
official visit to Bangladesh—the first-ever diplomatic visit
of a Pakistani leader. The Bangladesh government had
several concerns with Bhutto's visit, the primary one being
security, given the animosity many Bengalis harboured
towards Bhutto for his perceived role in the 1971 events.
At the same time, given the widespread cynicism over
the prevalent abysmal conditions in Bangladesh and
anticipation that renewed ties with Pakistan may promise
a better life, the government feared that Bhutto would
receive too warm a welcome.[33] Bhutto arrived in Dhaka
expecting to attend a banquet and civil reception arranged
for him; instead, the prime minister was met by hostile

---

[32] M. Asghar Khan, *We've Learnt Nothing From History: Pakistan: Politics and Military Power* (Karachi, Pakistan: Oxford University Press, 2006), 190.

[33] B.Z. Khasru, *The Bangladesh Military Coup and the CIA Link* (New Delhi: Rupa Publications, 2014), 152.

chants and verbal attacks by some members of the public, including the exceptionally denigrating, 'Butcher Bhutto, go home!' The Bengalis were reacting to Bhutto's remark, 'Thank God, Pakistan has been saved', which he had made at the start of the military offensive in East Pakistan on 26 March 1971.[34]

Discussions took place between Bhutto and Mujib one-on-one, in private; there was only one public meeting. At this meeting, Mujib acknowledged that he did not hold Bhutto responsible for the atrocities of 1971. He said Yahya Khan intended to finish him off first and then deal with Bhutto in a similar manner.[35] Despite the public's hostilities, Bhutto and Mujib attended the banquet together. Alluding to the day's earlier events, Mujib frankly reminded Bhutto, 'History could be [re]interpreted, but not rewritten.'[36] The schedule included a visit to the 1971 martyrs' monument to which Bhutto agreed reluctantly, overriding his security personnel. There were about a couple of thousand people present at the monument, most of them quiet. There were some others upfront chanting slogans and carrying posters against Bhutto.[37] At the official dinner, Mujib emphasised on the Bengalis' forgiveness for the past Pakistani misgivings and called on Pakistan to reciprocate. He suggested the repatriation of the Biharis and a reasonable division of assets was a fair solution.

Bhutto proposed to take 10,000 additional Biharis, much to Mujib's frustration. He neither rejected nor accepted it as it could form the basis for further discussions. Regarding the division of the assets, Bangladesh initially mentioned

---

[34] Ahmed Salahuddin, *Bangladesh: Past and Present* (New Delhi: APH Publishing, 2004), 210.

[35] B.Z. Khasru, *The Bangladesh Military Coup and the CIA Link* (New Delhi: Rupa Publications, 2014), 155.

[36] Ahmed Salahuddin, *Bangladesh: Past and Present* (New Delhi: APH Publishing, 2004), 210.

[37] B.Z. Khasru, *The Bangladesh Military Coup and the CIA Link* (New Delhi: Rupa Publications, 2014), 156.

56 per cent as its share, but later asked for equitable distribution. Pakistan proposed that a joint commission should decide on the assets and liabilities. Mujib suggested that transfer of easily identifiable assets, such as gold reserves, foreign exchange reserves, IMF balances and PIA planes, should be made within two months. Mujib also agreed to accept the corresponding share of liabilities.[38]

Overall, Bhutto's visit to Bangladesh and meeting with Mujib did not produce any tangible outcomes. Mujib used the meeting as an opportunity to negotiate the division of the assets held by united Pakistan before 1971 as well as a chance to discuss the admission of more non-Bengalis in Pakistan.[39] He accepted the invitation for a return visit, which was intended as a positive signal. Upon his return from Dhaka, Bhutto lauded the warmth of his welcome in Bangladesh. He described the talks with Mujib a success but expressed reservations regarding the discussion of financial topics. Hence, the status quo persisted. Mujib met Henry Kissinger on 30 September 1974 and shared his frustration, 'I have taken the liabilities. Why can't I have the assets? We received no gold, no planes and no ships. I have 75 million. I have returned the prisoners of war to Pakistan. I could have held back 4000 prisoners for bargaining, but I did not want to do that. I want good relations in South Asia. Bangladesh is a small country.'[40]

## INDIRA-BHUTTO RELATIONS POST-SIMLA

Prime Minister Indira Gandhi and President Zulfikar Ali Bhutto, both left Simla—historically a site of conflict

---

[38] Ibid., 53.

[39] Ahmed Salahuddin, *Bangladesh: Past and Present* (New Delhi: APH Publishing, 2004), 210.

[40] B.Z. Khasru, *The Bangladesh Military Coup and the CIA Link* (New Delhi: Rupa Publications, 2014), 122–23.

and clashes between the two countries—satisfied and optimistic. Although Indira herself had considered the Simla Agreement a 'real achievement' for India, political critics in India voiced concerns that the prime minister had made a 'fatal blunder' in falling prey to Bhutto's signature tactics in diplomacy.[41] Additionally, there were accusations that Indira and Bhutto had created a 'secret clause' in the Simla Agreement, which was not made public.[42] Around the same time, journalist Kuldip Nayar, a fierce critic of Indira in the past, wrote that Indira had 'won the war [with Pakistan]' and had also 'won the peace'. According to Nayar, in 1972, '[Indira] was the undisputed leader of the country; the cynicism of the intellectuals had given way to admiration; the masses were even more worshipful... [She] was hailed as the greatest leader India had ever had.'[43]

Under the patronage of Indira, India successfully tested a nuclear device code-named 'Smiling Buddha' on 18 May 1974. Since Buddha is considered a prophet of peace, India stressed that the experiment was for peaceful purposes; the difference between tests for peaceful and military purposes was indistinguishable. In reaction to India's successful nuclear tests, Prime Minister Bhutto stressed that the people of Pakistan would never accept Indian hegemony or succumb to its nuclear blackmail. Bhutto also said, 'If India builds the bomb, we will eat leaves or grass, even go hungry but we will have to get one of our own.'[44]

Subsequently, on 24 February 1975, Indira Gandhi announced the Kashmir Accord in the Indian Parliament, one day after the standing chief minister of Jammu and Kashmir had resigned. The Kashmir Accord was an

[41] Katherine Frank, *Indira: The Life of Indira Nehru Gandhi* (London: HarperCollins, 2001), 346–47.

[42] Ibid., 347.

[43] Ibid.

[44] G.W. Choudhury, *India, Pakistan, Bangladesh and the Major Powers* (New York, Macmillan Publishing, 1975), 239–40.

agreement between Kashmiri politician Sheikh Abdullah and Indian prime minister Indira Gandhi that allowed Sheikh Abdullah to become the chief minister of Jammu and Kashmir again after 11 years. As far as Prime Minister Indira was concerned, the Kashmir Accord removed the possibility of a plebiscite in Kashmir and put a stop to the growing movement for Kashmiri self-determination. In India, the Kashmir Accord was perceived as a confirmation of Kashmir's 'irrevocable accession' to India. Prime Minister Bhutto, who called the agreement a 'sell-out', insisting that it violated the terms of the 1972 Simla Agreement between India and Pakistan, rejected the Kashmir Accord.[45]

## SUMMARY

All three leaders were masters of posturing; they could carry a hostile demeanor and yet be generous whenever the situation demanded. Mujib and Bhutto resumed their mutual respect and dialogue after their political goals were achieved; i.e. getting rid of Yahya Khan and assuming power. Indira and Bhutto normalised their relation's post Bangladesh's independence and both developed friendly relations with Mujib.

[45] Katherine Frank, *Indira: The Life of Indira Nehru Gandhi* (London: HarperCollins, 2001), 366.

# 8

## How the Mighty Fall: Downfall and Martyrdom

*All prophets were leaders; should we expect all leaders to be prophets?*

—Dr Faisal Khosa[1]

'All the major actors of the period were creatures of a historic legacy and a psycho-political milieu which did not lend itself to accommodation and compromise, to bargaining and a reasonable settlement. Nurtured on conspiracy theories, they were all conditioned to act in a manner that neglected agreeable solutions and promoted violent judgments.'[2]

As S.M. Lipset has emphasised, the way that a nation is born conditions much of its later political development.[3] One of the ironies of the Indian subcontinent is that most elected leaders tried to assume absolute authority, and almost all dictators, after usurping power, tried to evolve into benevolent democratic leaders. Further, all three leaders discussed in the preceding chapters had an unshakable belief that a threat to them was a threat to their nation and its people. Each of these leaders successively garnered enough power to the extent that no one could question their

---

[1] https://www.goodreads.com/author/quotes/14927907.Faisal_Khosa (accessed 12 June 2019).
[2] Lawrence Ziring, *Pakistan: The Enigma of Political Development* (Colorado: Westview Press, 1980), 104.
[3] Talukder Maniruzzaman, 'Bangladesh in 1975: The Fall of the Mujib Regime and its Aftermath', *Asian Survey* (Volume 16, No. 2, 1976), 119–29.

authority, something, which, one could argue, produced in their minds an illusion of immortality. Moreover, each of these leaders' deaths captures moments of mythic courage, selfless acts which, when observed through the lens of the intellect, were indisputably irrational, but when observed through the heart, were the only choices worth considering.

## PART 1: BANGLADESH

*I have given you independence; now go and preserve it.*
—Sheikh Mujibur Rahman[4]

'In the thousand year history of Bengal, Sheikh Mujib is her only leader who has, in terms of blood, race, language, culture and birth, been a full blooded Bengali. His physical stature was immense. His voice was redolent of thunder. His charisma worked magic on people. The courage and charm that flowed from him made him a unique superman in these times,' said journalist Cyril Dunn.[5]

Although approximately 55 per cent of the people of Pakistan were Bengalis,[6] their rights and freedoms had been consistently denied by Pakistan's central government. In this light, Mujib emerged as the hero and saviour the Bengalis desired; without him, the fate of the people of East Bengal (East Pakistan) would be nothing more than austere and miserable.

In independent Bangladesh, natural calamities of massive floods and famines persisted. Despite his government's initial achievements in independent Bangladesh, Mujib struggled as an administrator. Even though a constitution was

---

[4] https://www.azquotes.com/quote/1194005 (accessed 12 June 2019).
[5] *Dhaka Tribune*, 'Bangabandhu: In their eyes' https://www.dhakatribune.com/feature/2016/08/15/bangabandhu-in-their-eyes (accessed 12 June 2019).
[6] Mujibur Sheikh Rahman, *The Unfinished Memoirs* (Karachi: Oxford University Press, 2012), 197.

adopted proclaiming a secular democracy, the country faced considerable challenges, including lack of infrastructure and resources, and repeated natural disasters.

According to a report in *Time* magazine of 1973:

> *Bangladesh had little reason to enjoy a happy first birthday. If it is not the 'basket case' that Henry Kissinger once called it, neither has it become the Shonar Bangla (Golden Bengal) envisioned by Mujib. How much this is the fault of Mujib is a moot question. It is true that he has had little time in which to combat some of Bangladesh's immense problems. Nevertheless, some critics contend that he has wasted some time playing the role of popular revolutionary figure (such as personally receiving virtually any of his people who call on him) when he should have been concentrating more on serious matters of state. If, as expected, he is elected in March, Mujib will face a clear test of whether he is not only the father of Bangladesh but also its savior.[7]*

Between 1974 and 1975, the economy of Bangladesh almost collapsed and famine was unavoidable. The infant and child mortality rate was at an all-time high and the estimated death toll crossed 100,000. These factors considerably undermined the morale in the country and gave way to feelings of anger and resentment against the ruling government.[8]

The first general elections in independent Bangladesh were held on 7 March 1973, which resulted in a sweeping victory for Mujib and his Awami League (allegedly 307 of the 315 seats; different sources vary). This landslide victory sparked unreal public expectations, which swiftly turned to growing discontent. Bangladesh's deteriorating economy and dissatisfaction with Mujib in every stratum of society,

---

[7] 'Bangladesh: Not Yet Shonar Bangla', *Time*, 1 January 1973, 32.
[8] William B. Milam, *Bangladesh and Pakistan Flirting with Failure in South Asia* (New York: Columbia University, 2009), 92.

including the army, made him opt for a more high-handed presidential form of government.[9] *The Financial Times* of 18 June 1974 reported, 'Bangladesh is losing its real battle – that of trying to conjure up some means of economic survival for the poorest and most over-crowded people in the world. No country so far, however poor, has reached the point where millions of its citizens actually die because they have nothing to eat. If there is a place on the planet facing that nightmare, this is it.'[10]

'When people are destined to self-destruct, they tend to make one mistake after another.'[11] Amid rising political and economic discontent and rampant unemployment, poverty and corruption, Mujib violated several principles of the Constitution, including constitutionalism, freedom of speech, the rule of law, the right to dissent and equal opportunity of employment.[12] As the polarisation between his centrist Awami League and the radical revolutionaries became more severe by the end of 1974, Sheikh Mujib 'gave up the façade' of parliamentary government.[13] On 28 December 1974, Mujib proclaimed a state of Emergency, suspending fundamental rights and completely stripping the courts of their power to intervene in any of his actions.[14]

In January 1975, he used his party's influence to amend the Constitution to establish a presidential system and Mujib was now the president. Using this executive power, Mujib banned

[9] Lawrence Ziring, *Bangladesh From Mujib to Ershad: An Interpretive Study* (Karachi: Oxford University Press, 1992), 96.
[10] G.W. Choudhury, *The Last Days of United Pakistan* (Bloomington: Indiana University Press, 1974), 242.
[11] Mujibur Sheikh Rahman, *The Unfinished Memoirs* (Karachi: Oxford University Press, 2012), 203.
[12] James Heitzman et al., *Bangladesh: A Country Study* (Washington: Federal Research Division, Library of Congress, 1989), 35.
[13] Talukder Maniruzzaman, 'Bangladesh in 1975: The Fall of the Mujib Regime and its Aftermath', *Asian Survey* (Volume 16, No. 2, 1976),119–29.
[14] Anthony Mascarenhas, *Bangladesh: A Legacy of Blood* (London: Hodder & Stoughton, 1986), 45.

all political parties and formed one single political party, to which all government employees were required to belong. The courts were enjoined to quit enforcing fundamental rights enumerated in the Constitution. The man who led its independence movement had now transformed Bangladesh from a democracy into personal dictatorship. A number of political leaders disliked the move towards dictatorship, but none could muster enough courage to object.[15]

Mujib's decision to alter the political process had the opposite effect and was perceived as a sign of weakness, not strength. His Emergency measures had the reverse effect of what was intended. Instead of calming a desperate situation, it provided those manipulating the chaos with the 'right' to continue with their activities. 'In such circumstances, rational minds become irrational, illogic becomes logic, the complex is made simple, and tragedy multiplies.'[16]

On 26 March 1975, Mujib announced sweeping reforms, setting up 61 districts with politically appointed governors aided by a council of people's representatives. The army, frontier guards (known as the Bangladesh Rifles), Rakkhi Bahini and the police were placed under the governor's control. Courts were set up in police districts and compulsory cooperatives were to be formed in every village without disturbing land ownership, although the produce was to be shared.[17] Mujib's fatal mistake was the fashioning of the Bangladesh Krishak Sramik Awami League (BaKSAL) on 7 June 1975.[18] He announced BaKSAL with the phrase 'second revolution' as it represented Mujib's answer to

---

[15] William B. Milam, *Bangladesh and Pakistan Flirting with Failure in South Asia* (New York: Columbia University, 2009), 38.

[16] Lawrence Ziring, *Bangladesh From Mujib to Ershad: An Interpretive Study* (Karachi: Oxford University Press, 1992), 102.

[17] B.Z. Khasru, *The Bangladesh Military Coup and the CIA Link* (New Delhi: Rupa Publications, 2014), 165.

[18] Lawrence Lifshultz, *Bangladesh: The Unfinished Revolution* (London: Zed Books, 1979), 117.

prevailing political challenges. Since he was imprisoned during the Bangladesh Liberation War, and as a result had missed the first revolution, he believed he had suffered because of it. The second revolution was one he would orchestrate and expected it to be a different story with a different outcome.[19]

Mujib was well aware of the criticism that BaKSAL was a totalitarian injunction. He told the BaKSAL central committee on 19 June 1975 that his move was necessary to combat corruption, bureaucratic ineptitude and unidentified foreign conspiracies. Since Mujib was well-versed in the art of politics of agitation, he recognised the kinds of situations and issues that would offer his opponents an opportunity to undermine his position. In his speech, Mujib presented a comprehensive explanation for his second revolution, which he defined as his new system of a one-party State and a revised administrative structure. There had been, he asserted, no possibility of the Awami League 'being thrown out of office'. BaKSAL was to end corruption and any foreign intervention to subvert independence. Despite Mujib's pronouncement that the BaKSAL was not to perpetuate his rule, the one-party structure lent no credibility to his claim. BaKSAL gave Mujib unlimited powers and no one could question his authority; in a sense, he became omnipotent. His word was the ultimate authority—he could choose his executive committee, fill cabinet posts, pick district governors and select candidates for the Parliament.[20]

If performance was to be the criterion, the first 100 days of the second revolution offered little comfort. The period demonstrated that its primary result had been a more personalised rule by Mujib. In dealing with

[19] Anthony Mascarenhas, *Bangladesh: A Legacy of Blood* (London: Hodder & Stoughton, 1986), 59.
[20] B.Z. Khasru, *The Bangladesh Military Coup and the CIA Link* (New Delhi: Rupa Publications, 2014), 166–69.

individuals, when all else failed, he would compromise through manipulation, promises and, at times, intimidation. Evidently, none of these tactics contributed to the country's progression. In the BaKSAL setting, Mujib's margin for error was narrower than ever since he himself had assumed the sole responsibility for any failings of the government. This eroded his support amongst the public and his burden of proving to be accomplished increased.[21]

The basic tenets of the Constitution, which came to be known as 'Mujibism' or 'Mujibbad', included the four pillars of nationalism, socialism, secularism and democracy. In effect, in the years following Bengali independence, Prime Minister Mujib cast-off everything that Bangladesh theoretically represented and after assuming power, he defied the very politics he himself had instilled.[22] Primary among those who took offence were a number of mid-level military officers who were already aggrieved by Mujib's actions toward the army, especially his creation of the national security force and its superiority to the army. They saw his moves towards dictatorship as harmful to their interests and the pretext for action to force a change.[23]

The sequence of events had been dramatic. In 1971 Mujib had spoken to crowds of over a million; from 1974 onwards, he rarely addressed open meetings as disturbances were expected.[24]

Among the notable achievements of Mujib's government were the total reconstruction and re-organisation of the administrative system, adoption of the Constitution, rehabilitation of millions of Bengali people, restoration

---

[21] Ibid., 182.

[22] James Heitzman et al., *Bangladesh: A Country Study* (Washington: Federal Research Division, Library of Congress, 1989), 32.

[23] William B. Milam, *Bangladesh and Pakistan Flirting with Failure in South Asia* (New York: Columbia University, 2009), 38.

[24] Lawrence Lifshultz, *Bangladesh: The Unfinished Revolution* (London: Zed Books, 1979), 46.

and development of a communication system and the expansion of education. He tried to normalise relations with Pakistan, forged new alliances on the international stage and cemented existing alliances with India. BaKSAL was scheduled to officially replace the political system in Bangladesh on 1 September 1975. The intervening period between the initial announcement and the official act provided Mujib's principal opponents with the time to not only plot their response but also seal alliances with others distressed by the manoeuvre.[25]

While the domineering prime ministers of both India and Pakistan were able to contain Opposition activity, the Opposition to President Mujib in Bangladesh launched a coup against its one-party leader. Two army officers— Major Farook Rahman and Major K.A. Rashid—planned and led the bloody murders of most of the family and closest friends of the man hailed three years earlier as the 'Nation-Unifier-Father'.

Khandaker Moshtaque Ahmed, Mujib's first minister for water resources and power and later, the minister for commerce and foreign trade, was privy to the conspiracy and immediately took over as the president after the slaughter of Mujib and his family on Dhaka's Dhanmandi Road on the morning of 15 August 1975. For a few moments, the charismatic president had managed with his defiant words to paralyse the first would-be-killer, who caught him on the stairs inside his home and softly requested, 'Sir, please come.' 'What do you want?' Mujib asked him scornfully in Bengali. 'Have you come here to kill me? Forget it; the Pakistan Army couldn't do it. Who are you that you think you can?' But the second intruder did what the first could not;

---

[25] Craig Baxter, *Bangladesh: A New Nation in an Old Setting* (Boulder: Westview Press, 1984), 56.

he fired 'a burst from his sten gun. Mujib didn't have a chance. The bullets tore a huge hole in his right side'[26].

R.N. Kao, India's first chief of the intelligence agency RAW, had information from 1974 onwards about plots against Mujib. Secret reports had reached him that plans of revolt were brewing in the Bangladesh defence services and he personally briefed Indira about these. She sent him to Dhaka to inform Mujib about the plot. 'We were walking in the garden. I told Mujib that we had information about a plot against him, but he was in a state of euphoria. "Nothing can happen to me," he said. "They are my people." This was even though I gave him details of the definite information we had received.' It was in March 1975 that information once again reached Kao that a plot against Mujib was being organised within the artillery. Indira was quick to inform Mujib, but he refused to believe her.[27]

Colonel Abu Taher of Bangladesh Army, who was a decorated war hero of 1971 liberation war and was later charged with treason and mutiny by the Government of Bangladesh, gave testimony to the Special Martial Law Tribunal in Dhaka (21 June 1976–17 July 1976). The following excerpt is from his testimony:

> It was really tragic and painful to see Sheikh Mujibur Rahman, the leading personality among the founders of this state, emerge as a dictator. Mujib in his chequered political career had never compromised with autocracy or dictatorship. He was once the symbol of democracy and the national independence movement... Sheikh Mujib was the leader of the masses. To deny this is to deny a fact. It is my firm conviction that the people who installed Mujib as their

---

[26] Anthony Mascarenhas, *Bangladesh: A Legacy of Blood* (London: Hodder & Stoughton, 1986), 73–74.

[27] Pupul Jayakar, *Indira Gandhi: An Intimate Biography* (New York: Pantheon Books, 1992), 220.

*leader would have destroyed Mujib the dictator. The people granted no rights to anyone to intrigue or conspire.*[28]

The widespread economic, social and political turmoil in the new Bengali nation state ultimately resulted in Mujib's martyrdom. The only surviving daughters of Mujib are Sheikh Rehana and Sheikh Hasina, who is the current prime minister of Bangladesh. With the elimination of Mujib, Bangladesh was brought under a military-backed political regime, which lasted until the restoration of parliamentary democracy in 1990. The second anniversary of Mujib's assassination (15 August 1977) was observed as a mourning day all over Bangladesh, defying all official restrictions and provocations. The nation pleaded on this memorable day to fight for the restoration of democracy as prayers were offered at Mujib's grave in his home village. Students, despite a ban on them, held public meetings and processions and police action against these students was widely condemned.[29]

Oriana Fallaci, the Italian journalist who had interviewed Indira and Bhutto, had also interviewed Mujib in February 1972; she had predicted Mujib's downfall to him at the end of her interview. Her interview of Mujib was not a pleasant experience since she received his scorn repeatedly, including when she questioned him about the atrocities committed by the Mukti Bahini on 18 December 1971 on those perceived supportive of Pakistan. During the interview, she questioned Mujib's claim of Pakistani authorities digging a grave for his burial during his imprisonment in Pakistan. Mujib also shouted at her when she wanted to discuss his meeting with Bhutto in the Pakistani jail. Mujib called Fallaci a liar several times and the acrimonious exchange continued. Mujib became more

[28] Lawrence Lifshultz, *Bangladesh: The Unfinished Revolution* (London: Zed Books, 1979), 86–87.
[29] S.R. Chakravarty, *Bangladesh under Mujib, Zia and Ershad* (New Delhi: Har-Anand Publications, 1995), 136.

and more agitated and finally accused Fallaci that she wasn't a journalist, she was instead a prosecutor. At this point, Fallaci's patience was exhausted; she got up and told Mujib that she was leaving Bangladesh and would never set foot in his country and that Mujib was a scoundrel, a mad hysterical and would end badly.[30]

Journalist Anthony Mascarenhas interviewed one of Mujib's assassins, Major Rashid. When asked why Mujib was murdered and not unseated, he replied, 'There was no other way. He had the capacity for mischief and given the chance would have turned the tables on us.'[31]

Mujib's Cardinal Sins:

- Progressively assuming an autocratic style of leadership
- Ignoring warnings of conspiracies leading to assassination

## PART 2: PAKISTAN

*The paradise of God lies under the feet of your mother. The paradise of politics lies under the feet of the people.*

—Zulfikar Ali Bhutto[32]

'If you were an American, you would be in my cabinet.'

'Be careful, Mr. President. If I were an American, I would be in your place,' said Bhutto to US president John F. Kennedy.[33]

---

[30] Oriana Fallaci, 'The True Face of the Tiger of Bengala', *L' Europeo* (Volume 28, No. 8, 1972), 26–33.

[31] Anthony Mascarenhas, *Bangladesh: A Legacy of Blood* (London: Hodder & Stoughton, 1986), 33.

[32] Zulfikar Ali Bhutto, *My Dearest Daughter: A Letter from the Death Cell* (Shanawaz Bhutto Trust, 1989), 12.

[33] Stanley A. Wolpert, *Bhutto of Pakistan: His Life and Times* (New York: Oxford University Press, 1993), 76.

Zulfikar Ali Bhutto was a brilliant politician and skilled diplomat who knew exactly when and how to appeal and appease his supporters as well as his enemies. Even though Bhutto was in power for just six years, he left a noticeable and enduring impression on Pakistan's history and politics. Under Bhutto, Pakistan experienced its 'second birth'.[34] The country transformed politically, culturally and geographically. The unusual 'dual State' of East Pakistan and West Pakistan became simply 'Pakistan'—a single territorial State extending along the Indus River Basin. What was once a socially homogenous western region progressively transitioned into a conglomerate of different ethnic and social groups.[35]

The stupendous defeat of the army in the brief 1971 war with India and the traumatic loss of the eastern half of united Pakistan had undermined the Pakistan Army's reputation and influence. The army might have been accustomed to ruling the nation, but its claim to remain a legitimate player in governance was torpedoed by unadulterated bungling, which led to the disaster and the military regime's outright prevarication to the Pakistani public before and during the war.

The new civilian government dominated the military and bureaucracy. The problem Bhutto faced was to consolidate this state of affairs by institutionalising the democratic reforms and inclusive governance, which Pakistan's divided ethnic polity needed in order to create a sense of nationalism. Bhutto's use of the army to settle political issues restored its reputation and, thus, public support for its claim to be the only institution in Pakistan with national interest at heart.[36] The army had been 'the

---

[34] V.Y. Belokrenitsky and V.N. Moscalenko, *A Political History of Pakistan, 1947–2007* (Oxford: Oxford University Press, 2013), 206.

[35] *Times of Islamabad*, 'Pakistan Population Statistics', https://timesofislamabad.com/pakistan-population-statistics-in-2016/2016/08/25/ (accessed 29 December 2016).

[36] William B. Milam, *Bangladesh and Pakistan Flirting with Failure in South Asia* (New York: Columbia University, 2009), 31.

spinal cord of the state apparatus' in Pakistan and it had no intention of diffusing its role under Bhutto.[37] Though the army had obediently tolerated Bhutto and his widespread 'political stardom' for six years, it was during the 1977 general elections that the commanding officers decided enough was enough.

Pakistan held a general election on 7 March 1977. Bhutto's PPP won, but it is alleged that the election had been strategically manipulated to ensure a landslide victory (155 of 200 seats) for Bhutto. Despite the negative reaction to his policies, Bhutto's populist vision still enjoyed the support of a plurality of Pakistanis. The proximate cause of his downfall and the suspected rigging of the 1977 election need not, therefore, have happened. It is suspected that Bhutto and the PPP actually won the election legitimately, but overzealous PPP local leaders, especially in Punjab, are alleged to have rigged the polls in their districts in order to achieve a PPP majority. However, it is almost certain this did not affect the outcome of the election.[38] Indira Gandhi sent Bhutto a personal congratulatory message for his electoral success.[39] Immediately after the results were announced, riots broke out across Pakistan. As one of Bhutto's biographers put it, in 'the excess of victory... lay the time bomb of defeat' for Bhutto.[40] The situation began to get out of hand, and mass arrests were carried out across Pakistan; all of the men who had once pledged their loyalty to Bhutto and the PPP were now sent to jail.[41] The US hostility towards Pakistan's

[37] Katherine Frank, *Indira: The Life of Indira Nehru Gandhi* (London: HarperCollins, 2001), 438.

[38] William B. Milam, *Bangladesh and Pakistan Flirting with Failure in South Asia* (New York: Columbia University, 2009), 49.

[39] Stanley A. Wolpert, *Bhutto of Pakistan: His Life and Times* (New York: Oxford University Press, 1993), 286.

[40] Katherine Frank, *Indira: The Life of Indira Nehru Gandhi* (London: HarperCollins, 2001), 412.

[41] Fatima Bhutto, *Songs of Blood and Sword: A Daughter's Memoir* (New York: Nation Books, 2010), 123.

nuclear programme—specifically, the fear of building a 'Muslim bomb'—increased. Henry Kissinger, who had publicly admired Bhutto, warned him in private that if he did not put a stop to the nuclear programme, there would be dire consequences for Pakistan.

On 5 July 1977, General Zia ul Haq, chief of army staff, led the Pakistani army to seize power of Bhutto's government. The irony of these events was that Bhutto himself had selected General Zia over numerous, more experienced and qualified generals, believing that Zia would be a 'loyal and pliable' accomplice.[42] The plan backfired; the man Bhutto had chosen to be his puppet ended up paving the path for Bhutto's execution. Bhutto was offered clemency in return for accepting and becoming the signatory of a document prepared by the military government. He remained defiant and responded, 'I would rather be destroyed by the military than by history.' As the Supreme Court verdict was announced, Bhutto retorted, 'This is not a trial of murder – this is the murder of a trial.'

According to Roedad Khan, the interior secretary of Pakistan:

> *Bhutto was a doomed man once it became clear that he continued to remain popular with the masses even after loss of office and nothing could stop him from staging a comeback in the free, fair and impartial election which Zia had promised to the people of Pakistan. Bhutto was now like a wounded animal and his political opponents were mortally afraid of him. They dreaded the prospect of his return to power and were demanding his death in the name of justice.*[43]

---

[42] Inder Malhotra, *Indira Gandhi: A Personal and Political Biography* (London: Hodder & Stoughton, 1989), 19.

[43] Roedad Khan, *Pakistan – A Dream Gone Sour* (Karachi, Oxford, 1997), 69.

During Bhutto's pre-execution trial, every single Muslim head of State—including those heads of State that had attended the Islamic conference in Lahore—wrote to the martial law government and sought clemency for Bhutto. The appeals for Bhutto's release extended beyond Muslim and Arab regions of the world; the leaders of the US, Britain, France, Germany, Australia and the Pope, amongst others, attempted to reason with the martial law government in Pakistan and secure a release or at the very least, an honourable sentencing, for Bhutto. One of the most notable aspects of the case was Indira Gandhi's involvement. Despite Gandhi's contentious animosities with Bhutto, following the verdict of his trial, Indira publicly condemned the sentencing and contacted the martial law government in Pakistan, 'urging [them] to grant Bhutto clemency'[44].

The attempts for clemency were unsuccessful and Bhutto spent his 51st—and last—birthday in a prison cell at Rawalpindi jail, scarcely able to eat because of untreated gum disease.[45] The man who had once dined with kings and foreign dignitaries in their castles and been adorned in 'savile row suits and silk handkerchiefs'[46] was now starving and withering away in solitary confinement in a cold, dark prison cell. This Bhutto looked nothing like the poised world statesman who exuded confidence and commanded respect everywhere he went; this Bhutto was frail and weak, living out the last moments of his life at the mercy of his captors.

While in jail, Bhutto sent a letter to his daughter, Benazir Bhutto, in which he compared Benazir to Indira, writing, 'One thing you have in common: both of you are equally brave. Both of you are made of pure damascene steel. But

[44] Katherine Frank, *Indira: The Life of Indira Nehru Gandhi* (London: HarperCollins, 2001), 438.

[45] *The Guardian*, 'Pakistan's Zulfikar Ali Bhutto executed-archive', https://www.theguardian.com/world/2016/apr/05/pakistan-zulfikar-ali-bhutto-executed-1979 (accessed 12 June 2019).

[46] Ibid.

where will your talent take you? Normally, it should take you to the very top. But we are living in a society where talent is a drawback and suffocating mediocrity an asset.'[47]

In the early morning hours of 4 April 1979, Bhutto was executed by hanging at the Central Jail Rawalpindi in Pakistan for the murder of a political opponent. The murder trial was deemed widely as 'unfair'.[48] Sajjad Ali Shah and Saeeduzzaman Siddiqui, who are both former Supreme Court of Pakistan's chief justices, have called Bhutto's trial 'judicial murder'. Bhutto got hanged because of expectations of justice and fairness from the Supreme Court by his followers.

'*Ye mujhai*?' ('This to me?') According to the chief of Bhutto's security detail, Colonel M. Rafiuddin, these were some of Bhutto's final words before his execution, in addition to, 'God help me, for I am innocent!'[49]

While opinions about Bhutto's role and place in Pakistan's history differ violently, there is a general agreement that he continues to be the most dominant figure. He occupied the centre stage in power as well as out of power and continues to influence the course of events from his grave. He remains the gold standard for almost all Pakistanis including his critics and political opponents.[50] The oversight on part of Bhutto devotees was to fight Bhutto's case in court only. They thought that this murder case, like all others, would be decided on its merits. They did not comprehend that Bhutto's fate was going to be decided not in court but on

---

[47] Zulfikar Ali Bhutto, *My Dearest Daughter: A Letter from the Death Cell* (Shahnawaz Bhutto Trust, 1989), 12.

[48] *The Guardian*, 'Pakistan's Zulfikar Ali Bhutto executed-archive', https://www.theguardian.com/world/2016/apr/05/pakistan-zulfikar-ali-bhutto-executed-1979 (accessed 12 June 2019).

[49] Mary Anne Weaver, 'Bhutto's Fateful Moment', *The New Yorker*, 26 September 1993, http://www.newyorker.com/magazine/1993/10/04/bhuttos-fateful-moment (accessed 12 June 2019).

[50] Roedad Khan, *Pakistan – A Dream Gone Sour* (Karachi, Oxford, 1997), 74.

the streets of Pakistan. Mujib was released in the Agartala Conspiracy Case when over a million people came out on the streets of Dhaka and showed Ayub Khan's government who was in control in East Pakistan. Curfew was violated and the writ of the government was defied. Ayub Khan's government had no choice but to withdraw the case.[51]

In any case, the 'new' Pakistan recovered its equilibrium surprisingly quickly after the shattering separation in 1971. In Bhutto's early months, high expectations for Pakistan's future emerged from its people and the international community. Bhutto retained the support of most Pakistanis during his time in office but failed to capitalise on that support to consolidate political institutions that maintained civilian political superiority over the military. Within six years of its new beginning, Pakistan fell back into the political patterns of the 'old' united Pakistan.[52] This lasted until Zia's (the military dictator who overthrew Bhutto) plane crash on 17 August 1988, and Benazir Bhutto's electoral victory and return as prime minister of Pakistan in December, when she became the youngest prime minister anywhere and the first female to head the government of a Muslim country.

'I found him brilliant, charming, of global stature in his perceptions... He did not suffer fools gladly. Since he had many to contend with, this provided him with more than his ordinary share of enemies... In the days of his country's tragedy, he held the remnant of his nation together and restored its self-confidence. In its hour of greatest need, he saved his country from complete destruction...his courage and vision in 1971 should have earned him a better fate... ' Henry Kissinger had said about Bhutto.[53]

---

[51] Ibid., 69–70.

[52] William B. Milam, *Bangladesh and Pakistan Flirting with Failure in South Asia* (New York: Columbia University, 2009), 39.

[53] Henry Kissinger, *The White House Years* (Boston: Little, Brown and Co., 1979), 907.

General Zia who overthrew Bhutto and ensured his hanging had told Roedad Khan, 'Roedad Sahib, it is his (Bhutto's) neck or mine.'[54]

Bhutto's Cardinal Sins:

- Progressively assuming an autocratic style of leadership
- Delaying the signing of an agreement with the Opposition over re-election in 1977

## PART 3: INDIA

*I will miss Mrs. Indira Gandhi very much. She was a truly great leader.*

—Margaret Thatcher at Indira's funeral[55]

'Indira Gandhi was the toughest woman prime minister I have met. She was feminine, but there was nothing soft about her. She was a more determined and ruthless political leader than Margaret Thatcher,' Lee Kuan Yew, founding father and first prime minister of Singapore had said.[56]

Indira Gandhi was a confident and assertive leader, one who did not readily admit flaws or take criticism. She was a goddess to her admirers but a demon to her critics, who accused her of damaging the civil service and the independent judiciary and of almost destroying the Constitution during her proclaimed state of Emergency—21 months between 1975 and 1977. During her years in office, Mrs Gandhi had successfully fed India during the drought of 1966, heightened

[54] Roedad Khan, *Pakistan – A Dream Gone Sour* (Karachi: Oxford University Press, 1997), 69–70.

[55] *The Hindu*, '"I will miss Mrs Gandhi very much", said Thatcher', 8 April 2013 https://www.thehindu.com/news/international/world/i-will-miss-mrs-indira-gandhi-very-much-said-thatcher/article4595205.ece (accessed 12 June 2019).

[56] Priya S. Lekshmi, 'Indira Gandhi—the iron-willed stateswoman', *The Week*, 19 January 2017, https://www.theweek.in/webworld/features/society/indira-gandhi-iron-willed-stateswoman.html (accessed 12 June 2019).

national pride after the victorious 1971 Indo-Pak War and ushered in a technological revolution with the detonation of a nuclear device in 1974.[57] Indira had a sharp instinct for solving crucial problems in the rough times she lived in and an even sharper instinct for acquiring the requisite power to tackle them. She was a superb manager of crises and was seldom hesitant to act under conditions of uncertainty.[58]

On 12 June 1975, judge Jag Mohan Lal Sinha of the Allahabad High Court stunned the country when he set aside Indira's 1971 election and found the prime minister guilty of 2 out of 52 counts of campaign malpractice in her election against Raj Narain. He had filed the petition accusing the prime minister of an election infraction; her office had delayed the announcement of a government employee's resignation and the employee had worked for her campaign. The error was technical in nature and the British newspaper, *The Guardian*, in its 16 January 1975 publication compared it to a British prime minister sent to jail for a parking ticket.[59]

If substantiated, the charges, although minor, carried a mandatory penalty that would deprive Indira of her seat in the Parliament and bar her from holding any public office for six years.

Indira Gandhi's worst nightmare had just materialised. On 26 June 1975, at 6:00 a.m., Indira summoned her cabinet and declared a state of Emergency, suspending all civil rights, including those of habeas corpus, putting

[57] Leslie Derfler, *The Fall and Rise of Political Leaders: Olof Palme, Olusegun Obasanjo, and Indira Gandhi,* 1st edition (New York: Palgrave Macmillan, 2011),146–47.
[58] Srinath Raghavan, 'Indira Gandhi: India and the World in Transition' in Ramachandra Guha edited, *Makers of Modern Asia* (Cambridge: Harvard University Press, 2014), 242.
[59] Leslie Derfler, *The Fall and Rise of Political Leaders: Olof Palme, Olusegun Obasanjo, and Indira Gandhi,* 1st edition (New York: Palgrave Macmillan, 2011), 169–70.

a lid on the press, placing armoured units on alert and grounding air flights over Delhi. All was done with speed and determination.[60]

By August, the foreign press reported at least 10,000 political prisoners were being held. The Opposition estimated up to 50,000 and Indira's government admitted to 'a few thousand'. The world's largest democracy had become a virtual dictatorship.[61] This was the beginning of the period of Indira's authoritarian rule.[62] The order authorised the prime minister to rule by decree, resulting in almost two years of arrests, press censorship and severe restrictions on civil liberties. During this time, the Indian National Congress pursued a programme of intense economic development under the 1971 campaign slogan *'Garibi Hatao' (Remove Poverty)*.[63] The 21-month period, known in India as the 'Emergency', represents one of the darkest periods in India's history as an independent State.

Public reception on the Emergency was abysmal, both at the domestic and global scale. On 23 June 1975, *TIME* published an article on the situation in India under Indira, claiming '[not] since India gained its independence from Britain in 1947 had it faced a constitutional crisis of such magnitude'[64]. Rising oil prices and poor monsoons coincided with corruption scandals involving Congress members and, between 1974 and 1975, the socialist campaigner, Jayaprakash Narayan, led a popular anti-corruption

---

[60] Ibid., 172.

[61] Ibid.

[62] The Emergency was officially in effect from June 1975 until its withdrawal in March 1977.

[63] Leslie Derfler, *The Fall and Rise of Political Leaders: Olof Palme, Olusegun Obasanjo, and Indira Gandhi*, 1st edition (New York: Palgrave Macmillan, 2011),158.

[64] Rishi Iyengar, 'What *TIME* Said 40 Years Ago When Indira Gandhi Declared a State of Emergency in India,' *TIME*, 25 June 2015, http://time.com/3935184/indira-gandhi-emergency-40-years-1975/ (accessed 9 January 2017).

movement against Indira Gandhi's government. Narayan called for Gandhi to resign. The Opposition as well as several national newspapers reiterated his call. One cartoon in the *Washington Post* that was found especially upsetting depicted Indira as a witch holding an apple entitled, 'A State of Emergency'. The caption read—*Who were you expecting? Snow White?*[65]

Chile's coup unnerved not just Mujib but Gandhi too. Mujib himself, however, had ruled out the possibility of a coup to overthrow him. Speaking at a rally after the violent death of Chile's president, Salvador Allende, in a US-inspired putsch in 1973, Mujib confidently declared, 'Bangladesh will not be Chile.' He was proven wrong. On 9 September 1974, Gandhi told a Congress rally in Madras that there were 'powerful elements with considerable money and other resources within the country and outside it that want to stop [their] onward march to progress'[66].

Indira, in her usual style of defiance, used the Opposition movement as justification for proclaiming and sustaining a national state of Emergency for 21 months starting on 25 June 1975. Mujib's reasoning for the creation of the second revolution on 7 June 1975 bore striking similarities with the explanation Gandhi offered for imposing Emergency rule in India. Just like Mujib, she defended the harsh measures as a means to continue India's progress, which some outside powers—mainly the US—were out to undermine. She consistently denied that the court verdict nullifying her membership in the Parliament forced her to impose the Emergency. Virtually no politically sensitive person in India took this explanation seriously. Mujib similarly denied that

[65] Leslie Derfler, *The Fall and Rise of Political Leaders: Olof Palme, Olusegun Obasanjo, and Indira Gandhi,* 1st edition (New York: Palgrave Macmillan, 2011), 185.

[66] B.Z. Khasru, *The Bangladesh Military Coup and the CIA Link* (New Delhi: Rupa Publications, 2014), 261.

his new party was intended to perpetuate his rule and very few in Bangladesh took his denial seriously.[67]

When asked how he felt about Prime Minister Gandhi's conviction, Prime Minister Bhutto said, 'We do not gloat over the predicaments of others. We take a serious and long-term view of such situations... We have to be watchful, lest Mrs Indira Gandhi, bedevilled and bewildered by the present crisis, seeks to extricate herself from this mess by embarking upon an adventurist course against Pakistan.'[68] Following these events, on 1 July 1975, Gandhi announced the Twenty Point Programme, an economic programme that included measures to control the price of essential commodities, tackle rural indebtedness and increase production.[69] In a national radio broadcast, Gandhi referred to the Opposition movement as part of a 'deep and widespread conspiracy' that posed a 'threat to internal stability' in the country.[70]

By the autumn of 1976, Indira Gandhi ruled supremely. The country was peaceful for all intents and purposes. A vast number of smugglers and black marketers had all been arrested and foreign exchange reserves were at an all-time high. Underground conspiracies and plots were extricated; most voices of the revolts quieted and conspirators were behind bars. The news of Zulfikar Ali Bhutto's call for general elections in Pakistan triggered an enquiry in Indira, 'Could the image of India be that of a dictatorship while Pakistan continues as a democracy?'[71] The subsequent elections in 1977 resulted in the reversal of Indira's rule,

---

[67] Ibid., 170.

[68] Stanley A. Wolpert, *Bhutto of Pakistan: His Life and Times* (New York: Oxford University Press, 1993), 254.

[69] Leslie Derfler, *The Fall and Rise of Political Leaders: Olof Palme, Olusegun Obasanjo, and Indira Gandhi*, 1st edition (New York: Palgrave Macmillan, 2011), 178.

[70] Ibid., 172.

[71] Pupul Jayakar, *Indira Gandhi: An Intimate Biography* (New York: Pantheon Books, 1992), 235–36.

primarily as a backlash of the Emergency. In the haze of her defeat and the grace and dignity with which she accepted it, few people have acknowledged the nature of Indira Gandhi's action. No authoritarian ruler in supreme control had ever given up power or submitted to possible political extinction with such integrity.[72] On 6 January 1980, Indira made a comeback with a landslide victory (351 of 529 seats) and was elected leader of the victorious Congress (I) party. This was her fourth swearing-in as prime minister. 'In 1966, she had been apprehensive; in 1967, with a reduced majority in Lok Sabha (House of the People; the lower house of the Parliament elected by common suffrage every five years) and the old guard of Congress determined to obstruct her in every way, she had been grim; in 1971, she was filled with a wild euphoria; in 1980, she was somber, without a trace of her imperious arrogance.'[73]

In June 1984, she approved Operation Blue Star, a military operation aimed at clearing the Golden Temple of armed men who had taken refuge in the temple in Amritsar, resulting in many deaths and enraging Sikhs across the world. The temple also know as Harmandir Sahib, is the holiest shrine of the Sikh religion, and Indira understood that authorising an operation would have dire consequences. The Golden Temple for Sikhs is what Mecca is to Muslims and the Vatican is to Catholics. When Indira authorised Operation Blue Star in the first week of June 1984, she knew that she had also signed her own death warrant.[74] She had a long-held conviction that she was destined for a violent end. In as early as 1973, in a meeting with Fidel Castro, news arrived in New Delhi of president of Chile Allende's murder. Indira told the Cuban, 'What they've done to Allende they want

[72] Ibid., 251.
[73] Ibid., 311.
[74] Inder Malhotra, *Indira Gandhi: A Personal and Political Biography* (London: Hodder & Stoughton, 1989), 291.

to do to me also.' She repeated this publicly, in a sanitised version, after the 1975 massacre in Dhaka of President Sheikh Mujibur Rahman and his family members, and again after the Bhutto execution in 1979.[75]

Immediately after Operation Blue Star, it was decided by the senior officers of Indira's government to remove all Sikh guards in charge of the prime minister's security. But when they forwarded the proposal to the prime minister for approval, Indira refused, saying that she was the prime minister of a secular country and any attempt to exclude Sikh guards from their positions would only add to their humiliation and hurt. The compromise to post a non-Sikh with every Sikh officer was for some unknown reason never implemented.[76] She firmly rejected the proposal of her defence minister to have her security transferred from the police to the army. 'In a democracy,' she remonstrated, 'the armed forces were kept well out.'[77]

At a gathering at Bhubaneswar on 30 October 1984—the day before she was gunned down—she declared to the crowd:

*I am here today; I may not be here tomorrow. But the responsibility to look after national interest is on the shoulder of every citizen of India. I have often mentioned this earlier. Nobody knows how many attempts have been made to shoot me; sticks have been used to beat me. In Bhubaneswar itself, a brickbat hit me. They have attacked me in every possible manner. I do not care whether I live or die. I have lived a long life, and I am proud that I spent*

[75] Leslie Derfler, *The Fall and Rise of Political Leaders: Olof Palme, Olusegun Obasanjo, and Indira Gandhi*, 1st edition (New York: Palgrave Macmillan, 2011), 222.

[76] Pupul Jayakar, *Indira Gandhi: An Intimate Biography* (New York: Pantheon Books, 1992), 468.

[77] Leslie Derfler, *The Fall and Rise of Political Leaders: Olof Palme, Olusegun Obasanjo, and Indira Gandhi*, 1st edition (New York: Palgrave Macmillan, 2011), 223.

*the whole of my life in the service of my people. I am only*
*proud of this and nothing else. I shall continue to serve*
*until my last breath, and when I die, I can say that every*
*drop of my blood will invigorate India and strengthen it.*[78]

As threats to Indira's life escalated, those responsible for
her security had made suggestions for increasing her cover
and taking extraordinary measures. Indira's response was,
'When they come to kill me, nothing would help. Those
supposed to save me will be the first to run away.'[79] In the
early hours of 31 October 1984, two Sikh bodyguards
assigned to protect Indira assassinated her in her own
garden. Two men she had trusted with her life mercilessly
gunned down Indira, who had once been compared to the
invincible Hindu goddess, Durga. She was taken to the
All India Institute of Medical Sciences in Delhi, where she
underwent an emergency operation to remove the bullets,
but died just after an hour-and-a-half.[80] It is believed
that the Sikh guards were acting in retaliation to Indira's
initiation of the June 1984 storming of the Sikh holy shrine
at the Golden Temple. Indira had received death threats ever
since the Indian troops marched into the temple at Amritsar,
where almost 1,000 people died.[81]

In less than one hour of the official pronouncement of
Indira's martyrdom, her son Rajiv Gandhi became the
youngest prime minister of the world's largest democracy.
Almost immediately, he called for fresh elections, advancing
them by a few months and rejecting advice that these be
postponed. His victory in the elections was even more
spectacular than his mother's nearly two decades earlier.

[78] Inder Malhotra, *Indira Gandhi: A Personal and Political Biography* (London: Hodder & Stoughton, 1989), 304.
[79] Ibid., 19.
[80] BBC, '1984: Indian prime minister shot dead', http://news.bbc.co.uk/onthisday/hi/dates/stories/october/31/newsid_2464000/2464423.stm (accessed 12 June 2019).
[81] Ibid.

It was indeed staggering, for he won three-quarters of Lok Sabha seats and more than 48 per cent of the vote, the highest anyone in India has ever gotten.[82]

A few days after Indira's death, some sheets of paper covered with her spidery handwriting were found in a pile of notes and documents she had kept aside. It turned out that these pages comprised of her will. Undated but penned apparently not long before the assassination, her last testament began:

*I have never felt less like dying, and that calm and peace of mind is what prompts me to write what is in the nature of a will. If I die a violent death, as some fear and a few are plotting, I know that the violence will be in the thought and the actions of the assassin, not in my dying... No hate is dark enough to overshadow the extent of my love for my people and my country; no force is strong enough to divert me from my purpose and my endeavour to take this country forward... I cannot understand how anyone can be Indian and not be proud.*[83]

Indira's assassin Beant Singh, after dropping his gun, immediately retorted in Punjabi, 'I have done what I had to do. Now you do what you have to do.'[84]

Indira's Cardinal Sins:

- Progressively assuming an autocratic style of leadership.
- Infuriating Sikh community by authorising police action inside the Sikh Holy Shrine Harmandir Sahib.

---

[82] Inder Malhotra, *Dynasties of India and Beyond: Pakistan, Sri Lanka and Bangladesh* (New Delhi: HarperCollins. 2003), 128.

[83] Inder Malhotra, *Indira Gandhi: A Personal and Political Biography* (London: Hodder & Stoughton, 1989), 303–08.

[84] Katherine Frank, *Indira: The Life of Indira Nehru Gandhi* (London: HarperCollins, 2001), 493.

# EPILOGUE

*But now it is time to go away, I to die and you to*
*live. Which of us goes to a better thing is unclear to*
*everyone except to the god.*

—Plato's Apology[1]

In spite of their stark differences and antagonisms with each other, all three leaders followed through with populist initiatives, nationalising banks, industries and reallocating land and resources. Mujib, Indira and Bhutto shared similar experiences in their political careers. All three were victims of imprisonment. Mujib, during his political journey, spent almost 12 years in prison and faced the death sentence twice. Similarly, Bhutto had two attempts on his life for opposing Ayub Khan and was also imprisoned by Ayub Khan's government, and again towards the end of his life. Indira was 25 when she first experienced imprisonment in 1942 for participating in the Quit India Movement and she was imprisoned for her involvement in the Indian independence movement for 8 months from September 1942 to May 1943. Indira was imprisoned again for excesses during the Emergency after her subsequent election loss.

Mujib was on a hunger strike on several occasions, the longest being 13 consecutive days. Bhutto, too, had been on hunger strikes on several occasions throughout his life, including the nine days leading up to his hanging.

---

[1] *https://en.wikiquote.org/wiki/Apology_(Plato)* (accessed 12 June 2017).

Amongst the unique experiences that these leaders have shared throughout their political careers are calendric overlaps that connect their legacies. For instance, where Bhutto and Mujib are concerned, the national holidays in Pakistan and Bangladesh are only days apart. In Pakistan, 23 March is hailed as Pakistan Day because in 1940, the Lahore Resolution for the creation of Pakistan was passed on this historic day. The same is also the date when the people of East Bengal, under Mujib's instructions, defied the central government and declared it Resistance Day. In Bangladesh, the national holiday is on 26 March, commemorating the country's independence from Pakistan that occurred in the late hours of 25 March 1971 (declared by General Zia Rahman, who was acting on behalf of Mujib). The date 15 August marks another strange parallel between the leaders; it is celebrated as Independence Day in India and it is also the day Mujib was assassinated—though it is arguable that the date was deliberately chosen as a message to Indira, who was one of Mujib's closest political allies.

Furthermore, there is ample evidence that a combination of political turmoil, natural calamities and foreign intervention continue to play a role in all three nations. In Pakistan and Bangladesh's history, the groups responsible for colluding with non-democratic forces to oust the elected leaders' governments have flourished; the central governments following Mujib's assassination and Bhutto's execution are prime examples of this theory. In contrast, India has never had to succumb to military rule as an independent State. Despite the tumultuous issues in India during Indira's tenure—including the imposition of the Emergency, widespread famine due to lack of rains, the ever-increasing costs of war and the oil shock of 1973—there were no real attempts to replace the government by force.

# BIBLIOGRAPHY

Ahmad, Mushtaq. *Government and Politics in Pakistan*. First ed. Karachi: Pakistan Pub. House, 1959.

Al Mujahid, Sharif. 'Pakistan: First General Elections.' *Asian Survey*, Volume 11, No. 2 (1971), 159–71.

Ali, S.M. *After The Dark Night: Problems of Sheikh Mujibur Rahman*. Dehli: Thomson Press Limited, 1973.

Asghar, Nauman. 'ZAB – An assessment'. *The Nation*, 10 April 2015. http://nation.com.pk/columns/10-Apr-2015/zab-an-assessment (accessed 26 May,2016).

Bass, Gary Jonathan. *The Blood Telegram: Nixon, Kissinger, and a Forgotten Genocide*. First ed. New York: Alfred A Knopf, 2013.

Baxter, Craig. *Bangladesh: A New Nation in an Old Setting*. Boulder: Westview, 1984.

BBC. '1984: Indian prime minister shot dead'. http://news.bbc.co.uk/onthisday/hi/dates/stories/ october/31/ newsid_2464000/2464423.stm (accessed 12 June 2019).

Belokrenitsky V.Y. and V.N. Moscalenko. *A Political History of Pakistan, 1947–2007*. Oxford: Oxford University Press, 2013.

Bhatnagar, Yatindra. *Mujib: The Architect of Bangladesh*. New Delhi: R.K. Printers. 1971.

Bhutto, Fatima. *Songs of Blood and Sword: A Daughter's Memoir*. New York: Nation Books, 2010.

Bhutto, Zulfiqar Ali. *My Dearest Daughter: A Letter from the Death Cell*. Pakistan: Shahnawaz Bhutto Trust, 1989.

Biography.com. 'Indira Gandhi Biography'. http://www.biography.com/people/indira-gandhi-9305913 (accessed 29 December 2016).

BrainyQuote. 'Indira Gandhi Quotes'. https://www.brainyquote.com/quotes/indira_gandhi_389576 (accessed 30 April 2019).

BrainyQuote. 'Samuel Goldwyn Quotes'. https://www.
brainyquote.com/quotes/samuel_goldwyn_122394 (accessed
12 June 2019).

*BrainyQuote*. *'Theodore Hesburgh Quotes'*. https://www.
brainyquote.com/quotes/theodore_hesburgh_126341
(accessed 12 June 2019).

Burki, Shahid Javed. *Pakistan Under Bhutto, 1971–1977*. Second
ed. London: Macmillan, 1988.

Chakravarty, S.R. *Bangladesh under Mujib, Zia and Ershad*.
New Delhi: Har-Anand Publications, 1995.

Chari, P.R. and Pervaiz Iqbal Cheema. *The Simla Agreement
1972: Its Wasted Promise*. New Delhi: Manohar Publishers &
Distributors, 2001.

Choudhury, G.W. *India, Pakistan, Bangladesh and the Major
Powers*. New York: Macmillan Publishing, 1975.

Choudhury, G.W. *The Last Days of United Pakistan*.
Bloomington: Indiana University Press, 1974.

Chowdhury, Obaid. 'Was Sheikh Mujib for an Unbroken
Pakistan or Independent Bangladesh? Sensational Revelation
about Mujib in Pakistan in 1971'. *South Asia Journal*, 5
February 2019. http://southasiajournal.net/was-sheikh-
mujib-for-an-unbroken-pakistan-or-independent-bangladesh-
sensational-revelation-about-mujib-in-pakistan-in-1971-
%EF%BB%BF/ (accessed 12 June 2019).

Clarke, P.F. *The Last Thousand Days of the British Empire*.
London; Toronto: Allen Lane, 2007.

Collins, Larry and Dominique Lapierre. *Freedom at Midnight*.
New York: Simon and Schuster, 1975.

Colonial Williamsburg. 'Patrick Henry's "Give Me Liberty or
Give Me Death" Speech'. https://www.history.org/ almanack/
life/politics/giveme.cfm (accessed 12 June 2019).

Crum, Thomas. *The Magic of Conflict: Turning a Life of Work
into a Work of Art*. Toronto: Simon and Schuster, 1987.

Derfler, Leslie. *The Fall and Rise of Political Leaders: Olof
Palme, Olusegun Obasanjo, and Indira Gandhi*. First ed. New
York: Palgrave Macmillan, 2011.

Dhar, P.N. *Indira Gandhi, the 'Emergency', and Indian Democracy*.
New York; New Delhi: Oxford University Press, 2000.

Dixit, J.N. *India-Pakistan in War and Peace*. London: Routledge, 2002.

Dummett, Mark. 'Bangladesh War: The Article That Changed History'. BBC, 16 December 2011. http://www.bbc.com/news/world-asia-16207201 (accessed 12 June 2019).

Fakhruddin, Samina. 'Pakistan's Relation with India and Bangladesh.' *Pakistan Horizon*, Volume 27, No. 2 (1974).

Fallaci, Oriana. *Interview with History*. Boston: Houghton Mifflin, 1977.

Facllaci, Oriana. 'The True Face of the Tiger of Bengala', *L' Europeo*, Volume 28, No. 8, 26–33.

Frank, Katherine. *Indira: The Life of Indira Nehru Gandhi*. London: HarperCollins, 2001.

Gandhi, Rajmohan. *Mohandas: A True Story of a Man, His People and an Empire*. Haryana: Penguin Books India, 2007.

Ganguly, Sumit. 'Avoiding War in Kashmir'. *Foreign Affairs*, Volume 69, No. 5 (1990), 57–73.

Global Security. 'Indo-Pakistani War of 1971'. http://www.globalsecurity.org/org/overview/index.html (accessed 9 February 2017).

GoodReads. Honore de Balzac. https://www.goodreads.com/quotes/327664-le-secret-des-grandes-fortunes-sans-cause-apparente-est-un (accessed 12 June 2019).

GoodReads. Henry Kissinger. https://www.goodreads.com/quotes/59866-power-is-the-ultimate-aphrodisiac

Gopal, Sarvepalli. *Jawaharlal Nehru: A Biography*. New York: Oxford University Press, 2004.

Government of Bangladesh, National Encyclopedia of Bangladesh. 'Agartala Conspiracy Case'. http://en.banglapedia.org/index.php?title=Agartala_Conspiracy_Case (accessed 9 January 2017)

Guha, Ramachandra (Ed.). *Makers of Modern Asia*. Cambridge: Harvard University Press, 2014.

Gupta, Amit Kumar and Nehru Memorial Museum and Library. *The Agrarian Drama: The Leftists and the Rural Poor in India, 1934–1951*. New Delhi: Manohar, 1996.

Hajari, Nisid. *Midnight's Furies: The Deadly Legacy of India's Partition*. Gloucestershire: Amberley Publishing Limited, 2015.

Heitzman, James, et al. *Bangladesh: A Country Study*. Washington: Federal Research Division, Library of Congress, 1989.

Hiro, Dilip. *The Longest August: The Unflinching Rivalry Between India and Pakistan*. New York: Nation Books, 2015.

*History and General Studies*. 'Peasant Movements And Tribal Uprisings in the 18th and 19th Centuries: Indigo Rebellion (1859–1860)'. https://selfstudyhistory.com/2015/10/14/peasant-movements-and-tribal-uprisings-in-the-18th-and-19th-centuries-indigo-rebellion-1859-60/ (accessed 12 June 2019).

Horne, Alistair. *Kissinger: 1973, the Crucial Year*. Toronto: Simon & Schuster, 2009. https://www.nytimes.com/2009/07/19/books/excerpt-kissinger.html

Hossain, Ishtiaq. 'Bangladesh-India Relations: Issues and Problems'. *Asian Survey,* Volume 21, No. 11 (1981), 1,115–28.

*Introduction to Western Philosophy,* http://www2.hawaii.edu/~freeman/courses/phil100/04.%20Apology.pdf (accessed 12 June 2019).

Iyengar, Rishi. 'What *TIME* Said 40 Years Ago When Indira Gandhi Declared a State of Emergency in India'. *TIME,* 25 June 2015. http://time.com/3935184/indira-gandhi-emergency-40-years-1975/ (accessed 9 January 2017).

Jacques, Kathryn. *Bangladesh, India and Pakistan*. New York: St Martin's Press, 2000.

Jaffrelot, Christophe and Gillian Beaumont. *A History of Pakistan and its Origins*. London: Anthem Press, 2002.

James, Lawrence. *Raj: The Making and Unmaking of British India*. London: Little, Brown & Company, 1997.

Jayakar, Pupul. *Indira Gandhi: An Intimate Biography*. First American ed. New York: Pantheon Books, 1992.

Kapur, Ashok. *Pakistan in Crisis*. London: Routledge, 1991.

Kennedy, John F. 'Inaugural Address Transcript'. John F. Kennedy Presidential Library and Museum. https://www.jfklibrary.org/learn/about-jfk/historic-speeches/inaugural-address (accessed 12 June 2019).

Khan, M. Asghar. *We've Learnt Nothing From History: Pakistan: Politics and Military Power*. Pakistan: Oxford University Press, 2006.

Khan, Roedad. *Pakistan – A Dream Gone Sour*. Karachi: Oxford University Press, 1997.

Khan, Yasmin. *The Great Partition: The Making of India and Pakistan*. New Haven: Yale University Press, 2007.

Khasru, B.Z. *The Bangladesh Military Coup and the CIA Link*. New Delhi: Rupa Publications, 2014.

Kuwajima, Sho. *Muslims, Nationalism, and the Partition: 1946 Provincial Elections in India*. University of Michigan: Manohar, 1998.

Lifshultz, Lawrence. *Bangladesh: The Unfinished Revolution*. London: Zed Books, 1979.

Mahmood, Safdar. *The Deliberate Debacle*. First ed. Lahore: Sh. Muhammad Ashraf, 1976.

Malhotra, Inder. *Dynasties of India and Beyond: Pakistan, Sri Lanka and Bangladesh*. New Delhi: HarperCollins, 2003.

Malhotra, Inder. *Indira Gandhi: A Personal and Political Biography*. London: Hodder & Stoughton, 1989.

Maniruzzaman, Talukder. 'Bangladesh in 1975: The Fall of the Mujib Regime and its Aftermath'. *Asian Survey*, Volume 16, No. 2 (1976), 119–29.

Mascarenhas, Anthony. *Bangladesh: A Legacy of Blood*. London: Hodder & Stoughton, 1986.

Mascarenhas, Anthony. *The Rape of Bangladesh*. Delhi: Vikas Publications, 1971.

Mehdi, Tahir. 'Revisiting 1971: What if they elected traitors?' *DAWN*, 17 December 2012. http://www.dawn.com/news/771987 (accessed 12 June 2019).

Milam, William B. *Bangladesh and Pakistan Flirting with Failure in South Asia*. New York: Columbia University Press, 2009.

Ministry of Information and Broadcasting, Government of Pakistan. *Report on Islamic Summit 1974 Pakistan. Lahore, 22–24 February* Karachi: Ferozsons, 1974.

Misra, K.P. 'Totalitarianism in South-Asia'. *Asia Survey*, Volume XIV, No. 7.

Morris, Jan. *Farewell the Trumpets: An Imperial Retreat*. London: Faber and Faber, 1978.

Mosley, Leonard. *The Last Days of the British Raj*. London: Weidenfeld and Nicolson, 1961.

Mustafa, Ghulam and Qasim S. Gill. 'The Issue of POWS, 1971 and Recognition of Bangladesh'. *International Journal of Business and Social Research*, Volume 4, No. 3 (2014).

Mustafa, Zubeida. 'The Kashmir Dispute and the Simla Agreement'. *Pakistan Horizon*, Volume 25, No. 3 (1972).

Nair, P. Sukumaran. *Indo-Bangladesh Relations*. New Delhi: APH Publishing Corporation, 2008.

*Pakistan from 1947 to the Creation of Bangladesh*. New York: Charles Scribner's Sons, 1973.

Raghavan, Srinath. 'Indira Gandhi: India and the World in Transition' in Ramachandra Guha edited *Makers of Modern Asia*. Boston: Harvard University Press, 2014.

Rahman, Mashuqur and Mahbubur R. Jalal. 'Swadhin Bangla Betar Kendro and Bangladesh's Declaration of Independence'. *The Daily Star*, 25 November 2014. https://www.thedailystar.net/swadhin-bangla-betar-kendro-and-bangladeshs-declaration-of-independence-52001 (accessed 5 February 2017).

Rahman, Md. Sayedur, Md. Tanziul Islam, and Abu Reza Md. Towfiqul Islam, 'Evaluation of Charismatic Leader of Bangabandhu: Sheikh Mujibur Rahman'. *International Journal of Scientific and Research Publications*, Volume 4, Issue 5, May 2014.

Rahman, Mujibur Sheikh. *The Unfinished Memoirs*. Karachi: Oxford University Press, 2012.

Rushbrook Williams, L.F. *The East Pakistan Tragedy*. London: T. Stacey, 1972.

Salahuddin, Ahmed. *Bangladesh: Past and Present*. New Delhi: APH Publishing, 2004.

Salunke, S.P.x *Pakistani POWs in India*. New Delhi: Vikas Publishing House, 1977.

Sarkar, Sumit. *Modern India, 1885–1947*. Delhi: Macmillan, 1983.

Singh, Jaswant. *Jinnah: India, Partition, Independence*. New Delhi: Rupa Publications, 2010.

Singh, Sourabh. 'Unraveling the Enigma of Indira Gandhi's Rise in Indian Politics: A Woman Leader's Quest for Political Legitimacy'. *Theory and Society*, Volume 41, No. 5 (2012).

Sinha, Kamaleshwar. *Zulfikar Ali Bhutto: Six Steps to Summit.* Delhi: Indian School Supply Depot, Publication Division, 1972.

Sisson, Richard and Leo E. Rose. *War and Secession: Pakistan, India, and the Creation of Bangladesh.* Berkeley: University of California Press, 1990.

Smith, R.E. *The Failure of the Roman Republic.* New York; London: Cambridge University Press, 1955.

Taseer, Salmaan. *Bhutto: A Political Biography.* London: Ithaca Press, 1979; 1980.

*The Chicago Tribune.* 'Moslems Riot Over Theft of Sacred Relic'. 29 December 1963. http://archives.chicagotribune. com/1963/12/29/page/1/article/moslems-riot-over-theft-of-sacred-relic (accessed 31 October 2016).

*The Daily Star.* 'I haven't seen Himalayas but have seen Sheikh Mujib: Castro in 1973'. 26 November 2016. http://www. thedailystar.net/politics/i-havent-seen-himalayas-have-seen-sheikh-mujib-castro-1973-1320706 (accessed 7 April 2019).

*The Hindu.* 'Did Bhutto Outwit Indira Gandhi?' 6 February 2000. http://www.thehindu.com/2000/02/06/ stories/1306067g.htm (accessed 12 June 2019).

*The India-Pakistan Simla Agreement, 3 July 1972.* 3 March 2008. https://www.tandfonline.com/doi/abs/ 10.1080/00396337208441358 (accessed 14 January 2018).

*The Telegraph.* 'From Churchill to Corbyn: The 40 Most Brutal British Political Insults'. 15 March 2018. http://www. telegraph.co.uk/books/authors/the-best-british-political-insults-rows-and-putdowns/clement-attlee/ (accessed 12 June 2019).

*TIME.* 'Bangladesh: Not Yet Shonar Bangla'. 1 January 1973. http://content.time.com/time/subscriber/ article/0,33009,903638-2,00.html (accessed 12 June 2019).

Wolpert, Stanley A. *Bhutto of Pakistan: His Life and Times.* New York: Oxford University Press, 1993.

Yakowicz, Will. 'Lessons from Leadership Guru Warren Bennis'. *Inc.*, 4 August 2014. https://www.inc.com/will-yakowicz/7-leadership-lessons-from-late-warren-bennis.html (accessed 12 June 2019).

Zaheer, Sidrah. 'List of Prime Ministers of Pakistan Since 1947 (With Photos)'. *Pakistan Insider*, 5 April 2012. http://insider.pk/national/list-of-prime-ministers-of-pakistan-since-1947-with-photos/ (accessed 11 September 2016).

Ziring, Lawrence. *Bangladesh: From Mujib to Ershad: An Interpretive Study*. First ed. Karachi: Oxford University Press, 1992.

Ziring, Lawrence. *Pakistan at the Crosscurrent of History*. New Delhi: Manas Publications, 2005.

Ziring, Lawrence. *Pakistan in the Twentieth Century: A Political History*. Karachi: Oxford University Press, 1997.

Ziring, Lawrence. *Pakistan: The Enigma of Political Development*. Colorado: Westview Press, 1980.

Ziring, Lawrence. 'The Roots of Political Instability in Pakistan'. *Journal of South Asian and Middle Eastern Studies*, Volume 9, No. 1 & 2 (1987), 52–72.

# ABOUT THE AUTHOR

 Dr. Faisal Khosa is an award-winning scholar, author and mentor who has over 200 peer-reviewed publications, more than 250 invited lectures, published two dozen book chapters and has received six million dollars in collaborative grants.

He has mentored, supported and sponsored more than 700 students from minority and underrepresented groups and offers a needs-based mentoring program. He is invited to conduct workshops on equity, diversity & inclusion and has received awards of excellence in the USA, Europe, Canada, Middle East and South Asia:

Global Humanitarian Award – American College of Radiology
May Cohen Equity, Diversity & Gender Award – The Association of Faculties of Medicine of Canada
Outstanding Academic Performance Award – University of British Columbia
Dudley Pennell Award – Journal of Cardiovascular Magnetic Resonance
Young Investigator Award – Canadian Association of Radiologists
Rising Star Exchange Scholarship – French Society of Radiology

Humanitarian Award – Association of Physicians of Pakistani Descent of North America
Healthcare Hero Award – Vancouver Coastal Health
Leadership Scholarship – Canadian Radiological Foundation
People First Leadership Award – Vancouver Coastal Health
Examiner Award – College of Physicians and Surgeons
American Roentgen Ray Society Scholarship
Outstanding Young Investigator Award – USA
One in One Hundred Mentor Award – USA
Tamgha-i-Imtiaz – Government of Pakistan
Outstanding Service to Medicine Award – College of Physicians and Surgeons in Pakistan
Invest in Youth Award – Europe

Website: https://faisalkhosa.com
Twitter: @khosafaisal